DEAR VALUED REA

The Appalachian Mountain Club is ho...
journey as you discover the beauty of the...
Mountains. This region is home to unique recreational experiences, fragile ecosystems, and unparallelled views. We hope that this guide will prepare you for a an enjoyable experience in the Presidential Range.

Trails are the physical link that connects human experience to the outdoors. These experiences nurture our relationship to the land, challenge our limits, and leave us with memories that last a lifetime.

The trails described in this guidebook do not occur naturally, of course—they are the product of countless hours of passion, dedication, and hard work by many federal, state, non-profit, and volunteer stewards, as well as by a network of partners who share our belief that trails play a vital role in fostering a deeper connection between people and the outdoors. The Appalachian Mountain Club participates in and supports the efforts of this skilled and dedicated trail community to ensure a vibrant outdoor experience for hikers like you and me.

As you consider the next steps in your outdoor journey, we invite you to explore with us and become an active participant in the protection of these trails by volunteering your time and skills, by donating, or becoming a member of the Appalachian Mountain Club. Together, we can ensure that these trails continue to blaze a path of exploration, discovery, and appreciation for the natural world.

Wishing you many meaningful and memorable hiking experiences, and when the time is right, we hope to welcome you into our community of trails stewards.

With appreciation,

Alexander DeLucia
Director of Trails & Recreation Management
Appalachian Mountain Club

TRAIL GUIDE TO
MOUNT WASHINGTON
AND THE
PRESIDENTIAL RANGE

AN ABRIDGMENT OF AMC'S
***WHITE MOUNTAIN GUIDE*, FEATURING THE FULL**
PRESIDENTIAL RANGE AND GREAT GULF

Compiled and edited by
Ken MacGray and Steven D. Smith

Appalachian Mountain Club Books
Boston, Massachusetts

AMC is a 501(c)3 nonprofit, and sales of AMC Books fund our mission to foster the protection, enjoyment, and understanding of the outdoors. If you appreciate our efforts and would like to become a member or make a donation to AMC, visit outdoors.org, call 603-466-2727, or contact us at Appalachian Mountain Club, 10 City Square, Suite 2, Boston, MA 02129.

outdoors.org/books-maps

Distributed by National Book Network

Front cover photograph of hikers at Lakes of the Clouds hut © Corey David Photography

Page i photograph of a hiker on Mt. Washington © David Long

Back cover photograph of a hiker on Mt. Madison © Gina Hurley

Cover design by Katie Metz

Interior design by Abigail Coyle

ISBN 978-1-62842-191-0

Library of Congress Control Number: 2024934629

The paper used in this publication meets the minimum requirements of the American National Standard for Information Sciences-Permanence of Paper for Printed Library Materials, ANSI Z39.48-1984. ∞

Interior pages and cover are printed on responsibly harvested paper stock certified by The Forest Stewardship Council®, an independent auditor of responsible forestry practices.
Printed in the United States of America, using vegetable-based inks.

5 4 3 2 1   24 25 26 27 28

CONTENTS

Abbreviations and Acronyms   vi
Acknowledgments   vii
How to Use This Book   ix
Introduction   xiv

SECTION ONE: Mt. Washington and the Southern Ridges   1
Mt. Washington from Pinkham Notch   12
Upper Cone of Mt. Washington   22
North of Pinkham Notch Visitor Center   25
Main Ridge of the Southern Presidentials   28
Southern Presidentials from the West and South   34
Dry River Valley   43
Montalban Ridge   48
Jackson Area   61

SECTION TWO: Northern Presidentials and the Great Gulf   65
Main Ridge   70
Linking Trails on the North and West Slopes   78
Great Gulf Wilderness   82
Mt. Madison   93
Mt. Adams   102
Mt. Jefferson   118
Mt. Clay   123
Pine Mtn.   125
Pleasure Paths on the Lower North Slopes   128

Index   131

ABBREVIATIONS AND ACRONYMS

The following abbreviations are used in this book.

AMC Appalachian Mountain Club
AT Appalachian Trail
FPA Forest Protection Area
FPRT Friends of the Presidential Rail Trail
FR Forest Road (WMNF)
ft. foot, feet
GPS Global Positioning System
HC Horton Center
hr. hour(s)
in. inch(es)
jct. junction
mi. mile(s)
min. minutes(s)
MPH miles per hour
Mt. Mount

Mtn. Mountain
NHDP New Hampshire Department of Natural & Cultural Resources, Division of Parks and Recreation
Rd. Road
rev. reverse elevation
RMC Randolph Mountain Club
SSOC Sub Sig Outing Club
St. Street
USFS United States Forest Service
USGS United States Geological Survey
WMNF White Mountain National Forest
WMTC White Mountain Trail Collective
X-C cross-country
yd. yard(s)

A NOTE REGARDING MAPS

AMC offers maps to the region covered in this guide, as well as the entire White Mountain National Forest and beyond, for individual purchase. Maps are an important tool for any hiker, and as a "Ten Essentials" item, it is highly recommended that you bring one whenever you adventure outdoors. Full color, waterproof, and tear-resistant, these maps can be purchased from AMC at amcstore.outdoors.org or from your local bookstore or outdoor retailer.

ACKNOWLEDGMENTS

White Mountain Guide and this abridgment are the product of the efforts of many people.

We want to thank the dedicated staff of AMC Books, including Abigail Coyle, senior production manager, and Tim Mudie, senior books editor. Much gratitude is owed to AMC's cartographer, Larry Garland, who has ushered AMC's mapmaking into a new era and whose trail maps are justly renowned for their clarity, accuracy, and ease of use.

From Ken:
I would like to thank my family and friends, many of whom have accompanied me on numerous adventures in the mountains. My close friend and hiking partner Christine Welsh has been my trail companion for many years now, offering support, enthusiasm, a shared love of being in the woods, and an uncanny ability to spot the small details of the forest that are often missed by others.

A special thanks goes to my partner in this guidebook, Steve Smith, for bringing me onboard for the *White Mountain Guide*. I am forever grateful for the opportunity to be a part of such a prestigious publication. In addition, I am thankful to be in good company with all of the notable authors of previous editions; much of their work lives on in this edition.

Last, I would like to thank my dad, who, when I was a young child, introduced me to the neighboring town forest just down the street from our house. In reality, this forest is only a few square miles in size, but as a child it seemed like a vast wilderness and filled me with wonder. It was here where my love for being in the woods and my connection to nature was born.

From Steve:
I would like to thank my wife, Carol Smith. Without her encouragement and support, as well as her companionship on many hikes, I would never have been able to give this book the time and energy it deserved. My contributions to this edition I dedicate to her, with love and gratitude.

Many people from trail-maintaining agencies, organizations, and clubs provided invaluable information and advice. These include Dylan Alden, Cristin Bailey, Jasmine Faunce, John Marunowski, Mike Mosley, and Nate Peters from the White Mountain National Forest; Alex DeLucia, the late Andrew Norkin, and Zack Urgese from the Appalachian Mountain Club; Bob Drescher and Randy Meiklejohn from the Randolph Mountain Club; and John Dickerman from Crawford Notch State Park.

Many individual hikers provided comments, updates, and suggestions for the 31st edition. We thank Summerset Banks, Rudy Bourget, Jonathan Burroughs, Mike Cherim, Jeremy Clark, John Compton, Liam Cooney, Dr. Peter Crane, Ben English Jr., Keith Enman, Jay Espy, Georg Feichtinger, Rachel S. Flaksman, Andreas Frese, Per Frost, Andy Furey, Paul Gaitanis, Chris Garby, Cath Goodwin, Chris Gothberg, John Gutowski, Trish Herr, Chris Higgins, Sue Johnston, Michelle Kingsbury, Allen Koop, Fawn Langerman, Rachel Lewis, Raymond Merkh, Scott Monroe, Adam Mooshian, Tim Muskat, Gregory Naigles, B. K. Noonan, Amy Patenaude, Curly Perzel, Bruce Richards, Bill Robichaud, Eric Savage, John Sobetzer, Jim St. Cyr, J. R. Stockwell, Dana Thurston, Gary Tompkins, Spencer Weatherholt, and Philip Werner. The website newenglandtrailconditions.com provided much valuable information.

The current editors of *White Mountain Guide* feel connected to a long and cherished tradition handed down by a century's worth of editors and committee members. There are far too many names to list here—for a comprehensive history of the guidebook, see *White Mountain Guide: A Centennial Retrospective*, published by AMC Books—but we would like to acknowledge a few individuals whose contributions were especially noteworthy. These include Harland Perkins, who guided the book through its first three editions; Ralph Larrabee, whose meticulous editing graced the 4th through 9th editions; Howard M. Goff, guidebook committee chairman for the 11th through 21st editions, covering a period of more than 35 years; Eugene S. Daniell III, editor or co-editor for the 23rd through 28th editions, a quarter-century of service; Jonathan Burroughs, co-editor for the 25th and 26th editions, who wheeled all the trails in the guide and—together with Eugene S. Daniell III and Vera Smith (also co-editor for the 23rd edition)—made many improvements and transitioned the guidebook's editing format from its former committee structure to its current stewardship under a single editor or two co-editors; and Mike Dickerman, co-editor for the 29th edition. It was an honor for Steve to work with Gene on the 27th and 28th editions and with Mike on the 29th edition. Louis Cutter, whose maps graced the book for many decades, deserves special mention. Since its beginning in 1907, this beloved and trusted guidebook has been a truly collaborative effort, and the current editors are only building upon the outstanding body of work established by the many who have come before them.

Any errors of commission or omission are the sole responsibility of the editors.

HOW TO USE THIS BOOK

This book aims to provide complete coverage of hiking trails located in the area around Mt. Washington and along the Presidential Range, which are part of the White Mountain National Forest (WMNF). The complete *White Mountain Guide* (AMC Books, 2022) covers the entire WMNF in New Hampshire and Maine, as well as numerous trails outside the boundary of the forest—both in the Lakes region to the south and in northern New Hampshire and adjacent parts of Maine. For other regions in Maine, consult AMC's *Maine Mountain Guide,* 11th Edition, edited by Carey Kish (AMC Books, 2018). *White Mountain Guide* also covers the Appalachian Trail (AT) and its side trails from the New Hampshire–Vermont boundary at the Connecticut River to Grafton Notch in Maine, just east of the Maine–New Hampshire boundary. Hikers interested in the area south of NH 25, including the Belknap, Ossipee, Cardigan, Monadnock, and Sunapee regions, should consult AMC's *Southern New Hampshire Trail Guide,* 5th Edition, edited by Ken MacGray (AMC Books, 2021).

For convenience of use, the trails are divided into two geographic regions. More than 100 trails are covered, totaling more than 300 mi. They range from easy waterfall strolls to strenuous ridge traverses, with many options available for every level of hiker. It is our hope that the users of this book will safely enjoy many days of outdoor pleasure and healthful exercise in the beautiful White Mountains.

TRAIL DESCRIPTIONS

Each trail in this book is described individually, usually in the ascending direction. A reference to the map(s) that correspond to the trail is given in the parenthetical following each trail name. The acronym for the organization responsible for maintaining the trail is given at the beginning of each description. A typical trail description first provides an overview of the trail, including its origin, destination, and, if notable, its general character (gradient, roughness, and so on). Trailhead driving directions are then given, where appropriate, followed by concise directions for following the trail. The description notes important features, such as trail junctions, stream crossings, viewpoints, and any significant difficulties.

In cases where a hike uses a combination of trails, the hiker will need to refer to several trail descriptions, in combination with the appropriate trail map. For example, if one wanted to climb King Ravine (a rugged route to the summit of Mt. Adams), from the Appalachia parking area, the hiker would read and follow trail descriptions first for Air Line, then for Short Line, and finally for King Ravine Trail.

DISTANCES, ELEVATION GAINS, AND TIMES

The distances, elevation gains, and times that appear in the tables above trail descriptions are cumulative from the starting point listed at the head of each table. Nearly all of the trails fully described in this book have been measured with a surveyor's wheel and all have been checked with GPS; numerous mileages were adjusted for this edition using surficial distances derived from LiDAR 3D terrain models by AMC cartographer Larry Garland. Minor inconsistencies sometimes occur when measured distances are rounded, and the distances given often differ from those on trail signs. Elevation gains are given for the reverse direction only when these gains are 50 ft. or more; these gains are not cumulative and apply only to the interval between the current entry and the previous one. Reverse elevation gains are not given for trails that have summaries in both directions.

Time is given as hours and minutes, so 1:30 should be read as "one hour and thirty minutes."

The following example shows users how to read the tables at the beginning of trail descriptions.

BOOT SPUR LINK (MAP 1: F9)			
From Tuckerman Ravine Trail (3,875 ft. [*elevation*]) to:			
Boott Spur Trail (4,650 ft.)	0.6 mi.	850 ft. (rev. 50 ft.)	0:45
elevation	*distance*	*elevation gain* *(reverse elevation gain)*	*time* *[hr: min]*

Elevation gains are estimated and rounded to the nearest 50 ft.; in some places, such as where several minor ups and downs are traversed, they are only roughly accurate. U.S. Geological Survey (USGS) maps are used as the basis for all such information, except for the area covered by Bradford Washburn's map of the Presidential Range, where that map supersedes the USGS maps. Elevations for summits, roadside trailheads, backcountry facilities, and some selected features and trail junctions in this edition have been revised based on recently released LiDAR data, as interpreted by AMC cartographer Larry Garland. LiDAR (Light Detection and Ranging) uses laser light pulses from airborne sensors to collect very dense and accurate information about surface characteristics of a regional landscape. Current technology allows LiDAR measurements to be accurate to approximately 4 to 8 in. of elevation. With a nominal pulse density of 2 or more laser pulses per square meter, the data are aggregated to produce an assigned elevation for ground areas that are typically less than a square meter in size. Waveform and intensity values of each laser-pulse return can differentiate between vegetation, buildings, cars, water, and bare earth; summit elevations used in this guide are based on bare earth values.

The vast majority of LiDAR-derived summit elevations are within 20 ft. of pre-LiDAR elevations. Thus, estimated hiking times and elevation gains/losses are not significantly affected by these revisions. Most trail junctions and non-summit elevations (for example, viewpoints, cols, and other features) have not been reevaluated in this edition. Elevations of places are estimated as closely as possible when not given precisely by USGS source maps or updated LiDAR data.

No reliable method exists for predicting how much time a hiker or group of hikers will take to complete a particular hike on a particular day. The factors that influence the speed of an individual hiker or hiking group are simply too numerous and too complex. Most hikers will observe that individual speed varies from day to day, often by a significant amount, depending on a variety of factors, many of which—such as fatigue, weight of pack, and weather conditions—are fairly easy to identify. Also, a given segment of trail will usually require more time at the end of a strenuous day compared with what it might require if encountered at the start of the day.

To give hikers a rough basis for planning, however, estimated times have been calculated for this book by allowing 30 min. for each mile of distance or 1,000 ft. of climbing. These are known as "book times." No attempt has been made to adjust these times for the difficulties of specific trails. These times may be inadequate for steep or rough trails, for hikers with heavy packs, or for large groups, particularly those including inexperienced hikers.

Average descent times vary even more; the hiker's agility, the condition of the hiker's knees, and the roughness of the trail are the principal factors. Times for descending are given in this book only for segments of ridge crest trails that have substantial descents in both directions. In winter, times are even less predictable: on a snow-packed trail, travel may be faster than in summer, but with heavy packs or in deep snow it may take two or three times the summer estimate.

MAPS AND NAVIGATION

Hikers should always carry a map and compass and, if desired, a Global Positioning System (GPS) unit, and carefully keep track of their approximate location on the map. The maps that correspond to the areas .included with this guide are topographic maps (maps with the shape of the terrain represented by contour lines). Every mile of trail on these maps was hiked and electronically recorded with GPS technology, which was then processed and edited using GIS (geographic information system) technology. The resulting maps accurately depict trail locations. (Many previous maps, including USGS quadrangle maps, relied on less precise techniques to determine a trail's location.) They provide complete coverage of the WMNF, with a contour interval of 100 ft. These maps (except Map 1, Presidential Range, which has a larger scale for its dense trail network) are designed at the same size and scale, allowing the user to easily read from one map to the next. Latitude and longitude and Universal Transverse Mercator (UTM) grid coordinates are included on the map sheets to facilitate the use of GPS units in the field. Although the original GPS data are quite precise, certain features (including roads, streams, and trails) may have been digitized using older, less accurate methods and/or exaggerated to show their proper relationships at map scale.

Waterproof versions of these maps can be purchased at AMC's website (amcstore.outdoors.org), bookstores, many outdoor equipment stores, and AMC's information centers in Pinkham Notch and Crawford Notch. Other trail maps for specific areas are mentioned in the individual sections of this guide. These are particularly useful in places with extensive trail systems.

Maps with more topographic detail are available from the USGS. These maps are published in rectangles of several standard sizes called quadrangles ("quads"). All areas in the regions included in this guidebook are covered by detailed 7.5-min. quads, some of which are in metric format. Most of the 7.5-min. quads were produced in the 1980s and 1990s. Although topography on these maps is excellent (with 40- or 20-ft. contours), the locations of some trails are shown inaccurately, and many other trails are not shown at all. These maps can be obtained at various local outlets and from the USGS (888-ASK-USGS; usgsstore@usgs.gov; store.usgs.gov). Index maps showing the available USGS quads in any state and an informative pamphlet titled *Topographic Maps* are available free from the USGS upon request. The USGS quads for all of New England are also available through many online sources. The WMNF is also covered by two of National Geographic's Trails Illustrated maps: *White Mountain National Forest West* (no. 740) and *White Mountain National Forest East* (no. 741), which were produced in partnership with AMC.

A baseplate compass (a circular, liquid-filled compass that turns on a rectangular base made of clear plastic) is well suited for use by hikers. Set such a compass to the bearing you want to follow, and then it is simply a matter of keeping the compass needle aligned to north and following the arrow on the base. Compass directions given in the text are based on true north instead of magnetic north, unless otherwise specified. Magnetic north changes over time, but currently there is a deviation (usually called declination) of 14 to 15 degrees between true north and magnetic north in the White Mountains. This means true north will be about 15 degrees to the right of (clockwise from) the compass's north needle. If you take a bearing from a map, you should add 15 degrees to the bearing when you set your compass. On the maps included with this guide, the black lines that run from bottom to top are aligned with true north and south. The compass directions given in the text are also based on true north rather than magnetic north. For more instruction on how to use a compass and how to orient a compass to a map, refer to *AMC's Mountain Skills Manual*, by Christian Bisson and Jamie Hannon (AMC Books, 2017), available at amcstore.outdoors.org.

GPS units have become increasingly popular with hikers. These can be loaded with various versions of topographic maps. When used in conjunction with a printed map and a compass, a GPS unit can be a very useful tool in the woods, but it is not a satisfactory substitute for a map and a compass. GPS reception can be poor in deep valleys and under heavy foliage, and units may be subject to damage or battery failure. If you are going to use a GPS unit, we recommend preparing a list of coordinates for several useful landmarks before leaving for the trail and bringing a set of extra batteries. It is important to practice with a GPS unit to become familiar with its features before setting off on a trip.

In recent years, there has been a significant rise in the usage of smartphone apps for navigation. While these apps are popular and can be useful in certain situations, they should not be solely relied on. Much of the information contained within them is crowdsourced—submitted by hikers and not professional map-makers—and can often be inaccurate. Abandoned trails and trails leading into private land may be shown. Users can also create their own names for routes that don't actually exist in real life—one example being "Mt. Chocorua Loop Trail." This can create a problem not only for hikers looking for such a route but also for search-and-rescue teams who may need to locate a lost or injured hiker. The editors of this guide recommend using smartphone apps only to supplement an actual printed map of the area where you will be hiking and a detailed description of the route from this guidebook.

AMC offers a number of its guidebook maps in digital format on the AvenzaMaps platform. The map images are the same as the printed versions and contain the same professionally vetted content. The AvenzaMap smartphone app is free, and each AMC map can be downloaded for a modest charge. Please visit outdoors.org/maps or scan the QR code at right for more information.

INTRODUCTION

A BRIEF HISTORY OF THE WHITE MOUNTAINS

The White Mountains are a range rich in history, adding great interest to climbs in the high peaks. For centuries, American Indians have inhabited parts of the White Mountain region, primarily in valleys around the fringes of the peaks. It is thought that Paleoindian people arrived in the White Mountain region about 12,500 years ago. Driven by belief that evil spirits inhabited the mountains, Abenaki tribes who lived here at the time seldom visited the summits. Many White Mountain place names have Abenaki origins, and several mountains—including one 4,000-footer, Mt. Passaconaway—were named in honor of Abenaki chiefs.

White settlers arrived in the late 1700s and early 1800s and began occupying valleys around the mountains. The most famous family was perhaps the Crawfords, who established inns at Crawford Notch and essentially founded the tourist industry in the White Mountains. Many of the first recreational hikers in the region were lured by the guide service offered by the Crawfords and the trails they established on the Presidential Range. Small hostelries were also established in other areas of the White Mountains.

European colonists' exploration of the mountains began with Darby Field's bold ascent of Mt. Washington in 1642, aided by two American Indian guides. Numerous scientific explorations were conducted, primarily in the Presidential Range, in the late 1700s and early 1800s, including the notable Belknap-Cutler expedition in 1784, the first expedition to make scientific observations on Mt. Washington; it is likely that this group gave the mountain its name. Botanists poked into many nooks and crannies in the 1820s and 1830s, and several Presidential Range features are named after them.

The coming of the railroads and the construction of numerous hotels, many of the "grand" variety, launched the "golden era" of White Mountain tourism in the middle and late 1800s. Writers such as Thomas Starr King and Moses Sweetser inspired visitors to get out and explore what the mountains had to offer. Trails and bridle paths were built on several mountains, and in places such as Waterville Valley, Wonalancet, Randolph, and Shelburne, entire networks of hiking paths were laid out in the areas surrounding local inns. This golden era also resulted in a boom of exploration and trail-building. The founding of the Appalachian Mountain Club in 1876 fostered additional probing into remote corners of the White Mountains, along with another flurry of trail-building. By century's end, hundreds of miles of paths had been cut, most notably on the Northern Presidentials, by such trailblazers as J. Rayner Edmands (known for his comfortably graded paths), Eugene B. Cook, William H. Peek, and

William G. Nowell. In 1907, AMC published its first guide to the trails of the White Mountains, and that has been the standard-bearer ever since.

Logging in the White Mountains also exploded from the 1870s into the 1920s and 1930s, led by timber barons such as Lincoln's infamous James Everell Henry, who constructed logging railroads into remote corners of the mountains; many these old grades serve as hiking trails today. Several trails pass the sites of old logging camps; all artifacts are protected by law and should not be removed or disturbed. Significant fires resulted from clear-cutting, the worst of which occurred in 1903.

In response to abusive logging and the destructive fires that followed, conservation groups, led by the Society for the Protection of New Hampshire Forests, successfully lobbied Congress to pass the Weeks Act in 1911, authorizing the creation of National Forests in the East. The U.S. Forest Service soon acquired several hundred thousand acres for the White Mountain National Forest (WMNF). Today the WMNF spreads across some 796,000 acres. These lands are managed under the multiple use concept for recreation, water, timber, wildlife, and other uses. Six Wilderness Areas totaling 149,500 acres are left in an undisturbed state. About 45 percent of the WMNF is open to timber harvesting on a sustainable basis.

The years from about 1915 to the mid-1930s brought the expansion and unification of the White Mountains trail system and the development of the chain of AMC huts. Four AMC trail architects—Nathaniel L. Goodrich, Paul R. Jenks, Charles W. Blood, and Karl P. Harrington—were key figures in this era, along with the legendary hut system manager Joe Dodge.

In the late 1960s and early 1970s, a tremendous surge in hiking and backpacking brought intense pressure to bear on trails and backcountry facilities, forcing land managers to create new methods of coping with heavy use. The continued popularity of hiking and the wealth of information available on the internet into the twenty-first century has brought an increasing focus on trail maintenance. It has also fostered the development of a leave-no-trace wilderness ethic, encouraging hikers to tread lightly on the land.

For a comprehensive and fascinating history of hiking in the White Mountains and in the Northeast in general, we highly recommend Laura and Guy Waterman's Forest and Crag (SUNY Press, 2019). Find stories of the early trail builders in Mike Dickerman's *White Mountains Hiking History* (History Press, 2013). For an interesting history of the White Mountains with an environmental angle, see Christopher Johnson's *This Grand & Magnificent Place* (University Press of New England, 2006). A good general history of the region is Randall H. Bennett's *The White Mountains: Alps of New England* (Arcadia Publishing, 2003). A wealth of historical information on the White Mountains, including many vintage maps and photos, is on the website whitemountainhistory.org.

USE OF THE WHITE MOUNTAIN NATIONAL FOREST

Most of the higher peaks of the White Mountains are within the White Mountain National Forest (WMNF), which was authorized under the Weeks Act (1911) and now comprises roughly 796,000 acres, about 47,000 in Maine and the rest in New Hampshire. This is not a national park, but rather a national forest; parks are established primarily for preservation and recreation, whereas national forests are managed for multiple uses. In the administration of national forests, the following objectives are considered: recreation management, timber production, watershed protection, and wildlife habitat management. About 45 percent of the WMNF is open to timber harvesting on a carefully controlled basis. The boundaries of the WMNF are usually marked wherever they cross roads or trails, typically by red-painted corner posts and blazes. Hunting and fishing are permitted in the WMNF under state laws; state licenses are required. Organized groups, including those sponsored by nonprofit organizations, must apply for an outfitter-guide permit if they conduct trips on WMNF land for which they charge a fee; contact any WMNF office for details.

Much information about the WMNF has been published by the USFS and is available free of charge at the forest supervisor's office in Campton, New Hampshire; at ranger district offices; and at other information centers.

Camping is restricted in many areas under the Forest Protection Area program to protect vulnerable areas from damage. To preserve the rare alpine plants of the Presidential Range and other significant ecosystems within the entire WMNF, rules prohibit the removal of any tree, shrub, or plant without written permission. Federal law also protects cultural sites and artifacts (such as those found at sites of old logging camps) on public lands. If you discover such remains, please leave them undisturbed; it is illegal to remove them from the WMNF.

Pets are allowed on WMNF trails; however, be sure to control your pet so it won't be a nuisance to other hikers and to clean up after your pet along the trail.

AMC earnestly requests that those who use trails, shelters, and campsites heed the rules (especially those having to do with camping) of the WMNF and the New Hampshire Department of Natural and Cultural Resources, Division of Parks and Recreation. New trails may not be cut in the WMNF without the approval of the forest supervisor or elsewhere without the consent of the landowners and definite formal provision for maintenance.

Some trails in this guide cross private land, and the same consideration and respect should be shown to private landowners; trails can be closed forever if a landowner objects to the way the public treats the land.

WILDERNESS AND SCENIC AREAS IN THE WMNF

The initial National Wilderness Preservation System, which included the Great Gulf Wilderness, was established in 1964 with passage of the Wilderness Act. Since then, the Presidential Range–Dry River, Pemigewasset, Sandwich Range, Caribou–Speckled Mtn., and Wild River Wilderness Areas in the WMNF have been added to the system, bringing the WMNF's total Wilderness base to 149,500 acres, which is almost 19 percent of WMNF's total acreage. Regulations for these areas prohibit logging, road building, and using motorized equipment or mechanical transport, including bicycles. New Wilderness Areas are established by acts of Congress, with USFS recommendations providing critical input.

Management of these areas, in accordance with guidelines contained in the Wilderness Act, is entrusted to the USFS. Most important is the protection of the natural environment, but the USFS is also charged with preserving the opportunity for visitors to enjoy "solitude and challenge." For example, "structures for user convenience," such as shelters, are not permitted in Wilderness Areas. In general, visitors to Wilderness Areas should look forward to a rougher, wilder, more primitive experience than in other parts of the WMNF and should expect USFS regulations to emphasize the preservation of Wilderness qualities, even at substantial inconvenience to hikers. As a consequence, there are no mileages on signs and few, if any, blazes; "easy-over, easy-under" blown-down trees, or blowdowns, may be intentionally left in place to add to the wild character of the trail. Hiking and camping group size is limited to ten people in Wilderness Areas; specific camping and fire regulations vary by area. Wilderness regulations also prohibit storing equipment, personal property, or supplies, including geocaching and letter boxing.

The USFS has also established nine Scenic Areas in the WMNF to preserve lands of outstanding or rare natural beauty: Gibbs Brook, Greeley Ponds, Pinkham Notch, Lafayette Brook, Rocky Gorge, Lincoln Woods, Sawyer Pond, Mt. Chocorua, and Snyder Brook. Additionally, three Research Natural Areas—the Alpine Garden, the Bowl, and Nancy Brook—have been established as locations where "natural processes will predominate" and recreation use will be incidental.

PARKING FEES AND HIKER SHUTTLE

When parking at established WMNF trailhead parking sites with a posted fee sign ("Parked Vehicles Must Display a Recreation Pass"), hikers must display a WMNF Recreation Pass on their windshield or dashboard. If a

Recreation Pass is required (as of 2024), it is noted in this guide in the trailhead information in the individual trail description. Annual Recreation Passes for one car ($30 in 2024) or two cars ($40 in 2024) are available at WMNF ranger offices, information centers, and outdoor retail stores, as well as at AMC's information centers in Pinkham Notch and Crawford Notch. Visit the WMNF website (fs.usda.gov/whitemountain) for details. Daily parking passes ($5 in 2024) are available at trailheads where Recreation Passes are required. Almost all of the proceeds from these passes go toward improvements to the WMNF. If there is no posted fee sign at a WMNF trailhead, a Recreation Pass is not required. The Recreation Pass is not required at trailheads outside the WMNF.

Throughout the summer and on fall weekends, AMC offers a hiker shuttle service between Pinkham Notch Visitor Center, Highland Center at Crawford Notch, and several major trailheads, including those serving popular routes to the AMC huts. (The shuttle route extends into Lincoln, New Hampshire, to connect with bus service from Boston.) For trips beginning and ending at different trailheads, many hikers leave their cars at the final trailhead and take the shuttle to their starting trailhead. Reservations are strongly recommended, and a fee is charged. For information, contact AMC's reservations office (603-466-2727) or visit AMC's website (outdoors.org/shuttle).

A NOTE ON PARKING

Use of hiking trails in the White Mountains has increased dramatically over the last several years. Parking areas for popular trails fill up quickly on fine days in summer and fall, and even in winter. At some trailheads, roadside parking is prohibited once the designated lot fills up. Where roadside parking is permitted, vehicles must be parked completely off the traveled roadway. Other trailheads are on or near private property, where visitors should take great care not to block driveways or other access points. If planning to hike at one of the more popular trailheads, you should have a backup hike in mind in case the trailhead parking is full.

Parking information is given in the individual trail descriptions and, in a few instances for major trailheads, in the section introduction. Information about restroom availability and winter plowing and access is given, if known. Some restroom facilities may be seasonal and not available in winter, even if the trailhead is plowed.

APPALACHIAN TRAIL

With the passage of the National Trails System Act by Congress on October 2, 1968, the AT became the first federally protected footpath in the country and was officially designated the Appalachian National Scenic Trail. Under this act, the AT is administered primarily as a footpath by the Department of the Interior in consultation with the Department of Agriculture and representatives of the states through which the AT passes.

The white-blazed footpath runs more than 2,000 mi., from Springer Mtn. in Georgia to Katahdin in Maine. It traverses the White Mountains for about 160 mi. in a southwest to northeast direction, from Hanover, New Hampshire, on the New Hampshire–Vermont border in the Connecticut River valley, to Grafton Notch, a short distance into Maine from the Maine–New Hampshire border. The AT traverses many of the major peaks and ranges of the White Mountains.

Many of the trails that make up the AT in the White Mountains are described in this book. In each section of this guide, the AT's route is described in a separate paragraph in the section introduction.

TRIP PLANNING, WEATHER, AND SAFETY

The typical hiking season runs approximately from Memorial Day to mid-October. In some years, ice or snowdrifts may remain at higher elevations until the early part of June and possibly later in some of the major ravines, on north-facing slopes, and in other sheltered places, such as Mahoosuc Notch. Conditions can vary greatly from year to year and place to place. See Winter Considerations, p. xxviii for more information.

Winter-like conditions can occur above treeline in any month of the year. Keep in mind that air temperature will drop about 3 degrees Fahrenheit with each 1,000 ft. of elevation gain, without factoring in the impact of windchill. As a result, even on sunny days in midsummer, hikers above treeline should always be prepared for cold weather with at least a wool or synthetic fleece jacket or sweater, a hat, gloves, and a wind parka, which will give comfort on sunny but cool days and protection against sudden storms. Spring and fall are particularly difficult seasons in the mountains because the weather may be pleasant in the valleys but brutal on the summits and ridges. Many serious incidents in the mountains occur in spring and fall, when hikers deceived by mild conditions at home or even at trailheads find themselves facing unanticipated and severe—perhaps even life-threatening—hazards once on the trail.

Plan your trip schedule with safety in mind. Consider the strength of your party and the general strenuousness of the trip: the overall distance, the amount of climbing, and the roughness of the terrain. Get a weather report, but be aware that most forecasts are not intended to apply to the mountain region; a day that is sunny and pleasant in the lowlands may well be inclement in the mountains. The National Weather Service (NWS) in Gray, Maine, issues a recreational forecast for the White Mountain region's valleys and higher summits and broadcasts it on its shortwave radio station each morning (162.500 MHz for the Mt. Washington station; 162.550 MHz for the Holderness station). The forecast can be viewed on the NWS website (weather.gov/gyx); for the mountain forecast, choose Recreational Forecast from the menu. Both a Higher Summits Forecast and a Mt. Washington Valley Forecast from the Mt. Washington Observatory are posted at Pinkham Notch Visitor Center each morning. These are also available on the websites of both AMC (outdoors.org) and the Mt. Washington Observatory (mountwashington.org) and via the observatory's weather phone (603-356-2137, ext. 1; hikers can also send a text message to this number with the word "weather" to get the current weather conditions, or the word "forecast" to receive an abbreviated version of the Higher Summits Forecast). Another mountain weather resource is the Recreational Forecast from the Fairbanks Museum in St. Johnsbury, Vermont (fairbanksmuseum.org).

Plan to finish your hike with daylight to spare, and remember that days grow shorter rapidly in late summer and fall. Hiking after dark, even with flashlights or headlamps (which frequently fail), makes finding trails more difficult and crossing streams hazardous. Let someone else know where you will be hiking, and if you are with a group, make sure that hikers, especially inexperienced ones, don't get separated from the group. Learn best practices for leaving your trip plans with a third party in *AMC's Mountain Skills Manual*.

Many unpaved roads are not passable until about Memorial Day, and from November to May, the WMNF locks the gates to many of its roads that are open during the summer season. (Current road conditions are listed on the WMNF Facebook page facebook.com/WhiteMountainNF). The website TrailsNH (trailsnh.com) also provides a crowdsourced list of seasonal road closures provided by hikers in the field. Many trips are much longer when the roads are not open.

STORM DAMAGE TO TRAILS AND ROADS

Two major storms in recent years—Tropical Storm Irene in August 2011 and the "Halloween storm" in October 2017—caused sudden and extensive flooding in many areas of the White Mountains. Multiple trails and roads located along streams suffered severe damage in the form of washouts, eroded banks, altered stream locations, landslides, and fallen trees. Several trail bridges were washed away or badly damaged. In the wake of these storms, several trails and roads were found to be impassable and were closed to all use by the USFS. Since then, many trails and roads have been repaired (and where necessary relocated), and several bridges have been replaced. Some washed-out areas still require caution; these locations are mentioned in individual trail descriptions.

HIKESAFE HIKER RESPONSIBILITY CODE

You are responsible for yourself, so be prepared:

1. **With knowledge and gear.** Become self-reliant by learning about the terrain, conditions, local weather, and your equipment before you start.
2. **To leave your plans.** Tell someone where you are going, the trails you are hiking, when you will return, and your emergency plans.
3. **To stay together.** When you start as a group, hike as a group, end as a group. Pace your hike to the slowest person.
4. **To turn back.** Weather changes quickly in the mountains. Fatigue and unexpected conditions can also affect your hike. Know your limitations and when to postpone your hike. The mountains will be there another day.
5. **For emergencies.** Even if you are headed out for just an hour, an injury, severe weather, or a wrong turn could become life threatening. Don't assume you will be rescued; know how to rescue yourself.
6. **To share the hiker code with others.** HikeSafe: It's Your Responsibility. The Hiker Responsibility Code was developed and is endorsed by the WMNF and New Hampshire Fish and Game. For more information, visit hikesafe.com. Hikers in the White Mountains are encouraged to purchase a voluntary hikeSafe Card ($25 individual, $35 family in 2024) from New Hampshire Fish and Game at wildlife.state.nh.us/safe. *Every purchase supports New Hampshire Fish and Game search-and-rescue efforts.* The card is valuable for anyone hiking, paddling, cross-country skiing, or engaging in other outdoor recreation. People who obtain the cards are not liable to repay rescue costs if they need to be rescued. An individual may still be liable for response expenses if the need for the emergency response was created by actions that were negligent, as defined by criteria set forth by legislation (RSA 206:26-bb).

FOLLOWING TRAILS

In general, trails are maintained to provide a clear pathway while protecting the environment by minimizing erosion and other damage. Some trails may offer rough and difficult passage. Trails in officially designated Wilderness Areas, by policy, are managed to provide a more primitive experience. As a result, they are maintained to a lesser degree, are sparsely marked, and have few signs. Hikers entering Wilderness Areas must be prepared to make a greater effort to follow their chosen route.

Most hiking trails not in Wilderness Areas are marked by paint on trees or rocks, known as blazes, although a few have only ax notches cut into trees. The trails that compose the AT through the White Mountains are marked with vertical, rectangular, white-paint blazes. Side paths off the AT are usually marked with blue paint. Other trails are marked in different colors, the most popular being yellow, which is used on most trails in the WMNF that are not part of the AT system. Blazing along trails varies greatly in frequency—some trails are sparsely marked—and on other trails many of the blazes are faded. Above timberline, cairns (piles of rocks) mark the trails.

Below treeline, the treadway is usually visible except when covered by snow or fallen leaves. In winter, trail blazes and signs at trailheads and intersections are often obscured by snow. Trails following or crossing logging roads require special care at intersections to distinguish the trail from diverging roads, particularly because blazing is usually sparse where the trail follows the road. Around shelters or campsites, beaten paths may lead in all directions, so watch for signs and paint blazes.

Hikers should be aware that some trails in this book (as noted in descriptions) are more difficult to follow than others: The presence of signs and blazes varies—some trails are too new to have a well-beaten treadway; others have received very little use. Trails may not be cleared of fallen trees and brush until late summer, and not all trails are cleared every year. Inexperienced hikers should avoid trails that are described as being difficult to follow, and all hikers should observe and follow trail markings carefully.

Although trails vary greatly in the amount of use they receive and the ease with which they usually can be followed, almost any trail might be closed unexpectedly or suddenly become obscure or hazardous under certain conditions. Trails can be rerouted, abandoned, or closed by landowners. Signs are stolen or fall from their posts. Storms may cause blowdowns or landslides, which can obliterate a trail for an entire hiking season or longer. Logging operations can cover trails with slash and add a bewildering network of new roads.

Momentary inattention to trail markers—particularly arrows at sharp turns or signs at junctions—or misinterpretation of signs or guidebook descriptions can cause hikers to become separated from all but the most heavily traveled paths or can lead them into what may be a much longer or more difficult route. Please remember that this book is an aid to planning, not a substitute for observation and judgment. All trail-maintaining organizations, including AMC, reserve the right to discontinue any trail without notice and expressly disclaim any legal responsibility for the condition of any trail.

IF YOU'RE LOST

If you lose a trail, it is usually best to backtrack right away to the last marker seen and look again from there; this will be much easier if you keep track of where and how long ago you saw the most recent blaze. Many cases in which a person has become lost for any length of time involve panic and aimless wandering, so the proper order of operations is to stop and take a break, make an inventory of useful information, decide on a course of action, and stick to it. (The caution against allowing inexperienced persons to become separated from a group should be emphasized here because they are most likely to panic and wander aimlessly. Make sure that all party members are familiar with the route of the trip and the names of the trails to be used, so that if anyone does become separated, the lost member will have some prospect of rejoining the group.)

Even when the trail cannot immediately be found, it is a serious but not desperate situation. If you have carefully tracked your location on the map, you usually will be able to find a nearby stream, trail, or road to which a compass course may be followed. Most distances are short enough (except in the North Country, north of NH 110) that it is possible, in the absence of alternatives, to reach a highway in half a day, or at most in a whole day, simply by going downhill, carefully avoiding any dangerous cliffs, until you come upon a river or brook. Then follow the stream downward.

WHAT TO CARRY AND WEAR

Adequate equipment for a hike in the New Hampshire hills and forests varies greatly, depending on the length of the trip and the difficulty of getting to the nearest trailhead if trouble arises. For even short day hikes, AMC advocates preparedness. If you are going above treeline or on an exposed ridge and are not inclined to turn back at the first sign of questionable weather, you will need a pack filled with plenty of warm clothing and food for emergency use, along with the usual gear.

AMC recommends always carrying the ten essentials:

- guidebook (or pages of it or photographs of pages) and maps; don't rely on your phone or other electronics in the wilderness
- waterproof matches/fire starter
- compass
- first-aid and repair kits
- warm clothing, including hat and mittens

- whistle
- rain/wind gear
- extra food (high-energy snacks) and water (3 liters per hiker, per day; always treat water sourced in the woods before drinking)
- pocketknife or multitool
- flashlight or headlamp, with extra batteries and a spare bulb

You might also bring:

- watch
- personal medications
- nylon cord
- trash bag

- toilet paper
- extra shirts
- sunscreen and sunglasses or hat
- space blanket or bivy sack

Wear comfortable, broken-in hiking boots. Lightweight boots, which are sturdier than sneakers, provide ankle support on rough and rocky trails, of which there are an ample supply in the White Mountains. Two pairs of socks are recommended: a lightweight inner pair and a heavier outer pair that is at least partly wool. Adjustable trekking poles offer many advantages to hikers, especially on descents, traverses, and stream crossings.

Jeans, sweatshirts, and other cotton clothes are not recommended; once these become wet, they dry very slowly. In adverse weather conditions, they seriously drain a cold and tired hiker's heat reserves. Thus, the hiker's maxim "cotton kills." Synthetics and wool are superior materials for hiking apparel, especially for people who are planning to travel in adverse conditions, to remote places, or above treeline. Wool keeps much of its insulating value even when wet, and it (or one of several modern synthetic materials) is indispensable for hikers who want to visit places from which returning to civilization might require substantial time and effort if conditions turn bad. Hats, gloves, and other such gear provide safety in adverse conditions, and they allow one to enjoy the summits in comfort on crisp, clear days when the views are particularly fine. For more on essential clothing and gear, see *AMC's Mountain Skills Manual*.

HIKING WITH KIDS

Many trails in this book are suitable for hiking with children. It is important to choose a hike that suits the age, fitness, and agility of your child and to bring adequate gear, food, and water. *AMC's Best Day Hikes in the White Mountains*, 4th Edition, by Robert N. Buchsbaum (AMC Books, 2022), is an excellent resource for hiking with kids in the White Mountains. See also *Outdoors with Kids: Maine, New Hampshire, and Vermont*, by Ethan Hipple and Yemaya St. Clair (AMC Books, 2014). A wealth of additional information on family hiking is available at outdoors.org.

HIKING WITH DOGS

Many hikers enjoy the companionship of their dogs on the trail. Out of consideration for other hikers, please keep your dog under voice control at all times and on a leash, if necessary. Due to the fragile vegetation, dogs should be leashed in the alpine zone. Carry out or bury dog waste, and do not leave waste bags on the trail or at the trailhead. Choose a hike that matches your dog's fitness, age, and agility. Some trails—such as those with ladders or difficult boulder or ledge scrambling—are not suitable for dogs. The sharp rocks above treeline on the Presidential Range are extremely rough on a dog's paws. Be sure your dog has adequate water to drink, especially on hot summer days. Recommended hikes for dogs can be found in *AMC's Best Day Hikes in the White Mountains*, 4th Edition, by Robert N. Buchsbaum (AMC Books, 2022) and in *Best Hikes with Dogs: New Hampshire & Vermont*, by Lisa Densmore (Mountaineers Books, 2005). For more advice on hiking with kids and with dogs, see *AMC's Mountain Skills Manual.*

CAMPING

Those who camp overnight in the backcountry tend to have more of an impact on the land than day-hikers do. Backpacking hikers should take great care to minimize their effect on the mountains by practicing low-impact camping. If available on your chosen trip route, the best alternative is to use formally designated campsites to concentrate impact and to minimize damage to vegetation. Many popular campsites and shelters have caretakers. In other areas, choose previously established campsites to minimize the impact caused by the creation and proliferation of new campsites.

When selecting an established campsite, choose one that is farther from surface water to protect the water quality for future and downstream users. Several websites are devoted to Leave No Trace principles (see p. xxxvii).

More than 50 backcountry shelters and tentsites are in the White Mountain area, open on a first-come-first-serve basis. Some sites have summer caretakers who provide trail and shelter maintenance, educate hikers on low-impact camping methods, and oversee the environmentally sound disposal of human waste. An overnight fee is charged at these sites to help defray expenses. Some sites have shelters, others (called "tentsites") have only tent platforms or earthen pads, and some (called "campsites") have both. Shelters are intended as overnight accommodations for persons carrying their own bedding and cooking supplies. The more popular shelters are often full, so be prepared to camp at a legal site off-trail with tents or tarps. Make yourself aware of regulations and restrictions before your trip. Information on established backcountry shelters and tentsites and Forest Protection Areas is given in the introduction to each section in this guide.

AMC manages 14 backcountry sites in the White Mountains (outdoors .org/backcountry-campsites) and four more on the western section of Grafton Loop Trail. In addition to shelters, tent platforms, or tent pads, all AMC sites have bear boxes for food protection. Each year, these sites host an average of 20,000 overnight visitors. Nine of the most popular sites see a combined average of 11,000 visitors in the summer months. More than one-third of those visitors are part of an organized group. The heavy use of these sites can lead to the improper disposal of human waste, erosion of trails, and trampling of vegetation—all of which have an impact on the forest. AMC requires notification from large groups at least two weeks in advance concerning the sites they plan to use. If you are planning a group trip with six or more people during the summer or fall season, visit AMC's website for notification forms and updates on group availability at outdoors.org/backcountry-campsites-form.

If you camp away from established sites, look for a spot more than 200 ft. from the trail and from any surface water, and observe USFS camping regulations for the area. Bring all needed shelter, including whatever poles, stakes, ground insulation, and cords are required. Do not cut boughs or branches for bedding or firewood or young trees for poles. Avoid clearing vegetation, and never make a ditch around the tent. Wash your dishes and yourself 200 ft. away from streams, ponds, and springs. Bury human waste at least 200 ft. from the trail, the campsite, and any water sources. Heed the rules of neatness, sanitation, and fire prevention and carry out everything—food, paper, glass, cans—that you carry in. Do not keep food in your tent; hang food from a tree—use a high, sturdy branch at least 10 ft. off the ground and 4 ft. from the tree trunk—or store it in a bear canister to protect it from raccoons and bears.

In some popular camping areas, a "human browse line," where people have gathered firewood during the years, is quite evident: limbs are gone from trees, the ground is devoid of dead wood, and vegetation has been trampled. Please refrain from exacerbating this problem. The use of portable stoves is often mandatory in popular areas and is encouraged everywhere to prevent damage to vegetation. Do not make wood campfires unless ample dead and downed wood is available near your site and you are certain that fires are legal in the area. Where fires are allowed, clear a space at least 5 ft. in radius of all flammable material, down to the mineral soil, before you begin to build your fire. Under no circumstances should you leave a fire unattended. All fires must be completely extinguished with earth or water before you leave a campsite, even temporarily. Restore the campfire site to as natural an appearance as possible (unless using a preexisting fire ring) when you are ready to move on.

CAMPING REGULATIONS

Trailside camping is allowed only within the WMNF, with a few limited exceptions, such as the established campsites on the AT. Camping and campfires are not permitted in New Hampshire state parks except in campgrounds. The state laws of Maine and New Hampshire require that permission be obtained from the owner to camp on private land and that permits be obtained to build campfires anywhere outside the WMNF in the region covered by this guide, except at officially designated campsites.

Overnight camping is permitted in almost all of the WMNF. The USFS has adopted regulations for numerous areas in the WMNF that are threatened by overuse and misuse. The objective of the Forest Protection Area (FPA) program, formerly called the Restricted Use Area program, is to disperse use so that people can enjoy themselves in a clean and attractive environment without causing deterioration of natural resources. Because hikers and backpackers have cooperated with FPA rules, many areas once designated as FPAs have recovered and are no longer under formal restriction; however, common sense and self-imposed regulation are still necessary to prevent damage.

Stated briefly, the 2024 FPA rules prohibit camping (except on 2 ft. or more of snow, but not on frozen bodies of water) and wood or charcoal fires above timberline (where trees are less than 8 ft. in height); within 0.25 mi. of any trailhead, hut, shelter, developed tentsite, cabin, picnic area, developed day-use site, or campground; within certain special areas; or within a specified distance of certain roads, trails, bodies of water, and other locations, except at designated sites.

These restrictions are in effect year-round. This guide provides information on FPAs as of 2024 in each relevant section. Signs are usually posted where trails enter and leave FPAs. Because the list of restricted areas may change from year to year, hikers should seek current information from the WMNF headquarters in Campton, New Hampshire; from AMC's Pinkham Notch Visitor Center; or from any ranger district office. A brochure outlining the current backcountry camping rules is available at WMNF ranger stations, information centers, and fs.usda.gov/whitemountain.

ROADSIDE CAMPGROUNDS

The WMNF operates a number of roadside campgrounds with limited facilities; fees are charged, and most of these campgrounds are managed by private concessionaires. Consult the WMNF offices for details or call the campground hotline at 877-444-6777. Many of these campgrounds are full on summer weekends. Reservations for sites at some WMNF campgrounds can be made through the National Recreation Reservation Service. Several New Hampshire state parks also have campgrounds located conveniently for hikers in the White Mountains, and reservations can be made at all of these. Literature on state parks and state and private campgrounds is available at New Hampshire highway rest areas. (*Note*: Visitors are not permitted to bring out-of-state firewood to any of the campgrounds, due to the risk of the spread of invasive insects. Violators are subject to warnings, tickets, and fines.)

FIRE REGULATIONS

Campfire permits are no longer required in the WMNF, but hikers who build fires are still legally responsible for any damage they cause. Fires are forbidden in FPAs, above treeline (where trees are less than 8 ft. tall), and in the Great Gulf Wilderness and Cutler River drainage. Fires are not permitted on state lands except at explicitly designated sites; on private land the owner's permission is required. During periods when there is a high risk of wildfires, the forest supervisor may temporarily close the entire WMNF against public entry. Such closures are given wide publicity so that local residents and visitors alike may realize the danger of fires in the woods.

WINTER CONSIDERATIONS

This book describes trails in the snowless season, which can vary considerably from year to year; higher elevations have much shorter snowless seasons. Snowshoeing and winter hiking on White Mountain trails and peaks have steadily become more popular, however, so a few general considerations are given here.

Road access and parking are, in general, much more limited in winter. Most USFS access roads are unplowed, necessitating long road walks to reach trailheads that one can drive to in summer. Many parking areas along major roads are plowed within a day or two after a storm, but some parking areas are not plowed, and roadside parking is limited by snowbanks. To avoid ticketing or towing, all wheels of a parked vehicle must be outside the travel corridor. If no safe parking is available, consider an alternative hike. Hikers should make sure their vehicle is winter ready and should always have a shovel. Notes on winter road closures are included in Road Access subsections, and normal plowing status, when known, is mentioned in many individual trail descriptions.

Although travel on the lower trails in average conditions can be relatively safe, much more experience is required to foresee and avoid dangerous situations in winter than in summer. Summer hiking boots are inadequate; winter hikers should wear insulated boots that will function well with snowshoes and crampons or other traction systems. Flashlight and smartphone batteries fail quickly. LED headlamps work much better as a light source but may still fail. Drinking water freezes unless carried in an insulated container. The winter hiker needs good physical conditioning from regular exercise and must dress carefully to prevent overheating and excessive perspiration, which soaks clothing and soon leads to chilling. Avoid cotton clothes completely in winter; only wool and some synthetic fabrics retain their insulating values when wet. Increase fluid intake, as dehydration can be a serious problem in the dry winter air. Larger packs are needed to carry the extra clothing layers and gear required in winter.

Snow, ice, and weather conditions are constantly changing, and a relatively trivial error of judgment may have grave, even fatal, consequences. Conditions can vary greatly from day to day and from trail to trail. Trails to popular peaks and features are usually well-packed soon after a snowstorm. However, many other trails see little to no use in winter and will require trail-breaking and navigational skills. Days are very short, particularly in early winter, when darkness falls soon after 4 p.m. Trails are frequently difficult or impossible to follow in deep snow, and navigation skills are hard to use (or learn) in adverse weather conditions. (Thus, out-and-back hikes—where one retraces one's tracks—are preferable to loop hikes, where unknown conditions ahead could make completion of the trip much more difficult than anticipated.) Brook crossings can be difficult and potentially dangerous if the brooks are not well frozen.

Deep snow requires snowshoes or skis and the skill to use them efficiently. Breaking trail on snowshoes through new snow can be strenuous and exhausting work. Trail courtesy suggests that winter hikers wear snowshoes when trails are not solidly packed out; "barebooting" in soft snow is unnecessarily tiring and creates unpleasant and potentially dangerous "postholes" in the trail for those who follow.

When ice is present on trails, as it often is in late fall, early spring, and after winter thaw-freeze cycles, there is particular danger on mountains with steep, open slopes or ledges. If icy trail conditions are expected, hikers should bring traction footgear, such as MICROspikes (a popular brand of ice cleat), or if severe conditions prevail, full crampons, which require practice and care to use safely.

In spring, deep snowdrifts may remain on northern slopes and wooded ridge crests, even at lower elevations, after all snow is gone on southern exposures. Heavily used trails develop an unpleasant "monorail"—a hard-packed spine of snow down the middle of the corridor.

It is important to note that some trails go through areas that may pose a severe avalanche hazard. Gulfs, ravines, landslides, and open slopes are especially prone to avalanches, although they can also occur below treeline. Information on avalanche danger for the eastern slopes of Mt. Washington is posted daily at mountwashingtonavalanchecenter.org and also at Pinkham Notch Visitor Center and on the AMC and Mt. Washington Observatory websites. These areas should be regarded as technical terrain and strictly avoided unless group leaders have been trained in avalanche safety; avalanches have caused numerous deaths and serious injuries in the White Mountains, often due to inexperienced, untrained hikers wandering into dangerous terrain.

Above timberline, conditions often require specialized equipment and skills, as well as experience of a different magnitude. Winter conditions on the Presidential Range are as severe as any in North America south of the great mountains of Alaska and the Yukon Territory. On the summit of Mt. Washington in winter, winds average 44 MPH, and daily high temperatures average 15 degrees Fahrenheit. The summit sees only a few calm days, and even on an average day, conditions will probably be too severe for any but the most experienced and well-equipped climbers. The Mt. Washington Observatory routinely records wind velocities in excess of 100 MPH, and temperatures are often far below zero. The combination of high wind and low temperature has such a cooling effect that the worst conditions on Mt. Washington are approximately equal to the worst reported from Antarctica, despite the much greater cold in the latter region. The conditions can be nearly as severe on Franconia Ridge, Mt. Moosilauke, the Bond Range, and lower open summits, such as Mt. Chocorua and North and South Baldface.

Severe storms can develop suddenly and unexpectedly. Winter weather in the White Mountains is extremely variable: it is not unusual for a cold, penetrating, wind-driven rain to be followed within a few hours by a cold front that brings below-zero temperatures and high winds.

Hikers who are interested in extending their activities into the winter season, especially at higher elevations, are strongly advised to seek organized parties with leaders who have extensive winter experience. AMC and several of its chapters sponsor numerous evening and weekend workshops, in addition to introductory winter hikes, through which participants can gain experience. Information on winter skills workshops is available at activities.outdoors.org; enter the keyword "instruction." Much good advice is found in *Essential Guide to Winter Recreation*, by Andrew Vietze (AMC Books, 2019).

Obviously, obtaining a current mountain weather forecast is a critical component of trip planning in winter. The Mt. Washington Observatory posts both a Higher Summits Forecast and a Mt. Washington Valley Forecast early each morning at mountwashington.org. Both of these are also available via the observatory's weather phone at 603-356-2137, ext. 1. Trail, snow, and weather conditions for AMC lodges and winter huts are posted daily on outdoors.org/weather.

BACKCOUNTRY HAZARDS

Safe hiking means knowing how to avoid dangerous situations as well as being prepared to deal with problems when they do occur. AMC and many other outdoor organizations offer courses that teach the principles of backcountry safety, wilderness first aid, and incident management.

Dozens of books also are available on such subjects. The following section outlines some common hazards encountered in the Northeast outdoors and discusses how to approach them.

Search and Rescue

In emergencies, call 911 or the toll-free New Hampshire State Police number (800-525-5555) or *77 on a cell phone. Hikers should be aware that cell phone coverage in the backcountry can be very unreliable, particularly in deep valleys but also on some summits, and there is absolutely no assurance that a cell phone call will get through to authorities in an emergency. Both phones and their batteries can fail, often at inconvenient times.

By state law, the New Hampshire Fish and Game Department is responsible for search-and-rescue operations in the New Hampshire outdoors, with assistance from several volunteer search-and-rescue groups and local fire departments. It takes a fair amount of time to organize rescue parties, which normally require a minimum of 18 people for litter carries. In addition, an unnecessary rescue mission may leave no resources available if a real emergency occurs. Please make sure a situation is really an emergency before calling for help. All such operations are expensive, and they frequently put good people at risk. Also note that under New Hampshire law, hikers who require rescue because of "negligent" behavior may be billed by the state for the cost of their rescue.

Hikers who wish to make monetary contributions in support of New Hampshire search-and-rescue organizations may purchase a voluntary hikeSafe Card ($25 individual, $35 family in 2024) from New Hampshire

Fish and Game at wildlife.state.nh.us/safe. Or one may make a contribution to the New Hampshire Outdoor Council, whose mission is to support backcountry safety education and the operations of search-and-rescue teams and organizations (P.O. Box 157, Kearsarge, NH 03847; nhoutdoorcouncil.org). Also see the hikeSafe Hiker Responsibility Code on p. xxi.

Falls and Injuries

The remoteness of the backcountry makes any injury a potentially serious matter. Be alert for places where footing may be poor, especially in rainy weather and on steep, rough, or wet sections of trail. In autumn, wet leaves and hidden ice are particular hazards. Remember that carrying a heavy pack can affect your balance. Another possible cause of injury in certain areas is rockfall from ledges that rise above the trail.

In case of serious injury, apply first aid and keep the injured party warm and comfortable. Then take a minute to assess the situation before going or calling for help. Backcountry evacuation can take many hours, so don't rush. Write down your location, the condition of the injured person, and any other pertinent facts. If phone service is not available, at least one person should stay with the injured hiker while two others go for help. (Hence the maxim that it is safest to hike in the backcountry in groups of four or more.)

Hypothermia

Hypothermia, the most serious danger to hikers in the White Mountains, is the loss of ability to preserve body heat and can be caused by injury, exhaustion, lack of sufficient food, and inadequate or wet clothing. This often occurs on wet, windy days with temperatures between 32 and 50 degrees Fahrenheit.

Symptoms of moderate hypothermia include shivering, impaired speech and movement, lowered body temperature, and drowsiness. Be on the lookout for what current hypothermia education programs refer to as the *umbles*—stumbles, mumbles, and bumbles—which amount to a loss of agility, an inability to speak clearly, difficulty with knots and zippers, and similar issues that indicate loss of control over normal muscular and mental functions. A victim should be given dry clothing and placed in a sleeping bag, if available, then given quick-energy food (such as chocolate, raisins, or energy bars) to eat and something warm (not hot) to drink (avoiding alcohol and caffeine).

In cases of severe hypothermia, which occurs when body temperature reaches a point below 90 degrees Fahrenheit, shivering ceases, but a victim becomes afflicted by an obvious lack of coordination to the point that walking becomes impossible. Sure indicators are slurred speech, mental confusion, irrational behavior, disorientation, and unconsciousness. Only prompt evacuation to a hospital offers reasonable hope for recovery. Use extreme care in attempting to transport such a person to a trailhead because even a slight jar can bring on heart failure. Protect the victim from further heat loss as much as possible and handle with extreme gentleness; trained rescue personnel should be called for assistance.

Successful rescue of a profoundly hypothermic person from the backcountry is difficult, so prevention or early detection is essential. The advent of hypothermia is usually fairly slow, and in cold or wet weather, all members of a hiking group must be aware of the signs of developing hypothermia and pay constant attention to the first appearance of such signs—which may be fairly subtle—in all party members.

Heat Exhaustion

Excessive heat also can be a serious problem in the mountains, particularly in midsummer on hot, humid days. Heat exhaustion, usually in a mild form, is quite common. The hiker feels tired, perhaps light-headed or nauseous, and may have cramps in large muscles. The principal cause is dehydration and loss of electrolytes (mostly salt) through perspiration, often combined with overexertion. On a hot day, a hiker can be well along the way to serious dehydration before even feeling thirsty. To prevent heat exhaustion, hikers should carry plenty of water (or the means to treat water from natural sources en route) and drink copiously before thirst is evident. Wearing a hat to block sun is another preventive measure.

To treat heat exhaustion, provide adequate water and perhaps salt (salt without adequate water will make the situation worse), help the victim cool down (especially the head and torso), and minimize further exertion. Heat exhaustion must be taken seriously because it can proceed to life-threatening cardiac problems or heatstroke, a medical emergency where irreversible damage to the brain and other vital organs can quickly occur. Heatstroke requires immediate cooling of the victim.

Lightning

Lightning is another serious potential hazard on any bare ridge or summit. Avoid these dangerous places when thunderstorms are likely. Look for shelter in thick woods as quickly as possible if an unexpected "thumper" is detected. Most thunderstorms occur on very warm days or when a cold front passes; storms produced by cold fronts are typically more sudden and violent. Weather forecasts that mention cold fronts or predict temperatures much above 80 degrees Fahrenheit in the lowlands and valleys should arouse concern.

Wildlife

In recent years, there have been hundreds of collisions between automobiles and moose, most occurring in spring and early summer, although the hazard exists year-round. Motorists need to be aware of the seriousness of the problem, particularly at night when these huge, dark-colored animals are both active and very difficult to see. Instinct often causes them to face an auto rather than run from it, and they are apt to cross the road unpredictably as a car approaches. Slower driving speeds and use of high beams are recommended at night. Moose normally constitute little threat to hikers on foot, although it would be wise to give a wide berth to a cow with young or to a bull during the fall mating season.

Bears are common but tend to keep well out of sight. Several recent serious incidents have been unnecessarily provoked by deliberate feeding of bears or by harassment by a dog leading to an attack on people nearby. Bears are omnivorous opportunists, especially fond of nuts and berries. They have become a nuisance and even a hazard at some popular campsites; any bear that has lost its natural fear of humans and gotten used to living off them is extremely dangerous. Hikers confronted by a bear should attempt to appear neither threatened nor frightened and should back off slowly—never run. Do not abandon food unless the bear appears irresistibly aggressive. A loud noise, such as one made by a whistle or by banging metal pots, is often useful. Careful protection of food—and scented items such as toothpaste—at campsites is mandatory; these items must never be kept overnight in a tent but should be placed in a metal bear box (located at all AMC backcountry campsites) or a bear canister (available on a first-come-first-serve basis at WMNF offices and visitor centers), or hung between trees on branches well off the ground—at least 10 ft. high and 4 ft. away from the tree trunk.

No known poisonous snakes inhabit the White Mountains.

Hunting Seasons

New Hampshire moose-hunting season runs from middle to late October; deer-hunting season (with rifles) is in November and early December, at which time you'll probably see many more hunters than deer. Seasons for muzzle-loader and bow-and-arrow hunters extend from mid-September through mid-December. Most hunters usually stay fairly close to roads; in general, the harder it would be to haul a deer out of a given area, the lower the probability that you'll encounter hunters there. In any case, avoid wearing brown or anything that might give a hunter the impression of the white flash of a white-tailed deer running away.

Wearing bright-orange clothing, as is usually done by hunters, is strongly recommended. Hikers also should be aware of the wild turkey gobbler season in May, when authorities advise against wearing red, white, blue, or black clothing. For dates of New Hampshire hunting seasons, visit wildlife.state.nh.us or call 603-271-3211.

Mosquitoes, Blackflies, and Ticks

Mosquitoes and blackflies are the woodland residents most frequently encountered by hikers. Mosquitoes are worst throughout the summer in low, wet areas, and blackflies are most bloodthirsty in late May, June, and early July. Head nets can be useful. The most effective repellents are based on the active ingredient N,N-diethyl-meta-toluamide, generally known as DEET, but some people have doubts about its safety. Recently, repellents with the active ingredient Picaridin have been found to be nearly or equally as effective. Hikers should apply repellents to clothing rather than skin where possible and avoid using DEET on small children.

Ticks have become an increasing problem in woods and grassy or brushy areas at lower elevations, especially in oak forests. At present, the most feared tick—the tiny, easily overlooked deer tick, which can transmit Lyme disease—is not yet often seen in the White Mountains, although its range is steadily increasing. The common tick in the White Mountains is the larger wood tick (also known as the dog tick), which can also carry serious diseases, such as Rocky Mountain spotted fever.

Countermeasures include using insect repellent, wearing light-colored long pants tucked into socks, and frequently checking clothing and skin. Ticks wander for several hours before settling on a spot to bite, so they can be removed easily if found promptly. Once a tick is embedded, take care to remove it entirely; the head can detach and may remain in the skin, possibly producing infection.

Brook Crossings

Rivers and brooks are often crossable without bridges, and you can usually step from rock to rock; trekking poles, a hiking staff, or a simple stick can be a great aid to balance. Use caution: Several fatalities have resulted from hikers (particularly solo hikers) falling on slippery rocks and suffering an injury that rendered them unconscious, causing them to drown in relatively shallow streams. Often the safer course is to wade across a stream; if you do so, wearing boots without socks is recommended. If you suspect in advance that wading may be required, a good option is to bring lightweight sneakers or water footwear.

Many crossings that may only be nuisances in summer could be serious obstacles in cold weather when one's feet and boots must be kept dry. Another kind of hazard can occur in late fall, when cold nights may cause a treacherous thin layer of ice to coat exposed rocks. Higher waters, which can turn innocuous brooks into virtually uncrossable torrents, come in spring as snow melts, or after heavy rainstorms, particularly in fall when trees drop their leaves and take up less water. Avoid trails with potentially dangerous stream crossings during these high-water periods. If you are cut off from roads by swollen streams, it is better to make a long detour, even if you need to wait and spend a night in the woods. Rushing current can make wading extremely hazardous, and several deaths have resulted.

Floodwaters may subside within a few hours, especially in small brooks. It is particularly important not to camp on the far side of a brook from your exit point if the crossing is difficult and heavy rain is predicted.

A useful website for assessing real-time streamflow conditions in the mountains is USGS Current Water Data for New Hampshire, at water-data.usgs.gov/nh/nwis/rt. This site provides streamflow data for the Androscoggin, Ammonoosuc, East Branch Pemigewasset, Pemigewasset, Saco, Swift, Upper Ammonoosuc, and Wild rivers.

Drinking Water

The presence of cysts of the intestinal parasite *Giardia lamblia* in water sources in the White Mountains is thought to be common, although difficult to prove. It is impossible to be sure whether a given source is safe, no matter how clear the water or how remote the location. The safest course is for day-hikers to carry their own water; those who use sources in the woods should treat or filter the water before drinking it. If treating water, bring it to a rolling boil or disinfect it with an iodine-based disinfectant. Allow extra contact time (and use twice as many disinfectant tablets) if the water is very cold. Chlorine-based products are ineffective in water that contains organic impurities, and all water-purification chemicals tend to deteriorate quickly. Various kinds of filters are available; they also remove impurities from water, often making it look and taste better, so that sources that are unappealing in the untreated state can be made to produce drinkable water. For more on water treatment methods, see *AMC's Mountain Skills Manual*.

The symptoms of giardiasis are severe intestinal distress and diarrhea, but such discomforts can have many other causes, making the disease difficult to diagnose accurately. The principal cause of the spread of this noxious ailment in the woods is probably careless disposal of human waste. Keep it at least 200 ft. away from water sources. If no toilets are nearby, dig a hole 6 to 8 in. deep (but not below the organic layer of the soil) for a latrine and cover the hole completely after use. The bacteria in the organic layer of the soil will then decompose the waste naturally. Be scrupulous about washing hands after answering calls of nature.

Break-Ins
Cars parked at trailheads are frequently targets of break-ins, so never leave valuables or expensive equipment in cars while you are hiking, particularly overnight.

TRAIL MAINTENANCE
The trails that we use and enjoy are only in part the product of government agencies and nonprofit organizations. Many trails are cared for by one dedicated person or a small group. Funds for this work are scarce, and unless hikers contribute both time and money to the maintenance of trails, the diversity of trails available to the public may well decline. Every hiker can make some contribution to the improvement of the trails, if by nothing more than pushing a fallen limb or tree off the trail rather than walking around it. Write to AMC Trails, Pinkham Notch Visitor Center, P.O. Box 298, Gorham, NH 03581, for more information regarding volunteer trail maintenance activities or see outdoors.org/get-involved. In addition to its own active Adopt-a-Trail program, AMC has worked cooperatively with the WMNF, the White Mountain Trail Collective, and New Hampshire State Parks on Adopt-a-Trail programs in recent years. Another group that is very active in trail maintenance is Trailwrights (P.O. Box 1223, Concord, NH 03302; trailwrights.org; trailwrights@pobox.com).

LEAVE NO TRACE
 AMC is a national educational partner of Leave No Trace, a nonprofit organization dedicated to promoting and inspiring responsible outdoor recreation through education, research, and partnerships. The Leave No Trace program develops wild land ethics, or guidelines for ways people should think and act in the outdoors to minimize their impact on the areas they visit and to protect our natural resources for future enjoyment. Leave No Trace unites four federal land management agencies—the USFS, National Park Service, Bureau of Land Management, and U.S. Fish & Wildlife Service—with manufacturers, outdoor retailers, user groups, educators, organizations such as AMC, and individuals. The Leave No Trace ethic is guided by these seven principles:

- Plan ahead and prepare.
- Travel and camp on durable surfaces.
- Dispose of waste properly.
- Leave what you find.
- Minimize campfire impacts.
- Respect wildlife.
- Be considerate of other visitors.

AMC is a national provider of the Leave No Trace Master Educator course. AMC offers this five-day course, designed especially for outdoor professionals and land managers, as well as the shorter two-day Leave No Trace Trainer course at locations throughout the Northeast.

For Leave No Trace information and materials, contact the Leave No Trace Center for Outdoor Ethics, P.O. Box 997, Boulder, CO 80306; 800-332-4100 or 303-442-8222; lnt.org.

SECTION ONE

MT. WASHINGTON AND
THE SOUTHERN RIDGES

Introduction	1
Trail Descriptions	12
Mt. Washington from Pinkham Notch	12
Upper Cone of Mt. Washington	22
North of Pinkham Notch Visitor Center	25
Main Ridge of the Southern Presidentials	28
Southern Presidentials from the West and South	34
Dry River Valley	43
Montalban Ridge	48
Jackson Area	61

Map 1: Presidential Range
Map 3: Crawford Notch–Sandwich Range

INTRODUCTION

This section includes the summit of Mt. Washington and the major ridges that run south from it, which constitute the southern portion of the Presidential Range. The region is bounded approximately on the north by the Mt. Washington Cog Railway and Mt. Washington Auto Rd., on the east by NH 16, on the south by US 302, and on the west by US 302 and Cog Railway Base Rd. The northern portion of the Presidential Range, including Mts. Clay, Jefferson, Adams, and Madison and the Great Gulf, is covered in Section Two. Many of the trails described in Section Two also provide routes to Mt. Washington. AMC's *White Mountains Trail Map 1: Presidential Range* covers this entire section except for Iron Mtn. Trail and several trails in the southern Montalban region, in the south part of the section. All these trails (and much of the rest of this section) are covered by AMC's *White Mountains Trail Map 3: Crawford Notch–Sandwich Range*. Davis Path is the only trail not completely covered by one map or the other; however, all but the southern end is on Map 1 and all but the northern end is on Map 3.

In this section, the AT follows the entire Webster Cliff Trail from Crawford Notch to its intersection with Crawford Path, near the summit of Mt. Pierce, and then follows Crawford Path to the summit of Mt. Washington. On the way, the AT also crosses the summits of Mts. Webster, Jackson, and Pierce and passes near Mts. Eisenhower, Franklin, and Monroe. From Mt. Washington, the AT descends to Gulfside Trail (Section Two) via Trinity Heights Connector. Then, after passing over the ridge of the Northern Presidentials (although missing most of the summits) and through the Great Gulf—areas also covered in Section Two—the AT returns to Section One at Mt. Washington Auto Rd. and follows Old Jackson Road to AMC's Pinkham Notch Visitor Center and NH 16.

SAFETY ON MT. WASHINGTON

Mt. Washington has a well-earned reputation as the most dangerous small mountain in the world. As chronicled in *Not Without Peril*, by Nicholas Howe (AMC Books, 2009), more than 150 people have died on its slopes, many of them from exhaustion and exposure to the mountain's severe and rapidly changeable weather. Storms quickly increase in violence toward the summit. The second-greatest wind velocity ever recorded at any surface weather station was attained on Mt. Washington, clocking in at 231 MPH on April 12, 1934. (The fastest being the 1996 Typhoon Olivia, as recorded on Barrow Island, Australia, at 253 MPH.) Based on windchill temperatures, the worst conditions on Mt. Washington are approximately equal to the worst reported in Antarctica, although actual air temperatures on Mt. Washington are not as low.

Winter-like storms of incredible violence occur frequently, even during summer months. Winds of hurricane force exhaust even the strongest hiker, and drive cold rain horizontally, which penetrates clothing and drains heat from the body. When a person's body temperature falls, brain function quickly deteriorates; this is one of the first, and most insidious, effects of excessive heat loss (hypothermia). For more information on this potentially lethal condition, see Backcountry Hazards on p. xxxi. If you begin to experience difficulty from weather conditions, expect that the worst is yet to come and turn back, without shame, before it is too late.

Hikers planning to ascend Mt. Washington should always check the weather forecast before setting out. The Mt. Washington Observatory issues a Higher Summits Forecast each day, early in the morning; it is available at mountwashington.org and outdoors.org and by calling 603-356-2137, ext. 1. If the forecast is unfavorable, save the trip for a better day.

When traveling above treeline, be sure to bring rain and wind gear, extra layers, and a hat and gloves; avoid cotton clothes.

Inexperienced hikers sometimes misjudge the difficulty of climbing Mt. Washington by placing too much emphasis on the relatively short distance from the trailheads to the summit. To people used to walking around their neighborhoods, the trail distance of 4 mi. or so sounds rather tame. But the most important factor in the difficulty of the trip is the altitude gain of about 4,000 ft. from base to summit, give or take a few hundred feet depending on the route chosen. To a person unaccustomed to mountain trails or in less-than-excellent physical condition, this unrelenting uphill grind can be grueling and intensely discouraging. If you are not an experienced hiker or a trained athlete, build up to the ascent of Mt. Washington with easier climbs in areas with less exposure to potentially severe weather. You'll enjoy the experience a great deal more.

Visitors ascending the mountain on foot should carry a compass and a trail map and should take care to stay on the trails. If you are forced to travel in conditions of reduced visibility, favor the main trails with their large, readily visible cairns over the lesser-used connecting trails that are often far less clearly marked. It is a grave predicament when a hiker above treeline accidentally abandons a trail in dense fog or a whiteout, particularly if the weather is rapidly deteriorating. No completely satisfactory course of action exists in this situation because the objective is to get below treeline as quickly as possible—with or without a trail—but weather exposure is generally worse to the west, and cliffs are more prevalent in the ravines to the east. If you know where the nearest major trail should be, then it is probably best to try to find it. If you have adequate clothing, it may be best to find a scrub patch and shelter yourself in it. In the absence of alternatives, take note that the Cog Railway on the western slope and Mt. Washington Auto Rd. on the eastern slope make a line, although a rather crooked one, from west to east. These landmarks are difficult to miss in even the darkest night or the thickest fog, although in winter, snowdrifts may conceal them. Remember which side of the mountain you are on, and travel clockwise or counterclockwise, skirting the tops of the ravines; sooner or later you will reach either the Cog Railway or Mt. Washington Auto Rd. Given a choice, aim for the road, as the railway is on the side of the mountain that faces the prevailing winds.

Safe ascent of the mountain in winter requires much warm clothing; special equipment, such as crampons and an ice ax; considerable previous experience and training in winter hiking; and expert leadership. The worst winter conditions are inconceivably brutal and can materialize with little warning. From about mid-October to Memorial Day, no building is open to provide shelter or refuge to hikers. All water sources in this heavily used area should be considered unfit to drink; the safest course is to avoid drinking from trailside sources (see p. xxxvi). Water is available at the Sherman Adams summit building during the months in which it is open, roughly from Memorial Day to about mid-October.

SUMMIT BUILDINGS

No hotel or overnight lodging for the public is available on the summit of Mt. Washington. The principal summit building serving tourists and hikers was named to honor Sherman Adams, a former New Hampshire governor, special assistant to President Eisenhower, legendary White Mountains woodsman, and, in his youth, trailmaster of AMC's trail crew. Operated by the New Hampshire Division of Parks and Recreation during the summer season (mid-May to mid-October), the building has food service, a pack room, a souvenir shop, public restrooms, telephones, and a post office. It houses the Mt. Washington Observatory, the Mt. Washington Museum, and facilities for park personnel.

The first Summit House on Mt. Washington was built in 1852. The oldest building still standing on the summit is the Tip Top House, a hotel built in 1853 and rebuilt after it burned in 1915. This stone building, now owned by the state of New Hampshire and a part of Mt. Washington State Park, has been restored and is open to the public as a historical site when the public summit facilities are in operation, but it is not available for lodging or emergency shelter. The second Summit House, built in 1873, was destroyed by fire in 1908. The third Summit House was built in 1915 and razed in 1980 to make room for the Sherman Adams building.

Several other buildings are on the summit of Mt. Washington, but none of them are open to the general public.

Mt. Washington Observatory

There has been a year-round weather observatory on Mt. Washington from 1870 to 1892, and from 1932 onward. The observatory maintains museum exhibitions in the Sherman Adams summit building on Mt. Washington. The Mt. Washington Observatory is operated by a nonprofit corporation, and individuals are invited to become members and to contribute to the support of its important work. For details, visit mountwashington.org or call 603-356-2137.

MT. WASHINGTON AUTO RD.

This private road from the Glen House site on NH 16 to the summit, often called the Carriage Rd., was constructed from 1855 through 1861. Vehicles are charged a toll at the foot of the mountain. With long zigzags and an easy grade, the road climbs the prominent northeast ridge named for Benjamin Chandler, who died on the upper part from the effects of hypothermia in 1856. Hiking on the road is not allowed due to the danger from vehicle traffic. After dark, however, this road—easier to descend at night than the rough and rocky trails—may well be the best escape route for hikers faced with the onset of nightfall on the trails of Mt. Washington. The emergency shelters that were formerly located along the upper part of the road have been removed. The first 4.0 mi. of the road (below treeline) are officially maintained as part of the Great Glen cross-country ski trail network and receive considerable use by skiers and snowshoers. A Great Glen trail pass is required for winter access.

Limited parking is available at several trailheads for hikers who have paid the automobile toll. Please park only in turnouts and make sure your vehicle is not blocking traffic. Check at the Toll House for the gate-closing schedule so you don't get locked in. Because of the continual theft and destruction of trail signs, they are often placed on the trails at some distance from the Auto Rd. The names of some trails are painted on rocks at the point where they leave the road. The Auto Rd. offers a limited hiker shuttle service up to or down from the summit (first come, first served); reservations are not accepted and there is no guarantee of availability. For information, visit mt-washington.com.

The Auto Rd. leaves NH 16 opposite the Glen House site (elevation about 1,600 ft.), crosses Peabody River, and starts the long climb. Just above the 2-mi. mark, after sharp curves right and then left, the AT crosses the road. To the south, the AT follows Old Jackson Road (now a foot trail) past jcts. with Nelson Crag Trail and Raymond Path to Pinkham Notch Visitor Center. To the north, the AT follows Madison Gulf Trail toward the Great Gulf and the Northern Presidentials. Low's Bald Spot, a fine viewpoint, can be reached by an easy walk of about 0.3 mi. from the Auto Road via Madison Gulf Trail and a short side path.

The Auto Rd. continues to treeline, passing to the left of the site of the Halfway House (3,840 ft.), and soon swings around the Horn, skirting a prominent shoulder known as the Ledge, where you have a fine view to the north. A short distance above the Ledge, Chandler Brook Trail descends into the Great Gulf on the right, and soon the route used by snow vehicles in winter diverges right.

Just above the 5-mi. mark, on the right, exactly at the sharp turn, are some remarkable folded strata in the rocks beside the road. Here, near Cragway Spring, Nelson Crag Trail comes close to the left side of the road. At about 5.5 mi., the road passes through the patch of high scrub in which Dr. B. L. Ball survived two nights in a winter storm in October 1855.

(Dr. Ball's account of his ordeal, *Three Days on the White Mountains: The Perilous Adventure of Dr. B. L. Ball on Mount Washington*, published in 1856, is available in a reprint edition from Bondcliff Books.) A short distance above the 6-mi. mark, where the winter route rejoins, Wamsutta Trail descends on the right to the Great Gulf, and Alpine Garden Trail diverges left. The trench-like structures near the road are the remains of the old Glen House Bridle Path, built in 1853. The road soon makes a hairpin turn and circles the left edge of a lawn sometimes called the Cow Pasture, where Huntington Ravine Trail enters on the left. The remains of an old corral are visible on the right a little farther along. Beyond the 7-mi. post, the Mt. Washington Cog Railway approaches and runs above the Auto Rd. on the right; near the tracks, just below the summit, the Bourne monument stands at the spot where 23-year-old Lizzie Bourne perished in September 1855, the second recorded death on the mountain. Soon, the road crosses Nelson Crag Trail, which enters on the left and climbs to the summit from the right side. Tuckerman Ravine Trail enters on the left just below the parking lot complex at about 8 mi.; from the parking lots, the summit buildings are reached by a wooden stairway. For information on schedules and fares for passenger vehicles, guided stage tours, and the limited hiker shuttle service, visit mt-washington.com or call 603-466-3988.

MT. WASHINGTON COG RAILWAY

The Mt. Washington Cog Railway, an unusual artifact of nineteenth-century engineering with a fascinating history, was completed in 1869. The railway roughly follows the route of Ethan Allen Crawford's second trail up the mountain, which he cut to provide a shorter and more direct route to Mt. Washington than Crawford Path over the Southern Presidentials.

The Cog Railway usually operates to the summit from early May through mid-October. Through the winter it operates to Waumbek Station at about 4,000 ft. The Base Station facility is open year-round, 7 days a week. For a current schedule, visit thecog.com or call 603-278-5404.

ROAD ACCESS

Access to most of the trailheads in this section is from NH 16 or US 302, or from roads a short distance off these major highways. Other access roads include Cog Railway Base Rd. from US 302 at Bretton Woods; Mt. Clinton Rd. (not plowed in winter), which runs 3.6 mi. from Cog Railway Base Rd. opposite Jefferson Notch Rd. to US 302 just west of AMC's Highland Center at Crawford Notch; and Jericho Rd. (FR 27, also known as Rocky Branch Rd.), which starts from US 302 in Bartlett and runs 4.3 mi. up Rocky Branch valley. The upper part of this road was severely damaged by the October 2017 storm and has been permanently closed by the USFS, with vehicle access ending at a gate and parking area 2.5 mi. from US 302, requiring a 1.8-mi. road walk to the start of Rocky Branch Trail. The road is plowed to this point in winter. Other access roads are described in individual trail descriptions.

HUTS AND LODGES

For current information on AMC's huts, Pinkham Notch Visitor Center, Joe Dodge Lodge, and Highland Center at Crawford Notch, contact AMC's Reservation Office (603-466-2727) or visit outdoors.org/destinations.

Pinkham Notch Visitor Center and Joe Dodge Lodge (AMC)

Pinkham Notch Visitor Center (2,028 ft.) is a unique mountain recreation facility in the heart of the WMNF. The center, originally built in 1920 and greatly enlarged since then, is located on NH 16, practically at the height-of-land in Pinkham Notch, 11.8 mi. north of the jct. with US 302 in Glen and 10.6 mi. south of the eastern jct. with US 2 in Gorham. The center is also 0.7 mi. north of the Glen Ellis Falls parking area and 0.9 mi. south of the base of Wildcat Mtn. Ski Resort. Pinkham Notch Visitor Center provides food and lodging to the public throughout the year. Pets are not allowed inside any of the buildings. Concord Coach Lines offers daily bus service to and from Logan Airport and South Station in Boston (concordcoachlines.com), and AMC operates a hiker shuttle bus from the visitor center to many of the principal trailheads in the White Mountains during the summer.

Joe Dodge Lodge accommodates more than 100 guests in a variety of rooms, including bunkrooms and family rooms. It offers a library that commands a spectacular view of nearby Wildcat Ridge, and a space where visitors can share accounts of the day's activities around an open fireplace. The lodge also features a 65-seat conference room equipped with audiovisual facilities.

The Trading Post, a popular meeting place for hikers, has been a hub of AMC's educational and recreational activities since 1920. Weekend workshops, seminars, and lectures are conducted throughout the year. The building houses a dining room, an information desk, and a shop where basic equipment, guidebooks, maps, and other AMC publications are available. The pack room downstairs is open 24 hr. a day for hikers to stop in, relax, use the coin-operated showers, and repack their gear.

Pinkham Notch Visitor Center is the most important trailhead on the east side of Mt. Washington. Free public parking is available, although sleeping in cars is not permitted. Additional parking is available in designated areas along NH 16 in both directions, but a USFS Recreation Pass is required at some areas. Although the permit is not legally required for parking at Pinkham Notch Visitor Center, AMC requests that hikers purchase one to support the USFS recreation program. Tuckerman Ravine Trail, Lost Pond Trail, and Old Jackson Road all start at the visitor center, giving access to many more trails. In addition, quite a few walking trails have been constructed for shorter, easier trips in the Pinkham vicinity. Among these are Crew-Cut Trail, George's Gorge Trail, Liebeskind's Loop, and Square Ledge Trail.

Highland Center at Crawford Notch and Shapleigh Bunkhouse (AMC)

Located on 26 acres of AMC-owned land at the head of Crawford Notch, the Highland Center (1,910 ft.), opened in 2003, is a lodging and education center open to the public year-round. It is on the site of the former Crawford House hotel on US 302, 20.6 mi. west of the jct. with NH 16 in Glen and 8.7 mi. east of the traffic lights and jct. with US 3 in Twin Mountain. Highland Center is a stop on the AMC Hiker Shuttle routes during summer and on fall weekends.

The center contains 34 rooms, accommodating a total of 122 beds, including shared rooms with shared baths and private rooms with private baths. The adjacent Shapleigh Bunkhouse contains 16 beds in two bunkrooms, as well as a common room and pantry with a refrigerator and a microwave. Reservations are encouraged. The center was constructed using energy-efficient materials and is designed to complement the landscape while paying tribute to the intriguing human history in Crawford Notch. Meals consisting of hearty mountain fare are served in a family-style setting.

A wide variety of educational programs and skills training for children, teens, and adults is offered at AMC's Highland Center, helping participants increase their understanding of the natural environment and gain proficiency in outdoor skills, such as map and compass use or wilderness first aid. Day-hikers, backpackers, and other visitors can find trail and weather information at the center.

AMC's Macomber Family Information Center, open during summer and fall, is located in the historic Crawford Depot, a former train station renovated by AMC, and houses interpretive displays, an information desk, and a small store that stocks last-minute hiker supplies, guidebooks, AMC publications, and souvenir items. The center has a hiker parking area. In addition, it is a major stop and transfer point for the AMC Hiker Shuttle, which operates throughout the summer and on fall weekends, and it serves as a depot for the excursion trains that run on the Crawford Notch line during tourist season.

Many trails described in Section One can be reached from AMC's Crawford Notch property, including Crawford Path, Saco Lake Trail, and Webster–Jackson Trail. Parking for overnight guests is on the Highland Center property near the main building. Parking for Crawford Path is available in the USFS lot (Recreation Pass required), just off Mt. Clinton Rd. near its jct. with US 302.

Lakes of the Clouds Hut (AMC)

For more than 130 years, AMC's White Mountain hut system has offered hikers bunks for the night in spectacular locations, with home-cooked dinners and breakfasts, cold running water, and composting or waterless toilets. Originally built in 1915 and greatly enlarged since then, Lakes of the Clouds Hut is open to the public from June to mid-September and closed at all other times. The hut is on a shelf near the foot of Mt. Monroe, about 50 yd. west of the larger lake, at an elevation of 5,014 ft. The hut is reached by Crawford Path or Ammonoosuc Ravine Trail and has accommodations for 90 guests in bunkrooms for six, eight, twelve, and fifteen people. Pets are not permitted in the hut. Reservations are highly recommended (603-466-2727; outdoors.org/destinations). Small stocks of drinks, snacks, and gear are available for purchase by day visitors. A limited number of backpacker spaces are offered at a significantly reduced rate for AT thru-hikers only—first come, first served. A refuge room in the cellar is left open in winter for emergency use only.

Mizpah Spring Hut (AMC)

Completed in 1965, this hut is at an elevation of 3,793 ft. on the site formerly occupied by the Mizpah Spring Shelter, at the jct. of Webster Cliff Trail and Mt. Clinton Trail, near Mizpah Cutoff. The hut accommodates 60 guests, with sleeping quarters in eight rooms containing from four to ten bunks, and it is open to the public from mid-May to mid-October (caretaker basis in May). Lodging, with meals included, is available for a fee; reservations are highly recommended (603-466-2727; outdoors.org/destinations). Limited drinks, snacks, and gear are available for purchase by day visitors. Pets are not permitted in the hut. Tentsites are nearby (caretaker; fee charged).

CAMPING
Presidential Range–Dry River Wilderness

In accordance with USFS Wilderness policy, hiking group size may not exceed ten people, and no more than ten people may occupy any designated or non-designated campsite. Camping and wood or charcoal fires are not allowed within 200 ft. of any trail except at designated campsites, which are marked with small wooden posts along several trails in the Wilderness Area. Several shelters have been removed, and the remaining one will be dismantled when major maintenance is required. See p. xvii for more information about Wilderness Area regulations.

Forest Protection Areas

The WMNF has established a number of FPAs, where camping and wood or charcoal fires are prohibited throughout the year. See p. xxvii for general FPA regulations.

In the region covered by Section One, no camping is permitted regardless of snow cover on the east face of Mt. Washington's summit cone, from Boott Spur to Nelson Crag (the area above Tuckerman and Huntington ravines, including the Alpine Garden area and East Snowfields).

No camping is permitted within 0.25 mi. of any trailhead, picnic area, or any facility for overnight accommodation, such as a hut, cabin, shelter, tentsite, or campground, except as designated at the facility itself. In the region covered by Section One, camping is also forbidden within 0.25 mi. of Glen Ellis Falls.

No camping is permitted within 200 ft. of certain trails. In 2024, designated trails included Ammonoosuc Ravine Trail.

No camping is permitted on WMNF land within 0.25 mi. of certain roads (camping on private roadside land is illegal except by permission of the landowner). In 2024, these roads included US 302 (from the junction with NH 16 in Glen, to the junction with US 3 in Twin Mountain), NH 16 (from the junction with US 2 in Gorham to the junction with US 302 in Glen), Cog Railway Base Rd. (FR 173), Jefferson Notch Rd. (FR 220) from Cog Railway Base Rd. to the trailhead for Caps Ridge Trail, and Jericho Rd. (FR 27, a.k.a. Rocky Branch Rd.).

In Tuckerman and Huntington ravines (Cutler River drainage, including the Alpine Garden and the east face of the Mt. Washington summit cone), camping is prohibited throughout the year; the only year-round exception is AMC's Hermit Lake Shelters and adjoining tent platforms. Visitors in the ravine areas may not kindle charcoal or wood fires; people intending to cook must bring their own small stoves. Day visitors and shelter users alike are required to carry out all their own trash and garbage; no receptacles are provided. Updated information on these policies is available at Pinkham Notch Visitor Center, at the Tuckerman Ravine caretaker's residence, or from WMNF offices. No warming room is available to the public, and no refreshments are stocked.

Crawford Notch State Park

No camping is permitted in Crawford Notch State Park, except at Dry River Campground (NHDP; fee charged; nhstateparks.org) on US 302.

Established Trailside Campsites

To reduce overcrowding during peak summer and fall periods, groups of six or more planning to stay at AMC-managed backcountry campsites are required to use AMC's group notification system. For more information, visit outdoors.org/backcountry-campsites-form.

Hermit Lake Campsite (AMC/WMNF; 3,881 ft.), located in Tuckerman Ravine, consists of eight open-front shelters, with a total capacity of 86 persons, and three tent platforms open to the public. Tickets for shelter and tentsite space (nontransferable and nonrefundable) must be purchased in person for a fee at Pinkham Notch Visitor Center (first come, first served). Campers are limited to a maximum of seven consecutive nights, and pets are not allowed to stay overnight.

Nauman Tentsite (AMC; 3,792 ft.) consists of seven tent platforms near Mizpah Spring Hut. In summer, the site has a caretaker and a fee is charged.

Lakes of the Clouds Hut (AMC; 5,014 ft.) has limited space available for AT thru-hikers at a substantially reduced cost.

Rocky Branch Shelter #1 and Tentsite (WMNF; 1,424 ft.), with three tent platforms, is located near the jct. of Rocky Branch and Stairs Col trails, just outside the Presidential Range–Dry River Wilderness.

Rocky Branch Shelter #2 (WMNF; 2,807 ft.), formerly located at the jct. of Rocky Branch Trail and Isolation Trail, has been removed and will be replaced with primitive tentsites in the future.

Dry River Shelter #3 (WMNF; 3,121 ft.) is located on Dry River Trail, 6.3 mi. from US 302, within the Presidential Range–Dry River Wilderness. This shelter will be removed when major maintenance is required.

Resolution Shelter (AMC), formerly located on a spur path off Davis Path at its jct. with Mt. Parker Trail, has been removed.

Mt. Langdon Shelter (WMNF; 1,774 ft.) was located at the jct. of Mt. Langdon and Mt. Stanton trails, just outside the Presidential Range–Dry River Wilderness. The USFS removed this shelter in 2022 and established primitive tentsites at the location.

Wilderness Tentsites (WMNF): Several designated tentsites are located along trails in the Presidential Range–Dry River Wilderness. These are marked with small wooden posts. They are not shown on the maps in this guide and are not indicated in the text because the USFS may relocate some of these sites periodically.

TRAIL DESCRIPTIONS

MT. WASHINGTON FROM PINKHAM NOTCH

TUCKERMAN RAVINE TRAIL (MAP 1: F9)

Cumulative from Pinkham Notch Visitor Center (2,028 ft.) to:

Boott Spur Trail (2,275 ft.)	0.4 mi.	250 ft.	0:20
Huntington Ravine Trail (3,031 ft.)	1.3 mi.	1,000 ft.	1:10
Huntington Ravine Fire Road (3,425 ft.)	1.7 mi.	1,400 ft.	1:35
Raymond Path (3,700 ft.)	2.1 mi.	1,650 ft.	1:55
Lion Head Trail (3,825 ft.)	2.3 mi.	1,800 ft.	2:05
Boott Spur Link and Hermit Lake shelters (3,875 ft.)	2.4 mi.	1,850 ft.	2:10
Foot of headwall (4,490 ft.)	3.0 mi.	2,450 ft.	2:45
Alpine Garden Trail (5,150 ft.)	3.4 mi.	3,100 ft.	3:15
Tuckerman Junction (5,383 ft.)	3.6 mi.	3,350 ft.	3:30
Lion Head Trail, upper jct. (5,675 ft.)	3.8 mi.	3,650 ft.	3:45
Mt. Washington summit (6,288 ft.)	4.2 mi.	4,250 ft.	4:15

WMNF This trail to the summit of Mt. Washington from NH 16 at Pinkham Notch Visitor Center (ample parking, plowed in winter) is probably the most popular route of ascent on the mountain. Pinkham Notch Visitor Center is on the west side of NH 16 near the height-of-land in Pinkham Notch, 11.8 mi. north of the jct. with US 302 in Glen and 10.6 mi. south of the eastern jct. with US 2 in Gorham. From Pinkham Notch Visitor Center, the trail follows a wide, rocky tractor road up to the floor of Tuckerman Ravine. From there to the top of the headwall, the trail is well graded, steady, but not excessively steep. The section on the headwall underwent major reconstruction by the AMC trail crew in 2011, including the placement of many new rock steps. The trail's final section ascends the cone of Mt. Washington steeply over fragments of rock. In spring and early summer, the WMNF often closes the section of trail on the ravine headwall due to snow and ice hazards, including dangerous crevasses, and notice is posted at Pinkham Notch Visitor Center. In these circumstances, Lion Head Trail is usually the most convenient alternative. In winter conditions, the headwall is usually impassable except by experienced and well-equipped technical snow and ice climbers, and it is frequently closed by the WMNF even to such climbers due to avalanche and icefall hazards. The winter route of Lion Head Trail, which begins on Huntington Ravine Fire Rd. 0.1 mi. from Tuckerman Ravine Trail, bypasses the headwall and usually provides the easiest and safest route for ascending Mt. Washington from the east in winter, although it is very steep. This route is closed at other times of the year.

Tuckerman Ravine Trail starts near information boards behind the Trading Post at Pinkham Notch Visitor Center; Old Jackson Road diverges right 50 yd. from here. At first the grade is easy and the footing is good. Be careful to avoid several side paths, including Blanchard Ski Trail, in this area. In 0.3 mi., Tuckerman Ravine Trail crosses a bridge to the south bank of Cutler River, with cascades below and above, begins its moderate but relentless and rocky climb, and soon passes a side path leading 20 yd. right up rock steps to the best viewpoint for Crystal Cascade. Boott Spur Trail diverges left at a sharp curve to the right, 0.4 mi. from Pinkham Notch Visitor Center, and at 1.3 mi., Huntington Ravine Trail diverges right. At 1.5 mi., Tuckerman Ravine Trail crosses a tributary and then, at 1.6 mi., the main branch of Cutler River, both on bridges. At 1.7 mi., Huntington Ravine Fire Road, which is the easiest route to Huntington Ravine in winter but offers very rough footing on some parts in summer, leaves on the right (no sign). The Lion Head Trail winter route (signed only in the winter season) begins about 0.1 mi. up this road. At 2.1 mi., Raymond Path enters on the right where Tuckerman Ravine Trail turns sharply left, and at 2.3 mi., Lion Head Trail leaves on the right. In another 0.1 mi., Boott Spur Link leaves on the left, opposite the buildings located at the floor of Tuckerman Ravine, near Hermit Lake. Views from the floor of the ravine are impressive: the cliff on the right is Lion Head, and the more distant crags on the left are the Hanging Cliffs of Boott Spur.

Tuckerman Ravine Trail keeps to the right (north) of the main stream and ascends a well-constructed footway into the upper floor of the ravine. At the foot of the headwall, at 3.0 mi., the trail bears right and ascends a steep slope, where the Snow Arch can be seen on the left in spring and early summer of most years. In the early part of the hiking season, the snowfield above the Snow Arch usually extends across the trail, and the trail is often closed to hiking until this potentially hazardous snow slope has melted away. Some snow may persist in the ravine until late summer. The arch (which does not always form) is carved by a stream of snowmelt water that flows under the snowfield. (*Caution*: Do not get too close to the arch, and under no circumstances cross over it or venture beneath it because sections weighing many tons may break off at any moment. One death and several narrow escapes—the most recent escape in July 2020—have occurred as a result of falling ice.) When ascending the headwall, be careful not to dislodge rocks and start them rolling; doing so would put hikers below you in serious danger. Several serious accidents in recent years have involved hikers who slipped off the side of the trail on the upper part of the headwall, often in adverse weather conditions, especially when the trail was slippery. Although the yellow-blazed trail itself is relatively easy and quite safe when the footing is dry, it passes within a very short distance of some extremely dangerous terrain, so a minor misstep off the side of the trail can have grave consequences.

Turning sharply left at the top of the debris slope and passing under a cliff, the trail emerges from the ravine and climbs almost straight west up a grassy, ledgy slope. At 3.4 mi., a short distance above the top of the headwall, Alpine Garden Trail diverges right. At Tuckerman Junction, located on the lower edge of Bigelow Lawn at 3.6 mi., Tuckerman Crossover leads almost straight ahead (southwest) to Crawford Path near Lakes of the Clouds Hut; Southside Trail diverges from Tuckerman Crossover in 30 yd. and leads northwest, skirting Mt. Washington's cone to Davis Path; and Lawn Cutoff leads left (south) toward Boott Spur. Tuckerman Ravine Trail turns sharply right (north) at this jct. and ascends the steep rocks, marked by cairns. At 3.8 mi., at Cloudwater Spring (unreliable) about a third of the way up the cone, Lion Head Trail reenters on the right. Tuckerman Ravine Trail continues to ascend to Mt. Washington Auto Rd. a few yards below the lower parking area, from which crosswalks and wooden stairways lead to the summit area.

Descending, Tuckerman Ravine Trail leaves the Auto Rd. at a sign a short distance below the lower parking area (sign and large cairn).

LION HEAD TRAIL (MAP 1: F9)
Cumulative from lower jct. with Tuckerman Ravine Trail (3,825 ft.) to:

Alpine Garden Trail (5,175 ft.)	1.1 mi.	1,350 ft.	1:15
Upper jct. with Tuckerman Ravine Trail (5,675 ft.)	1.6 mi.	1,850 ft.	1:45
From Pinkham Notch Visitor Center (2,028 ft.) to:			
Mt. Washington summit (6,288 ft.) via Lion Head Trail and Tuckerman Ravine Trail	4.3 mi.	4,250 ft.	4:15

AMC Lion Head Trail follows the steep-ended ridge—aptly named for the appearance of its upper portion when viewed from points on NH 16 north of Pinkham Notch Visitor Center—that forms the north wall of Tuckerman Ravine. The trail begins and ends on Tuckerman Ravine Trail and thus provides an alternative, although much steeper, route to that heavily used trail. Lion Head Trail is especially important as an option when Tuckerman Ravine Trail over the headwall is closed during the spring or at other times when snow and ice create hazardous conditions on that trail. The winter route of Lion Head Trail is considered the least dangerous (although still quite difficult) way to ascend the east side of

Mt. Washington in winter conditions and is the most frequently used winter ascent route from that side. An avalanche in 1995 destroyed the former winter route, and a new winter route was constructed; this route leaves Huntington Ravine Fire Road just past the crossing of Raymond Path, about 0.1 mi. from Tuckerman Ravine Trail, and rejoins the summer Lion Head Trail at treeline. The winter route is very steep, ascending 950 ft. in 0.4 mi., and usually requires use of full crampons and an ice ax. The signs and markings are changed by the USFS according to prevailing conditions at the beginning and end of the winter season (which on Mt. Washington extends from late fall through much of the spring in most years) to ensure that climbers take the proper route. The winter route is closed when it is not signed and marked as the currently open route.

Yellow-blazed Lion Head Trail diverges right from Tuckerman Ravine Trail 2.3 mi. from Pinkham Notch Visitor Center and 0.1 mi. below Hermit Lake. Running north, Lion Head Trail passes a side path on the left to one of the Hermit Lake shelters and crosses the outlet of Hermit Lake. The trail soon begins to climb the steep slope with rough footing and then makes several switchbacks, scrambling up several small ledges and one ladder. It reaches treeline at 0.4 mi., where the winter route enters on the right as the main trail bears left. (Descending, the summer route turns right and the winter route descends almost straight ahead.) The trail then ascends an open slope to lower Lion Head and continues to upper Lion Head at 0.9 mi., where it runs mostly level (with impressive views from the open spur) until it crosses Alpine Garden Trail at 1.1 mi. After passing through a belt of scrub, Lion Head Trail ascends steadily, then steeply, through an area of crags, with some short scrambles and a passage through a crack. The trail reaches its upper jct. with Tuckerman Ravine Trail at Cloudwater Spring (unreliable), about a third of the way up the cone of Mt. Washington, 0.4 mi. and 600 ft. below the summit.

HUNTINGTON RAVINE TRAIL (MAP 1: F9)
Cumulative from Tuckerman Ravine Trail (3,031 ft.) to:

Raymond Path (3,425 ft.)	0.5 mi.	400 ft.	0:25
First-aid cache on ravine floor (4,075 ft.)	1.2 mi.	1,050 ft.	1:10
Alpine Garden Trail crossing (5,475 ft.)	2.1 mi.	2,450 ft.	2:15
Mt. Washington Auto Rd. (5,725 ft.)	2.4 mi.	2,700 ft.	2:35
From Pinkham Notch Visitor Center (2,028 ft.) to:			
Mt. Washington summit (6,288 ft.) via Tuckerman Ravine, Huntington Ravine, and Nelson Crag trails	4.4 mi.	4,300 ft. (rev. 50 ft.)	4:20

AMC *Caution*: As noted on a USFS warning sign at the start of the trail, this is the most difficult regular hiking trail in the White Mountains. Many of the ledges demand proper use of handholds for safe passage, and hikers must exercise extreme caution at all times. Although experienced hikers who are reasonably comfortable on steep rock will probably encounter little difficulty when conditions are good, the exposure on several of the steepest ledges is likely to prove extremely unnerving to novices and to those who are uncomfortable in steep places. Do not attempt this trail if you have difficulty on ledges on ordinary trails. Hikers encumbered with large or heavy packs may experience great difficulty in some places. This trail is very dangerous when wet or icy, and its use for descent at any time is strongly discouraged. Retreat under unfavorable conditions can be extremely difficult and hazardous, so one should never venture beyond the boulder slope known as the Fan in deteriorating conditions or when weather on the Alpine Garden is likely to be severe. During late fall, winter, and early spring, this trail (and any part of the ravine headwall) should be attempted only by those with full technical ice-climbing training and equipment. In particular, the ravine must not be regarded as a feasible escape route from the Alpine Garden in severe winter conditions.

Yellow-blazed Huntington Ravine Trail diverges right from Tuckerman Ravine Trail 1.3 mi. from Pinkham Notch Visitor Center. It begins at an easy grade but with rough and rocky footing. In 0.2 mi., Huntington Ravine Trail crosses Cutler River on large rocks, and at 0.3 mi., it crosses the brook that drains Huntington Ravine. The trail then climbs steeply, and at 0.5 mi. it goes straight across Raymond Path. The grade eases, and in another 0.1 mi. Huntington Ravine Trail crosses Huntington Ravine Fire Road and then climbs a rocky section to meet the road again at 0.8 mi. The trail turns left on the road, and they coincide for 0.1 mi. on a wide, wet section; at this jct., a fine view of the ravine can be obtained by following the road to a small rise about 100 yd. in the opposite direction. At 0.9 mi. the road diverges left and the trail continues ahead, climbing moderately and crossing a brook twice. The road rejoins from the left in another 0.15 mi., and they again coincide, crossing a brook and reaching the Albert Dow Memorial first-aid cache (left) on the floor of the ravine at 1.2 mi. Huntington Ravine Trail now ascends a rocky stretch where a brook runs in the trail, then narrows to a rough footpath, and ascends into an area of large boulders. At 1.4 mi. it passes a boulder on the left whose top, reached by a scramble, affords a good view of the ravine. Beyond the scrubby trees is a steep slope covered with broken rock, known as the Fan. The tip of the

Fan lies at the foot of the deepest gully. To the left of this gully are precipices; the lower one is called the Pinnacle.

After passing through the boulders, with several scrambles, Huntington Ravine Trail ascends to the left side of the Fan and, marked by yellow blazes on the rocks, crosses the talus diagonally. The trail then turns left and ascends in scrub along the north (right) side of the Fan to its tip at 1.8 mi., crossing a small brook about two-thirds of the way up. It then recrosses the brooklet and immediately attacks the rocks to the right of the main gully, swinging right and climbing about 650 ft. in 0.3 mi. The marked route up the headwall takes the line of least difficulty and should be followed carefully over the ledges, which are dangerous, especially when wet. The first pitch above the Fan—a large, fairly smooth, steeply sloping ledge—is probably the most difficult scramble on the trail. Above the first ledges, the trail climbs steeply through scrub and over short sections of rock, including some fairly difficult scrambles; one high rock chimney is particularly challenging. About two-thirds of the way up, the trail turns sharply left at a promontory with a good view and then continues to the top of the headwall, where it crosses Alpine Garden Trail at 2.1 mi. From this point, Huntington Ravine Trail ascends moderately, and at 2.3 mi., it crosses Nelson Crag Trail; the summit can be reached in 0.8 mi. by turning left at this jct. Soon, Huntington Ravine Trail reaches Mt. Washington Auto Rd. just below the 7-mi. mark, 1.1 mi. below the summit.

HUNTINGTON RAVINE FIRE ROAD (MAP 1: F9)
From Tuckerman Ravine Trail (3,425 ft.) to:

First-aid cache on ravine floor (4,075 ft.)	1.1 mi.	50 ft.	0:50

WMNF This road, rough in places, is used by the USFS for snowcat access in winter. It is the preferred hiking route into Huntington Ravine during that season, when it is used primarily by technical climbers. It also provides access to the winter route of Lion Head Trail. It links Tuckerman Ravine Trail with Huntington Ravine Trail and then leads into the floor of the ravine, coinciding with the latter trail in two sections. Parts of it are sometimes used by summer hikers as an alternative to Huntington Ravine Trail, particularly in times of high water because the road's stream crossings are bridged. Huntington Ravine Fire Road diverges right from Tuckerman Ravine Trail (no sign in 2023) 1.7 mi. from Pinkham Notch Visitor Center and in 125 yd. crosses Raymond Path. In another 60 yd. the winter route of Lion Head Trail (closed and unsigned in other seasons) diverges left. The road runs at easy grades, passing a spur path to Harvard Cabin (open

December 1 to April 1 only) on the right at 0.3 mi. It crosses two bridges and then crosses Huntington Ravine Trail at 0.4 mi.

The next section is lightly used but offers easier grades and better footing than the hiking trail. It runs east for 0.1 mi. and then turns sharply left (northwest); at this turn there is a view back to Boott Spur. The road ascends gradually to the top of a rise with a view of Huntington Ravine ahead, and in another 100 yd., at 0.7 mi., Huntington Ravine Trail joins from the left. The road and trail coincide for 0.1 mi., and then the road diverges left, crosses a bridge, and ascends a very rough and rocky pitch. It crosses another bridge and rejoins the trail at 0.95 mi. The road ends at 1.1 mi. at the Albert Dow Memorial first-aid cache (left) as Huntington Ravine Trail continues ahead.

NELSON CRAG TRAIL (MAP 1: F9)
Cumulative from Old Jackson Road (2,625 ft.) to:

Closest approach to Mt. Washington Auto Rd. near Cragway Spring (4,825 ft.)	1.7 mi.	2,200 ft.	1:55
Huntington Ravine Trail (5,725 ft.)	2.8 mi.	3,150 ft. (rev. 50 ft.)	3:00
Mt. Washington summit (6,288 ft.)	3.6 mi.	3,750 ft. (rev. 50 ft.)	3:40

AMC This trail begins on Old Jackson Road, 1.7 mi. from Pinkham Notch Visitor Center and 0.2 mi. from the Auto Rd., and ascends to the summit of Mt. Washington. This is an attractive trail, relatively lightly used, fairly steep, rough in the lower part, and greatly exposed to weather in the upper part.

Leaving Old Jackson Road, Nelson Crag Trail follows and soon crosses a small brook, then climbs steadily west, quickly becoming quite steep and rough. At about 1.1 mi., the trail rises out of the scrub, emerging on the crest of Chandler Ridge, from which hikers have an unusual view of Pinkham Notch in both directions. From this point, the trail is above treeline and very exposed to the northwest winds. It bears northwest, climbs moderately over open ledges, and passes close by the Auto Rd. near Cragway Spring (unreliable) at the sharp turn about 0.3 mi. above the 5-mi. mark. The trail then climbs steeply southwest to the crest of the ridge. It passes over Nelson Crag and crosses Alpine Garden Trail, swings left, skirts the south side of a rocky bump recently named Agiocochook Crag (5,735 ft.), and crosses Huntington Ravine Trail at 2.8 mi. Nelson Crag Trail climbs up the rocks to Ball Crag (6,112 ft.), descends briefly, runs across the Auto Rd. and the Cog Railway, and finally ascends to the summit, passing to the left of the Sherman Adams summit building. To descend on this trail, follow the walkway down along the lower (east) side of the Sherman Adams building.

BOOT SPUR TRAIL (MAP 1: F9)
Cumulative from Tuckerman Ravine Trail (2,275 ft.) to:

Harvard Rock (4,046 ft.)	1.7 mi.	1,750 ft.	1:45
Split Rock (4,337 ft.)	2.0 mi.	2,050 ft.	2:00
Boott Spur Link (4,650 ft.)	2.2 mi.	2,400 ft.	2:20
Davis Path jct. (5,450 ft.)	2.9 mi.	3,200 ft.	3:05
Cumulative from Pinkham Notch Visitor Center (2,028 ft.) to:			
Davis Path jct. (5,450 ft.)	3.3 mi.	3,400 ft.	3:20
Mt. Washington summit (6,288 ft.) via Davis and Crawford paths	5.3 mi.	4,400 ft. (rev. 150 ft.)	4:50

AMC This trail runs from Tuckerman Ravine Trail, near Pinkham Notch Visitor Center, to Davis Path, near the summit of Boott Spur. Boott Spur Trail follows the long ridge that forms the south wall of Tuckerman Ravine and affords fine views. Grades are mostly moderate, but the trail has some rough footing. Much of this trail is above treeline and thus greatly exposed to any bad weather for a considerable distance.

Yellow-blazed Boott Spur Trail diverges left from Tuckerman Ravine Trail at a sharp right turn 0.4 mi. from Pinkham Notch Visitor Center, about 150 yd. above the side path to Crystal Cascade. Boott Spur Trail immediately crosses John Sherburne Ski Trail and then climbs through a ledgy area, crosses a tiny brook, and climbs steeply up a ladder to the ridge crest. At 0.5 mi., Boott Spur Trail climbs over a ledge with a vista of Huntington Ravine and then turns sharply right, where a side path (left) leads in 50 yd. to a very limited view east. Boott Spur Trail next crosses a level, muddy area and then ascends northwest up a steeper, rougher slope toward a craggy shoulder. Halfway up this section, an obscure, overgrown side path leads left 100 yd. to a small brook (last water). At the ridge crest, 1.0 mi. from Tuckerman Ravine Trail, Boott Spur Trail turns left, and a side path leads right (east) 25 yd. to an interesting although restricted outlook to Huntington Ravine. The main trail continues upward at moderate grades with several short scrambles, reaching a ledgy ridge crest that affords some views; at 1.7 mi., a side path on the right leads in 30 yd. to Harvard Rock, which provides an excellent view of Tuckerman Ravine and of Lion Head directly in front of the summit of Mt. Washington.

Boott Spur Trail emerges from the scrub at 1.9 mi., soon bears left, and then angles up the slope to Split Rock, which one can pass through or go around, at 2.0 mi. The trail turns right, passes through a final patch of fairly high scrub, and rises steeply over two minor humps to a broad, flat ridge, where, at 2.2 mi., Boott Spur Link descends on the right to Tuckerman Ravine Trail near Hermit Lake. Above this point, Boott Spur Trail follows the broad, open ridge, which consists of a series of alternating steplike levels and steep slopes. After passing just to the right (north) of the summit of Boott Spur, the trail descends slightly and ends at Davis Path.

BOOTT SPUR LINK (MAP 1: F9)
From Tuckerman Ravine Trail (3,875 ft.) to:

Boott Spur Trail (4,650 ft.)	0.6 mi.	850 ft. (rev. 50 ft.)	0:45

AMC This steep and rough but interesting trail climbs the south wall of Tuckerman Ravine, connecting the main floor of the ravine with the upper part of Boott Spur Trail. The link trail leaves the south side of Tuckerman Ravine Trail at the southeast corner of the clearing opposite the buildings at Hermit Lake, 2.4 mi. from Pinkham Notch Visitor Center. From this clearing, yellow-blazed Boott Spur Link descends south-southeast and soon crosses Cutler River on a bridge, then crosses John Sherburne Ski Trail and swings to the left, descending to a jct. with a former route of Boott Spur Link at 0.2 mi. Here, Boott Spur Link turns right and climbs very steeply straight up the slope through woods and scrub, with rapidly improving views back into the ravine. It continues to climb steeply over open rocks to the crest of Boott Spur, where it meets Boott Spur Trail.

GLEN BOULDER TRAIL (MAP 1: G9)
Cumulative from Glen Ellis Falls parking area on NH 16 (1,957 ft.) to:

The Direttissima (2,300 ft.)	0.4 mi.	350 ft.	0:25
Avalanche Brook Ski Trail (2,600 ft.)	0.8 mi.	650 ft.	0:45
Glen Boulder (3,729 ft.)	1.6 mi.	1,750 ft.	1:40
Slide Peak (4,804 ft.)	2.6 mi.	2,850 ft.	2:45
Davis Path jct. (5,175 ft.)	3.2 mi.	3,200 ft.	3:10
Boott Spur Trail (5,450 ft.) via Davis Path	3.7 mi.	3,500 ft.	3:35
Mt. Washington summit (6,288 ft.) via Davis and Crawford paths	5.7 mi.	4,450 ft. (rev. 150 ft.)	5:05

AMC This trail ascends past the famous Glen Boulder and over Slide Peak to Davis Path 0.5 mi. below Boott Spur. The trail begins on the west side of NH 16 at the Glen Ellis Falls parking area (WMNF Scenic Area sign; Recreation Pass required; restrooms; not plowed in winter; nearby roadside parking may be available). The parking area entrance is 0.7 mi. south of Pinkham Notch Visitor Center and 8.9 mi. north of the red covered bridge (NH 16A) in Jackson. Parts of the trail are steep and rough, but it reaches treeline and views relatively quickly.

Yellow-blazed Glen Boulder Trail leaves the south end of the parking area (sign) and ascends gradually for about 0.4 mi. southwest to the base of a small cliff. It climbs steeply around to the right of the cliff and meets the trail known as the Direttissima, which enters from the right (north) coming from Pinkham Notch Visitor Center. At this jct., Glen Boulder Trail turns sharply left (south) and soon passes a short branch that leads left to an outlook on the brink of a cliff, which commands a fine view of Wildcat Mtn. and Pinkham Notch. The main trail swings west, rises gradually, and then becomes steeper. At 0.8 mi., it crosses Avalanche Brook Ski Trail, which is marked with blue plastic markers (but not maintained for hiking). Glen Boulder Trail soon reaches the north bank of a brook draining the minor ravine south of the Gulf of Slides. After following the brook, which soon divides, the trail turns southwest and crosses both branches. The trail is level for 200 yd. and then rapidly climbs the northeast side of a spur of Slide Peak through conifers, giving views of the minor ravine and spur south of the Gulf of Slides. Leaving the trees, the trail climbs over open rocks with one fairly difficult scramble and, at 1.6 mi., reaches Glen Boulder, an immense rock perched on the end of the spur that is a familiar landmark for travelers through Pinkham Notch. The wide vista stretches from Mt. Chocorua around to Mt. Washington, with the view of Wildcat Mtn. being particularly fine.

From the boulder, the trail climbs steeply up the open ridge crest to its top at 2.0 mi., reenters high scrub, and ascends moderately. At 2.3 mi., a side path descends right about 60 yd. to a fine spring. Glen Boulder Trail continues to Slide Peak (also called Gulf Peak) at 2.6 mi.; this rather insignificant peak at the head of the Gulf of Slides offers fine views. The trail then turns north and descends slightly, leaving the scrub, and runs entirely above treeline—greatly exposed to the weather—and climbs moderately to Davis Path just below a minor crag.

GLEN ELLIS FALLS TRAIL (MAP 1: G9)
From Glen Ellis Falls parking area (1,957 ft.) to:

Base of Glen Ellis Falls (1,830 ft.)	0.2 mi.	0 ft. (rev. 125 ft.)	0:10

WMNF This short, popular path to a scenic waterfall was partly reconstructed with impressive stonework in 2020 by the WMNF and WMTC. The trail begins at the Glen Ellis Falls parking lot (WMNF Scenic Area sign; Recreation Pass required; restrooms; not plowed in winter, when the descent of the stone steps can be dangerous) on NH 16. The parking lot entrance is 0.7 mi. south of Pinkham Notch Visitor Center and 8.9 mi. north of the red covered bridge (NH 16A) in Jackson. The trail leaves from the south end of the parking area (sign for Glen Ellis Falls Trail and Wildcat Ridge Trail) and descends stone steps to a pedestrian underpass beneath the highway. (The USFS was in the process of constructing an accessible path down to the tunnel as of this writing.) On the far side of the underpass, Wildcat Ridge Trail diverges left at a sign, and Glen Ellis Falls Trail turns right and leads south along Ellis River. The first 300 ft. beyond the tunnel has been improved for accessibility to a widened pullout with a vista of Ellis River and Wildcat Ridge. From here the trail descends over many stone steps with wooden handrails and passes several cascades and WMNF informational panels. After a steeper descent over more stone steps, it makes a hairpin turn to the left (north) and continues down to a fine view of Glen Ellis Falls.

THE DIRETTISSIMA (MAP 1: F9–G9)
From NH 16 near Cutler River bridge (2,026 ft.) to:

Glen Boulder Trail (2,300 ft.)	1.0 mi.	400 ft. (rev. 100 ft.)	0:40

AMC For hikers desiring access to Glen Boulder Trail from Pinkham Notch Visitor Center, the Direttissima eliminates a road walk on NH 16. Although in general the trail is almost level, it is somewhat rough in places, with several significant ups and downs. The Direttissima begins 0.15 mi. south of Pinkham Notch Visitor Center (best winter parking), at a parking area just south of the highway bridge over Cutler River, indicated by a sign at the north end of the parking area. The yellow-blazed trail turns sharply left about 30 yd. into the woods and winds generally south, crossing a small brook. It skirts the upper (west) end of a gorge and then crosses the gorge on a bridge at 0.5 mi. The trail continues past a viewpoint looking down Pinkham Notch, runs along the top of one cliff and the bottom of another cliff, and ends at Glen Boulder Trail.

UPPER CONE OF MT. WASHINGTON
ALPINE GARDEN TRAIL (MAP 1: F9)
Cumulative from Tuckerman Ravine Trail (5,150 ft.) to:

Lion Head Trail (5,175 ft.)	0.3 mi.	50 ft. (rev. 50 ft.)	0:10
Huntington Ravine Trail (5,475 ft.)	1.2 mi.	350 ft.	0:45
Nelson Crag Trail (5,575 ft.)	1.4 mi.	450 ft.	0:55
Mt. Washington Auto Rd. jct. (5,305 ft.)	1.8 mi.	450 ft. (rev. 250 ft.)	1:10

AMC This trail leads from Tuckerman Ravine Trail to Mt. Washington Auto Rd. through the grassy lawn called the Alpine Garden. Although Alpine Garden Trail's chief value is the beauty of the flowers (in season) and the views, it is also a convenient connecting link between the trails on the east side of the mountain, making up a part of various routes for hikers who do not wish to visit the summit. The trail is completely above treeline and exposed to bad weather, although it is on the mountain's east side, which usually bears somewhat less of the brunt of the mountain's worst weather.

The tiny alpine flowers that grow here are best seen in middle to late June. Especially prominent are the five-petaled white diapensia; the bell-shaped, pink-magenta Lapland rosebay; and the very small pink blossoms of the alpine azalea. (For more details, see the *AMC Field Guide to the New England Alpine Summits*, AMC Books.) No plants should ever be picked or otherwise damaged. Hikers are urged to stay on trails or walk very carefully on rocks so as not to kill the fragile alpine vegetation.

Alpine Garden Trail diverges right (northeast) from Tuckerman Ravine Trail a short distance above the ravine headwall, 0.2 mi. below Tuckerman Junction. It leads northeast, descending and then ascending and, bearing toward Lion Head, crosses Lion Head Trail at 0.3 mi. Beyond this jct., Alpine Garden Trail ascends gradually northward. The trail traverses the Alpine Garden and crosses a tiny stream that is the headwater of Raymond Cataract. (This water may be contaminated by drainage from the summit buildings.) The trail soon approaches the top of Huntington Ravine and crosses Huntington Ravine Trail at 1.2 mi. (In winter and spring, take care not to approach too close to the icy gullies that drop precipitously from the edge of the Alpine Garden.) Rising to the top of the ridge leading from Nelson Crag, the trail crosses Nelson Crag Trail at 1.4 mi. and then descends and soon enters the old Glen House Bridle Path, constructed in 1851, whose course is still plain although it was abandoned more than 170 years ago. In a short distance, Alpine Garden Trail turns left and soon enters the Auto Rd. just above the 6-mi. mark, opposite the upper terminus of Wamsutta Trail.

TUCKERMAN CROSSOVER (MAP 1: F9)
Cumulative from Tuckerman Junction (5,383 ft.) to:

Davis Path (5,475 ft.)	0.3 mi.	100 ft.	0:10
Crawford Path (5,100 ft.)	0.8 mi.	100 ft. (rev. 400 ft.)	0:25
Lakes of the Clouds Hut (5,012 ft.) via Crawford Path	1.0 mi.	100 ft. (rev. 100 ft.)	0:35

AMC This trail connects Tuckerman Ravine with Lakes of the Clouds Hut. It is totally above treeline and crosses a high ridge where there is much exposure to westerly winds. Tuckerman Crossover leaves Tuckerman Ravine Trail left (southwest) at Tuckerman Junction, where the latter trail turns sharply right to ascend the cone. In 30 yd., Southside Trail diverges right. Tuckerman Crossover then rises gradually across Bigelow Lawn, crosses Davis Path, and descends moderately to Crawford Path, which it meets (along with Camel Trail) a short distance above the upper Lake of the Clouds. After a left turn on Crawford Path, Lakes of the Clouds Hut is reached in 0.2 mi. In the reverse direction, Tuckerman Crossover is the left-hand trail of two trails that diverge to the right (east) from Crawford Path, 0.2 mi. above the hut; Camel Trail is the right-hand trail of the two.

SOUTHSIDE TRAIL (MAP 1: F9)
From Tuckerman Junction (5,383 ft.) to:

Davis Path (5,575 ft.)	0.3 mi.	200 ft.	0:15

AMC This trail, completely above treeline, forms a direct link between Tuckerman Ravine and Crawford Path and Westside Trail. Southside Trail diverges right (northwest) from Tuckerman Crossover about 30 yd. southwest of Tuckerman Ravine Trail at Tuckerman Junction and climbs moderately. Southside Trail then skirts the southwest side of Mt. Washington's summit cone and enters Davis Path 0.1 mi. south of its jct. with Crawford Path.

LAWN CUTOFF (MAP 1: F9)
From Tuckerman Junction (5,383 ft.) to:

Davis Path (5,475 ft.)	0.4 mi.	100 ft.	0:15

AMC This trail provides a direct route between Tuckerman Junction and Boott Spur, entirely above treeline. It leaves Tuckerman Ravine Trail on the left (south) at Tuckerman Junction and ascends gradually southward across Bigelow Lawn to Davis Path 0.6 mi. north of Boott Spur.

CAMEL TRAIL (MAP 1: F9)
From Crawford Path (5,100 ft.) to:

Davis Path (5,465 ft.)	0.7 mi.	350 ft.	0:30

AMC This trail, connecting Boott Spur with Lakes of the Clouds Hut, is named for ledges on Boott Spur that resemble a kneeling camel when seen against the skyline. This is the right-hand trail of the two that diverge right (east) from Crawford Path 0.2 mi. northeast of Lakes of the Clouds Hut (Tuckerman Crossover is the left-hand trail). Camel Trail ascends easy grassy slopes, crosses the old location of Crawford Path, and continues in a nearly straight line eastward across the level stretch of Bigelow Lawn. Camel Trail aims directly toward the ledges that form the camel, passes under the camel's "nose," and joins Davis Path about 250 yd. northwest of Lawn Cutoff.

WESTSIDE TRAIL (MAP 1: F9)
From Crawford Path (5,625 ft.) to:

Gulfside Trail (5,500 ft.)	0.9 mi.	100 ft. (rev. 200 ft.)	0:30

WMNF This trail was partly constructed by pioneer trail maker J. Rayner Edmands; as was Edmands's practice, many segments are paved with carefully placed stones. The trail is wholly above timberline, very much exposed to the prevailing west and northwest winds. As a shortcut between Gulfside Trail and Crawford Path that avoids the summit of Mt. Washington, it saves about 0.7 mi. in distance and 600 ft. in elevation between objectives in the Northern and Southern Presidentials. Westside Trail diverges left (northwest) from Crawford Path at the point where Crawford Path begins to climb the steep part of the cone of Mt. Washington. Westside Trail skirts the cone, climbing for 0.6 mi. at an easy grade, then descends moderately, passes under the tracks of the Mt. Washington Cog Railway, and soon ends at Gulfside Trail.

TRINITY HEIGHTS CONNECTOR (MAP 1: F9)
From summit of Mt. Washington (6,288 ft.) to:

Gulfside Trail (6,100 ft.)	0.2 mi.	0 ft. (rev. 200 ft.)	0:05

AMC This trail was created to allow the AT to make a loop over the summit of Mt. Washington; formerly the true summit was a side trip, albeit a very short one, from the AT, so technically the AT did not pass over the summit. Trinity Heights is a name previously used for the summit region of Mt. Washington. From the true summit (a rock outcropping, marked by a sign, between the Tip Top House and the Sherman Adams summit building), the trail leaves at a sign to the right of the Tip Top House and runs northwest, descending moderately over the rocks to Gulfside Trail, less than 0.1 mi. to the north of its jct. with Crawford Path.

NORTH OF PINKHAM NOTCH VISITOR CENTER
RAYMOND PATH (MAP 1: F9)
Cumulative from Old Jackson Road (2,650 ft.) to:

Huntington Ravine Trail (3,425 ft.)	1.8 mi.	900 ft. (rev. 100 ft.)	1:20
Tuckerman Ravine Trail (3,700 ft.)	2.4 mi.	1,200 ft. (rev. 50 ft.)	1:50
Hermit Lake (3,850 ft.) via Tuckerman Ravine Trail	2.7 mi.	1,350 ft.	2:00

AMC Raymond Path, one of the older trails in the region, begins on Old Jackson Road 1.7 mi. from Pinkham Notch Visitor Center and 0.2 mi. from Mt. Washington Auto Rd., about 100 yd. south of the beginning of Nelson Crag Trail. Raymond Path ends at Tuckerman Ravine Trail about 0.3 mi. below Hermit Lake. Grades are mostly easy to moderate.

Leaving Old Jackson Road, blue-blazed Raymond Path crosses several small branches of Peabody River, climbing moderately to the crest of a small ridge at 0.8 mi., which offers a restricted view of Lion Head and Boott Spur. The trail descends moderately for a short distance to a small mossy brook and then begins an easy ascent, crossing Nelson Brook at 1.2 mi. and Huntington Ravine Trail at 1.8 mi. From here, Raymond Path drops down a steep slope to cross the brook that drains Huntington Ravine on a ledge at the brink of Vesper Falls; use great care here in high water or icy conditions, and perhaps consider a detour upstream. (*Note*: This crossing can be avoided entirely by following Huntington Ravine Trail north 0.1 mi. to Huntington Ravine Fire Road and then following the road 0.3 mi. south until it crosses Raymond Path.) Soon the trail crosses the brook coming from the Ravine of Raymond Cataract (sign) and then Huntington Ravine Fire Road before climbing 0.3 mi. at a moderate grade to Tuckerman Ravine Trail.

OLD JACKSON ROAD (MAP 1: F9)
From Pinkham Notch Visitor Center (2,028 ft.) to:

Mt. Washington Auto Rd. (2,675 ft.)	1.9 mi.	750 ft. (rev. 100 ft.)	1:20

AMC This trail runs north from Pinkham Notch Visitor Center to Mt. Washington Auto Rd., providing access to a variety of other trails, along with the most direct route from the visitor center to the Great Gulf. Old Jackson Road is part of the AT and is blazed in white. Because the trail is used as a cross-country ski trail in winter, it is usually also marked with blue diamonds year-round.

Old Jackson Road diverges right from Tuckerman Ravine Trail about 50 yd. from the trailhead at the rear of the Trading Post. After about 0.3 mi., Blanchard and Connie's Way ski trails cross, and at 0.4 mi., Link Ski Trail enters right, just before a bridge; Crew-Cut Trail leaves right (east) just after the bridge. Soon, Old Jackson Road begins to ascend moderately and crosses a small brook that runs in an interesting gorge with a small waterfall just above the trail. At 0.9 mi., George's Gorge Trail enters on the right (east), and Old Jackson Road rises easily across the flat divide between the Saco and Androscoggin drainages and then descends gradually, crossing several small brooks. Just before reaching a larger brook, the trail makes a sharp left turn uphill, and after a short and steep climb, it turns right and runs nearly level. At 1.7 mi., Raymond Path leaves on the left, and in another 100 yd., just after a small brook crossing, Nelson Crag Trail leaves on the left. Continuing north, Old Jackson Road climbs slightly up an interesting little rocky hogback, passes through an old gravel pit, and meets the Auto Rd. just above the 2-mi. mark, at a small parking area opposite the trailhead for Madison Gulf Trail.

CREW-CUT TRAIL (MAP 1: F9–F10)
Cumulative from Old Jackson Road (2,075 ft.) to:

Liebeskind's Loop (2,330 ft.)	0.5 mi.	250 ft.	0:25
NH 16 (1,961 ft.)	1.0 mi.	250 ft. (rev. 400 ft.)	0:40

AMC Crew-Cut Trail, George's Gorge Trail, and Liebeskind's Loop, a small network of paths in the region north of Pinkham Notch Visitor Center, were originally located and cut by Bradford Swan. These trails provide pleasant walking at a modest expenditure of effort, passing through pleasant woods with small ravines and ledges.

Blue-blazed Crew-Cut Trail leaves Old Jackson Road on the right 0.4 mi. from the visitor center, just after a bridged stream crossing and just before the point where Old Jackson Road starts to climb more steeply. After crossing a stony, dry brook bed, Crew-Cut Trail runs generally northeast, crossing two small brooks. On the east bank of the second brook, at 0.2 mi., George's Gorge Trail leaves left. Crew-Cut Trail continues generally east-northeast, rising moderately and at times steeply, up the slope through open woods, crossing several gullies. It skirts southeast of the steeper rocky outcroppings until, at 0.5 mi. from Old Jackson Road, Liebeskind's Loop enters left, coming down from George's Gorge Trail. The spur path to Lila's Ledge, an excellent viewpoint, leaves Liebeskind's Loop less than 0.1 mi. from this jct. Crew-Cut Trail travels along the base of a cliff, turns right, and then descends steeply over a few small ledges and through open woods until it passes east of a small, high-level bog formed by an old beaver dam. Shortly thereafter, the trail crosses a small stream and Connie's Way Ski Trail and goes through open woods again, emerging at the top of the grassy embankment on NH 16, 0.1 mi. south of the entrance to Wildcat Mtn. Ski Resort (best parking year-round).

GEORGE'S GORGE TRAIL (MAP 1: F9)
From Crew-Cut Trail (2,065 ft.) to:

Old Jackson Road (2,525 ft.)	0.8 mi.	600 ft. (rev. 150 ft.)	0:40

AMC This blue-blazed trail leaves Crew-Cut Trail on the left, 0.2 mi. from Old Jackson Road on the east bank of a small brook (the infant Peabody River). George's Gorge Trail leads north up the brook—steeply in places—passing Chudacoff Falls (often dry), and crossing the brook twice before swinging sharply right away from the water. Liebeskind's Loop leaves on the right at 0.5 mi., and George's Gorge Trail then climbs nearly to the top of a knob. It descends west by switchbacks, crosses a small brook, and rises slightly to Old Jackson Road in the flat section near that trail's halfway point, 0.9 mi. from Pinkham Notch Visitor Center.

LIEBESKIND'S LOOP (MAP 1: F9–F10)
From George's Gorge Trail (2,575 ft.) to:

Crew-Cut Trail (2,350 ft.)	0.6 mi.	50 ft. (rev. 250 ft.)	0:20
From Pinkham Notch Visitor Center (2,028 ft.):			
Complete loop via Old Jackson Road, Crew-Cut Trail, George's Gorge Trail, Liebeskind's Loop (including side trip to Lila's Ledge), Crew-Cut Trail, and Old Jackson Road	2.8 mi.	650 ft.	1:45

AMC Yellow-blazed Liebeskind's Loop makes possible an interesting loop hike starting on Old Jackson Road 0.4 mi. from Pinkham Notch Visitor Center (using Crew-Cut and George's Gorge trails, Liebeskind's Loop, and Crew-Cut Trail). This trip is best made in the sequence noted above because George's Gorge is more interesting on the ascent, and Liebeskind's Loop is more interesting on the descent.

Liebeskind's Loop leaves right (east) near the high point of George's Gorge Trail, 0.3 mi. from Old Jackson Road, and descends to a swampy flat. It then rises through a spruce thicket to the top of a cliff and a fine lookout called Brad's Bluff, with a clear view to the south down Pinkham Notch. Here, the trail turns left and runs along the edge of the cliff, finally descending by an easy zigzag in a gully to a beautiful open grove of birches. Liebeskind's Loop continues east, descending through a small gorge and skirting the east end of several small swells, until it swings south and descends to a small notch in the ridge crest. Here, a spur path leads left 0.1 mi. (50-ft. ascent) to Lila's Ledge (named by Brad Swan in memory of his wife), which affords excellent views of Pinkham Notch and the eastern slope of Mt. Washington; the lower ledge is reached by a short, steep descent that may be dangerous in wet or icy conditions. Liebeskind's Loop descends on the other side of the ridge to meet Crew-Cut Trail, which can then be followed back to the starting point by turning right (west-southwest).

MAIN RIDGE OF THE SOUTHERN PRESIDENTIALS
CRAWFORD PATH (MAP 1: G8–F9)
Cumulative from Mt. Clinton Rd. parking area (1,884 ft.) via Crawford Connector to:

Mizpah Cutoff (3,490 ft.)	1.9 mi.	1,600 ft.	1:45
Webster Cliff Trail (4,250 ft.)	3.1 mi.	2,350 ft.	2:45
South end of Mt. Eisenhower Loop (4,425 ft.)	4.3 mi.	2,750 ft.	3:30
Mt. Eisenhower Trail (4,465 ft.)	5.0 mi.	2,900 ft.	3:55

South end of Mt. Monroe Loop (5,075 ft.)	6.2 mi.	3,550 ft.	4:55
Lakes of the Clouds Hut (5,014 ft.)	7.0 mi.	3,600 ft.	5:20
Westside Trail (5,625 ft.)	7.9 mi.	4,200 ft.	6:05
Gulfside Trail (6,150 ft.)	8.3 mi.	4,750 ft.	6:30
Mt. Washington summit (6,288 ft.)	8.5 mi.	4,900 ft.	6:40

CRAWFORD PATH, IN REVERSE (MAP 1: G8–F9)
Cumulative from the summit of Mt. Washington (6,288 ft.) to:

Gulfside Trail (6,150 ft.)	0.2 mi.	0 ft.	0:05
Westside Trail (5,625 ft.)	0.6 mi.	0 ft.	0:20
Lakes of the Clouds Hut (5,012 ft.)	1.5 mi.	0 ft.	0:45
South end of Mt. Monroe Loop (5,075 ft.)	2.3 mi.	150 ft.	1:10
Mt. Eisenhower Trail (4,465 ft.)	3.5 mi.	200 ft.	1:50
South end of Mt. Eisenhower Loop (4,425 ft.)	4.2 mi.	300 ft.	2:15
Webster Cliff Trail (4,250 ft.)	5.4 mi.	500 ft.	2:55
Mizpah Cutoff (3,490 ft.)	6.6 mi.	500 ft.	3:35
Mt. Clinton Rd. parking area (1,884 ft.) via Crawford Connector	8.5 mi.	500 ft.	4:30

WMNF This trail is considered the oldest continuously maintained footpath in the United States. The first section, leading up Mt. Pierce (Mt. Clinton), was cut in 1819 by Abel Crawford and his son Ethan Allen Crawford. In 1840, Thomas J. Crawford, a younger son of Abel, converted the footpath into a bridle path, but more than a century has passed since it was used regularly for ascents on horseback. The trail still mostly follows the original path, except for the section between Mt. Monroe and Westside Trail, which was relocated to take Crawford Path off the windswept ridge and down past the shelter at Lakes of the Clouds. From the jct. just north of Mt. Pierce to the summit of Mt. Washington, Crawford Path is part of the AT and is blazed in white; the lower part is blazed in blue. In 1994, on its 175th anniversary, Crawford Path was designated as a National Recreation Trail. In 2018 and 2019, in conjunction with the trail's 200th anniversary, extensive improvements were made on Crawford Path under the direction of the WMTC, partnering with the WMNF, AMC, and several other organizations and trail clubs. Many rock steps and drainages were constructed along the section leading up to Mt. Pierce. Above treeline, sections of the trail were more clearly defined with the building of cairns and scree walls, especially in the vicinity of Mt. Franklin and Mt. Monroe. Funding was provided by WMTC with support from the National Forest Foundation and outdoor retailer REI.

Caution: Parts of this trail are dangerous in bad weather. Several lives have been lost on Crawford Path because of failure to observe proper precautions. Between Mt. Pierce and Mt. Eisenhower, numerous ledges are exposed to the weather, but they are scattered, and shelter is usually available in nearby scrub. From the Eisenhower–Franklin col, the trail runs completely above treeline, exposed to the full force of storms. The most dangerous section is on the cone of Mt. Washington, beyond Lakes of the Clouds Hut. Always carry a compass and study the map before starting. If trouble arises on or above Mt. Monroe, take refuge at Lakes of the Clouds Hut or go down Ammonoosuc Ravine Trail. Crawford Path is well marked above treeline with large cairns; in poor visibility, take great care to stay on the main trail because many of the other paths in the vicinity are much less clearly marked. Hikers who lose the main trail in bad weather and cannot find it again after diligent effort should travel west, descending into the woods and following streams downhill to the roads. On the southeast side of the ridge, toward the Dry River valley, nearly all the slopes are more precipitous, the river crossings are potentially dangerous, and the distance to a highway is much greater.

The main parking area (Recreation Pass required; restrooms; plowed in winter), at the south end of Crawford Path, is on the west side of Mt. Clinton Rd., 0.1 mi. north of its jct. with US 302. The former parking lot on US 302 has been closed, and Crawford Path hikers are requested to use the Mt. Clinton Rd. lot because the parking spaces at other lots in the area are needed for the trails that originate from those lots. For historical reasons, the name Crawford Path continues to be attached to the old route of the trail that leads directly from US 302, and the short path that connects Crawford Path to the Mt. Clinton Rd. parking lot is called Crawford Connector. In the descriptions that follow, the main route will be described and distances given starting from Mt. Clinton Rd. via Crawford Connector, which is the route for most hikers using this trail.

The path is described in the northbound direction (toward Mt. Washington). Distances, elevation gains, and times are also given in the reverse direction.

Leaving the parking lot and soon crossing Mt. Clinton Rd., blue-blazed Crawford Connector climbs gradually for 0.4 mi. until it reaches the bridge over Gibbs Brook. Here, Crawford Cliff Spur diverges left.

Crawford Cliff Spur, a short side path with yellow blazes, leaves Crawford Connector at the west end of the bridge over Gibbs Brook and follows the brook to a small flume and pool. Crawford Cliff Spur turns left and climbs steeply above the brook, then turns left again, becomes very rough, and reaches Crawford Cliff (2,400 ft.), a ledge with an outlook over Crawford

Notch, the Willey Range, and Highland Center, 0.4 mi. (350-ft. ascent, 0:20) from Crawford Connector.

Crawford Connector, meanwhile, continues across the bridge and ends at **Crawford Path** 0.2 mi. from the latter trail's trailhead on US 302, opposite AMC's Highland Center at Crawford Notch. To continue ascending on Crawford Path, turn left. Crawford Path follows the south bank of Gibbs Brook, passing a National Recreation Trail plaque and an old dam on the brook, and at 0.6 mi. from Mt. Clinton Rd., a side path (sign) leads 40 yd. left, dropping steeply to the base of Gibbs Falls. Soon Crawford Path enters the 900-acre Gibbs Brook Scenic Area, with old-growth red spruce and yellow birch, and ascends moderately but steadily, using many recently placed rock steps. At about 1.2 mi. from Mt. Clinton Rd., the trail begins to climb away from the brook, angling southeast up the side of the valley. At 1.9 mi., Mizpah Cutoff diverges right (east) for Mizpah Spring Hut. Crawford Path continues to ascend at easy to moderate grades, crossing several small brooks. It reaches its high point on the shoulder of Mt. Pierce and runs almost level through scrub, breaking into the open with fine views shortly before reaching the jct. with Webster Cliff Trail at 3.1 mi. Webster Cliff Trail leads right (south) to the summit of Mt. Pierce in 0.1 mi. (*Caution*: In winter, Crawford Path can be very difficult to follow in the reverse direction where it enters the snow-packed scrub; in windy conditions, tracks may be quickly covered with snowdrifts.)

From Mt. Pierce to Mt. Eisenhower, Crawford Path runs through patches of scrub and woods with many open ledges that allow for magnificent views in all directions. Cairns and the marks left by many feet on the rocks indicate the route. The path winds about, heading generally northeast, staying fairly near the poorly defined crest of the broad ridge, which is composed of several rounded humps. The trail descends at easy to moderate grades over several ledgy bumps with views and crosses the Pierce–Eisenhower col on bog bridges at 3.6 mi. At 3.8 mi., it crosses a small stream and then ascends mostly on ledges to the jct. with Mt. Eisenhower Loop, which diverges left at 4.3 mi. The trip over this summit adds only 0.3 mi. and 300 ft. of climbing and provides excellent views in good weather. Crawford Path bears somewhat to the right at this jct. and runs nearly level, with minor ups and downs—although with rough footing—through scrub on the steep southeast side of the mountain. (Crawford Path is a better route in bad weather compared with Mt. Eisenhower Loop.) Mt. Eisenhower Loop rejoins Crawford Path on the left at 4.8 mi., just above the sag between Mt. Eisenhower and Mt. Franklin. Edmands Path can be reached from this jct. by following Mt. Eisenhower Loop to the left for 35 yd.

At 5.0 mi., Mt. Eisenhower Trail from the Dry River valley enters right. Crawford Path then begins the ascent of the shoulder southwest of Mt. Franklin, first moderately, passing ledges with excellent views back to the Dry River valley and Mt. Eisenhower, and then steeply for a short distance near the top. At 5.5 mi., the trail reaches the relatively level shoulder, where it is defined by recently built scree walls and cairns. It continues, with minor descents and ascents, to a jct. at 6.0 mi. Here, an unmarked but well-worn path diverges sharply right and in 130 yd. leads to the barely noticeable summit of Mt. Franklin (cairn), which provides a particularly good look into Oakes Gulf. (In the reverse direction, bear right and downhill at this jct., as the side path diverges left and uphill.) At 6.2 mi., Mt. Monroe Loop diverges left to cross both summits of Monroe, affording excellent views. The loop is about the same length as the parallel section of Crawford Path but requires about 350 ft. more climbing with rougher footing. Crawford Path is safer in inclement conditions because it is much less exposed to the weather. Crawford Path continues along the edge of the precipice that forms the northwest wall of Oakes Gulf and then follows a relocated section, passing to the left of an area that has been closed to public entry to preserve the habitat of the dwarf cinquefoil, an endangered species of plant. (*Note*: The area between the two ends of Mt. Monroe Loop is one of great fragility and botanical importance. To protect this area—probably the most significant tract of rare vegetation in the entire White Mountain region—hikers should take great care to stay on the defined trail.) At 6.9 mi., Mt. Monroe Loop rejoins on the left, and Crawford Path descends easily to Lakes of the Clouds Hut at 7.0 mi.

Ammonoosuc Ravine Trail enters on the left at the corner of the hut, and in another 30 yd., Dry River Trail enters on the right. Crawford Path crosses the outlet of the lower, larger Lake of the Clouds and passes between it and the smaller, upper lake. In a short distance, at 7.2 mi., Camel Trail (leading southeast, then east to Boott Spur) and Tuckerman Crossover (leading northeast to Tuckerman Junction) diverge right at the same point. Crawford Path then ascends moderately on the northwest side of the ridge, always some distance below the crest. Davis Path, which has been following the original, less-sheltered location of Crawford Path, enters on the right at 7.9 mi., at the foot of the cone of Mt. Washington. In another 50 yd., Westside Trail, a shortcut to the Northern Presidentials, diverges left. Crawford Path runs generally north, switching back and forth as it climbs the steep cone through a trench in the rocks. At the plateau west of the summit, Crawford Path meets Gulfside Trail at 8.3 mi. Now coinciding with Gulfside Trail, Crawford Path turns right and passes through the old corral (outlined by rock walls) in which saddle horses from the Glen House were kept. The combined trails then swing left (northeast) and lead between the Yankee Building and the Tip Top House on the left and the Stage Office and Cog Railway track on the right. Follow the sign "Crawford Path to Summit." The summit, also marked by a sign, is an outcropping between the Tip Top House and the Sherman Adams summit building.

Descending from the summit of Mt. Washington, the combined Crawford Path and Gulfside Trail are on the right (west) side of the Cog Railway track. They lead southwest between the buildings and then swing to the right (northwest) at a sign and large cairn (avoid random side paths to the south). After passing through the old corral, the combined trails reach a jct. where Gulfside Trail turns sharply right. Here, Crawford Path turns left (southwest) and zigzags downward through a trench in the rocks.

MT. EISENHOWER LOOP (MAP 1: G8)
Cumulative from south jct. with Crawford Path (4,425 ft.) to:

Mt. Eisenhower summit (4,763 ft.)	0.4 mi.	350 ft.	0:25
North jct. with Crawford Path (4,475 ft.)	0.8 mi.	350 ft. (rev. 300 ft.)	0:35

AMC This trail parallels Crawford Path, climbing over the bare, flat summit of Mt. Eisenhower, which provides magnificent views. Mt. Eisenhower Loop diverges from Crawford Path 4.3 mi. from Mt. Clinton Rd. at the south edge of the summit dome, climbs easily through scrub for 0.1 mi., turns sharply left in a flat area, and ascends rather steeply via wooden and rock steps and two short ladders. It swings right at an easy grade, with views over the Dry River valley, and then bears left to the summit at 0.4 mi. Here there is a large cairn and a defined circular viewing area to protect surrounding alpine vegetation. Mt. Eisenhower Loop then descends moderately northeast to a ledge overlooking Red Pond (more a small alpine bog than a pond) before dropping steeply by switchbacks over ledges. It passes through a grassy sag to the left of Red Pond, climbs briefly past a jct. on the left with Edmands Path, and in another 35 yd. rejoins Crawford Path, just above the sag between Mt. Eisenhower and Mt. Franklin.

MT. MONROE LOOP (MAP 1: F9)
Cumulative from south jct. with Crawford Path (5,075 ft.) to:

Summit of Mt. Monroe (5,369 ft.)	0.4 mi.	350 ft. (rev. 50 ft.)	0:20
North jct. with Crawford Path (5,075 ft.)	0.7 mi.	350 ft. (rev. 300 ft.)	0:30

AMC This short trail runs parallel to Crawford Path and passes over the summits of Little Monroe and Mt. Monroe. The views are fine, but parts of Mt. Monroe Loop are rough, and the summits are very exposed to the weather. The trail diverges from Crawford Path 6.2 mi. from Mt. Clinton Rd. It quickly ascends the minor crag called Little Monroe and then descends into the shallow, grassy sag beyond. Mt. Monroe Loop climbs steeply over boulder fields to the summit of Mt. Monroe at 0.4 mi., follows the northeast ridge to the end of the shoulder, and drops sharply to Crawford Path 0.1 mi. south of Lakes of the Clouds Hut.

SOUTHERN PRESIDENTIALS FROM THE WEST AND SOUTH

AMMONOOSUC RAVINE TRAIL (MAP 1: F8–F9)

Cumulative from Cog Railway Base Rd. parking lot (2,495 ft.) to:

Ammonoosuc Link (2,870 ft.)	1.0 mi.	400 ft. (rev. 50 ft.)	0:40
Gem Pool (3,450 ft.)	2.1 mi.	1,000 ft.	1:35
Brook crossing on flat ledges (4,175 ft.)	2.5 mi.	1,750 ft.	2:05
Lakes of the Clouds Hut (5,012 ft.)	3.1 mi.	2,550 ft.	2:50
Mt. Washington summit (6,288 ft.) via Crawford Path	4.6 mi.	3,850 ft.	4:15
Mt. Monroe summit (5,369 ft.) via Crawford Path and Mt. Monroe Loop	3.5 mi.	2,950 ft.	3:15

WMNF Ammonoosuc Ravine Trail ascends to Lakes of the Clouds Hut from a parking lot (Recreation Pass required; restrooms; plowed in winter) on Cog Railway Base Rd., 1.1 mi. east of its jct. with Mt. Clinton Rd. and Jefferson Notch Rd. The parking area is a stop for the AMC Hiker Shuttle. The trail can also be reached on foot from Jefferson Notch Rd. via Boundary Line and Jewell trails (Section Two). Together with the upper section of Crawford Path, Ammonoosuc Ravine Trail provides the shortest route to Mt. Washington from the west. The trail follows the headwaters of the Ammonoosuc River, with many fine falls, cascades, and pools, and affords excellent views from its upper section. This is the most direct route to Lakes of the Clouds Hut and the best route to or from the hut in bad weather because the trail lies in woods or scrub except for the last 0.2 mi. to the hut. The section above Gem Pool is very steep and rough and is likely to prove arduous to many hikers, particularly those with limited trail-walking experience. Many hikers also find it somewhat unpleasant to descend this section due to the steep, often slippery rocks and ledges. Follow the trail with care on the ledges, where it is not always marked well.

Leaving the parking lot, the blue-blazed trail follows a path through the woods, descending to cross Franklin Brook at 0.3 mi. and then passing over a double pipeline as the trail skirts the Base Station area at mostly easy grades. The trail joins an older route at the edge of the Ammonoosuc River at 1.0 mi., after a slight descent. Here a link trail from the Cog Railway joins from the left (signs: "Cog R.R.," "Lakes of the Clouds Hut"). Descending, bear left here to return to the WMNF parking area.

Ammonoosuc Link. Ammonoosuc Ravine Trail can be accessed from the Cog Railway Base Station by this link path. Parking (fee charged, $10 per person in 2024; plowed in winter) is available in a designated lower gravel lot on the right (south) side of Cog Railway Base Rd. (sign: "Hiker Parking"), 0.4 mi. east of the WMNF trailhead parking area. Elevation is 2,630 ft. (The upper lots are reserved for Cog Railway customers.) Proceed on foot up the access loop road and through a parking lot to a sign ("Ammonoosuc Ravine Trail") behind the main Base Station building on the right. The route turns right on a paved driveway, passes between two cabins, and enters the woods at a trail sign to the right of a third cabin, 0.2 mi. from hiker parking (elevation 2,720 ft.). The link passes a WMNF kiosk and ascends moderately with good footing to meet Ammonoosuc Ravine Trail, 0.3 mi. from the Base Station (elevation gain 150 ft., 0:15). From hiker parking: 0.5 mi., 250 ft., 0:25.

From this jct., **Ammonoosuc Ravine Trail** bears right along the attractive river. It ascends by easy to moderate grades, although with much rough and rocky footing. This section offers numerous views of the river, which was widened by heavy rainfall and landslides in October 2017. After passing a memorial plaque for Herbert Judson Young, a Dartmouth student who perished from hypothermia near here in 1928, the trail traverses a gravelly washout, where caution is needed. It crosses Monroe Brook at 1.7 mi., and at 1.9 mi., at an open spot along the river, there is a good view of the headwall of Ammonoosuc Ravine a few steps left of the trail. Soon the trail skirts an area that was severely damaged by a large avalanche in 2010; the avalanche track can be seen to the left of the trail. It then follows the main branch of the river away from the avalanche track, and at 2.1 mi., the trail crosses the outlet of Gem Pool, a beautiful emerald pool at the foot of a cascade.

Now the very steep, rough ascent begins, with many rock steps. At 2.3 mi., a side path (sign) descends right about 80 yd. to a spectacular viewpoint at the foot of the gorge. Above this point, the main brook falls about 600 ft. down a steep trough in the mountainside at an average angle of 45 degrees; another brook a short distance to the north does the same—and these two spectacular waterslides meet in a pool at the foot of the gorge. Ammonoosuc Ravine Trail continues its steep ascent, crossing a side stream and ascending steep, often slippery ledges, one by means of a short ladder. The trail passes an outlook over the cascades to the right and, at 2.5 mi., crosses the main brook on flat ledges at the head of the highest fall, a striking viewpoint. (When descending, turn left after crossing the brook and descend over ledges; avoid a beaten path leading ahead into the woods.) The grade now begins to ease, and the trail makes several more brook crossings; follow the trail with care where it crosses a brook and continues up ledges between that brook and another brook on the right. As the ascent continues, ledges become more frequent, and the scrub becomes smaller and more sparse. At 3.0 mi., the trail emerges from the scrub and follows a line of cairns directly up some rock slabs (which are slippery when wet), passes through one last patch of scrub, and reaches Crawford Path at the south side of Lakes of the Clouds Hut.

EDMANDS PATH (MAP 1: G8)
Cumulative from Mt. Clinton Rd. (2,039 ft.) to:

Stone gateway (4,000 ft.)	2.2 mi.	1,950 ft.	2:05
Mt. Eisenhower Loop jct. (4,450 ft.)	2.9 mi.	2,400 ft.	2:40
Mt. Eisenhower summit (4,763 ft.) via Mt. Eisenhower Loop	3.3 mi.	2,750 ft.	3:00

WMNF Edmands Path climbs to Mt. Eisenhower Loop near its jct. with Crawford Path in the Eisenhower–Franklin col, starting from a parking lot on the east side of Mt. Clinton Rd., 2.3 mi. north of its jct. with US 302 and 1.3 mi. south of its jct. with Cog Railway Base Rd. and Jefferson Notch Rd. Mt. Clinton Rd. is not plowed in winter. Edmands Path provides the shortest route to the summit of Mt. Eisenhower and a relatively easy access to the middle portion of Crawford Path and the Southern Presidentials. The last 0.1-mi. segment before Edmands Path joins Mt. Eisenhower Loop and Crawford Path and is very exposed to northwest winds, and, although short, can create a serious problem in bad weather. The ledgy brook crossings in the upper part of the trail can be treacherous in icy conditions.

J. Rayner Edmands, the pioneer trail maker, relocated and reconstructed this trail in 1909. The rock cribbing and paving in the middle and upper sections of the trail testify to the diligent labor that Edmands devoted to constructing a trail with constant comfortable grades in difficult terrain. Erosion from the weather and hiker traffic of many decades has made the footing significantly rougher in recent years; in many places above 3,000 ft. the footway has been eroded to bedrock. Still, this blue-blazed trail retains what is probably the most moderate grade of any comparable trail in the Presidential Range.

From its trailhead, Edmands Path runs nearly level and crosses a small brook on a log bridge, then swings left to cross a second, gullied brook. At 0.4 mi., the trail crosses Abenaki Brook on rocks and turns sharply right onto an old logging road on the far bank. At 0.7 mi., the trail turns left off the old road and crosses a wet area. Soon the trail begins to climb steadily up the west ridge of Mt. Eisenhower, with rougher footing. The grade remains comfortable, although erosion has created some short ledge scrambles. At 2.0 mi., the trail turns sharply left and ascends through a blowdown patch from the October 2017 storm; at the top of the patch there is a partial view west that should endure for a few years. After a short zigzag, the trail swings left at 2.2. mi. through a tiny stone gateway. At 2.4 mi., it crosses a small brook running over a ledge and climbs a short, steep, ledgy pitch with water running down the trail. Soon the grade becomes almost level, even descending slightly, as the trail contours around the north slope of Mt. Eisenhower, affording partial views out through a fringe of trees. The footing becomes quite rough and rocky, and at 2.8 mi., Edmands Path breaks into the open, crosses the nose of a ridge on a talus slope with rough, loose footing, and ascends moderately to Mt. Eisenhower Loop 35 yd. west of Crawford Path.

WEBSTER–JACKSON TRAIL (MAP 1: G8)
Cumulative from US 302 (1,892 ft.) to:

Bugle Cliff (2,450 ft.)	0.6 mi.	550 ft.	0:35
Flume Cascade Brook (2,500 ft.)	0.9 mi.	650 ft. (rev. 50 ft.)	0:45
Mt. Webster-Mt. Jackson fork (2,800 ft.)	1.4 mi.	950 ft.	1:10
Webster Cliff Trail (3,800 ft.) via Webster branch	2.4 mi.	2,000 ft. (rev. 50 ft.)	2:10
Summit of Mt. Webster (3,910 ft.) via Webster Cliff Trail	2.5 mi.	2,100 ft.	2:20
Summit of Mt. Jackson (4,052 ft.) via Jackson branch	2.6 mi.	2,200 ft.	2:25
Loop trip over summits of Webster and Jackson (via Webster Cliff Trail)	6.5 mi.	2,550 ft.	4:30

AMC Webster–Jackson Trail connects US 302 across from a parking area (plowed in winter) on the highway's west side—0.25 mi. south of AMC's Macomber Family Information Center (at Crawford Depot) and 0.1 mi. north of the Gate of the Notch—with the summits of both Mt. Webster and Mt. Jackson. It provides the opportunity for an interesting loop trip, as the two summits are linked by Webster Cliff Trail. Sections of Webster–Jackson Trail are steep and rough.

The blue-blazed trail leaves the east side of US 302, 50 yd. north of the parking area, runs through a clearing, enters the woods, and, at 0.1 mi. from US 302, passes the side path leading right to Elephant Head.

Elephant Head Spur. Elephant Head is an interesting ledge on a knob that forms the east side of the Gate of the Notch. This mass of gray rock striped with veins of white quartz has a remarkable likeness to an elephant's head and trunk. Elephant Head Spur runs through the woods parallel to the highway at an easy grade and then ascends across the summit of the knob and descends 40 yd. to the top of the ledge, which overlooks Crawford Notch and affords fine views. It is 0.2 mi., 100-ft. elevation gain, rev. 30 ft., 0:10, from Webster–Jackson Trail.

Webster–Jackson Trail climbs steadily along the south bank of Elephant Head Brook, well above the stream, and turns right, away from the brook, at 0.2 mi. The trail angles up the mountainside roughly parallel to the highway, consisting of nearly level stretches alternating with steep, rocky pitches. At 0.6 mi. from US 302, a side path leads right 60 yd. to Bugle Cliff. This massive ledge overlooks Crawford Notch, and the view is well worth the slight extra effort required; if ice is present, use extreme caution. Webster–Jackson Trail ascends another steep, rocky pitch, continues climbing across the slope, with two short descents, and then crosses Flume Cascade Brook on a smooth, slippery ledge at 0.9 mi. It soon makes one more short descent, and at 1.4 mi., after a mostly gradual ascent, the trail divides within sound of Silver Cascade Brook, the left branch for Mt. Jackson and the right for Mt. Webster.

Mt. Webster Branch

The Mt. Webster (right) branch immediately descends very steeply to Silver Cascade Brook, crosses it on rocks just below a beautiful cascade and pool, and then climbs a very steep, rough, washed-out pitch up the bank; use caution, especially when descending. The trail then ascends steadily south for 1.0 mi., often with wet, rough footing, including many ledge slabs in the upper half. It meets Webster Cliff Trail on the high plateau northwest of the summit of Mt. Webster, 2.4 mi. from US 302. The ledgy summit of Mt. Webster, with an excellent view of Crawford Notch and the mountains to the west and south, is 0.1 mi. right (south) via Webster Cliff Trail. For Mt. Jackson and Mizpah Spring Hut, turn left.

Mt. Jackson Branch

The Mt. Jackson (left) branch ascends gradually until it comes within sight of Silver Cascade Brook and then begins to climb moderately, with rough, wet footing. About 0.5 mi. above the jct., the trail crosses three branches of the brook in quick succession. At 1.0 mi. from the jct., a short distance below the base of the rocky summit cone, the trail swings left and soon passes Tisdale Spring (unreliable, often scanty and muddy). The trail then swings right and ascends steep ledges, with several fairly difficult scrambles, to the open summit, 2.6 mi. from US 302, where the Mt. Jackson branch meets Webster Cliff Trail. The last ledgy pitch is often icy in winter. Descending, the trail leads west down the right edge of a steep, open ledge slab.

WEBSTER CLIFF TRAIL (MAP 1: G8)
Cumulative from US 302 (1,278 ft.) to:

First open ledge (3,025 ft.)	1.8 mi.	1,750 ft.	1:45
Summit of Mt. Webster (3,910 ft.)	3.3 mi.	2,750 ft. (rev. 100 ft.)	3:00
Summit of Mt. Jackson (4,052 ft.)	4.7 mi.	3,150 ft. (rev. 250 ft.)	3:55
Mizpah Spring Hut (3,793 ft.)	6.4 mi.	3,400 ft. (rev. 500 ft.)	4:55
Crawford Path (4,250 ft.)	7.3 mi.	3,950 ft. (rev. 100 ft.)	5:40

AMC This trail, a part of the white-blazed AT, leaves the east side of US 302 diagonally across from Willey House Station Rd. (signs for Ripley Falls and Ethan Pond Trail), 1.0 mi. south of the Willey House site and 1.8 mi. north of Dry River Campground. The parking area at the jct. of US 302 and Willey House Station Rd. is a stop for the AMC Hiker Shuttle and is plowed in winter. The trail ascends along the edge of the spectacular cliffs that form the east wall of Crawford Notch, passing numerous viewpoints, and then leads over Mts. Webster, Jackson, and Pierce to Crawford Path, 0.1 mi. north of Mt. Pierce. The section of trail ascending to Mt. Webster is more difficult and tiring than the statistics would suggest, with various ledge scrambles interspersed through the ascent along the top of the cliffs.

From US 302, Webster Cliff Trail enters the woods (signs for Webster Cliff Trail and Appalachian Trail) and runs east 0.1 mi. to a bridge (built in memory of Albert and Priscilla Robertson, founding members of the AMC Four Thousand Footer Club) on which the trail crosses the Saco River. Blue-blazed Saco River Trail joins from the left (sign) at 0.2 mi. and departs on the right at 0.3 mi. (no sign in 2021). Webster Cliff Trail climbs steadily up the south end of the ridge, winding up the steep slope, swinging more to the north and growing steeper as the trail approaches the cliffs. At 1.4 mi., after an easier section, the trail crosses the remains of a small 2009 landslide and then makes a tricky ledge scramble across the top of an older slide. It climbs a very steep pitch and then ascends moderately. At 1.8 mi. from US 302, at a sharp bend to the right, the trail reaches the first open ledge with wide views west and south (a good objective for a shorter hike). From here, as the trail ascends north up the ridge at easier grades with occasional sharp pitches, frequent outlook ledges provide ever-changing perspectives of the notch and the mountains to the south and west. The trail passes through a small col, and at 2.4 mi., a ledge affords a view straight down to the state park buildings. After a scramble up open rock, the trail reaches a ledge with a large cairn and an outlook to Mt. Washington; it turns left 15 yd. behind the cairn, where a false path leads to the right. Beyond another col, the trail crosses an outcropping with a view east to Montalban Ridge. After a sharp, ledgy drop to another col, the trail climbs at varying grades with several short scrambles, crosses an open ledge with a perched boulder at 2.9 mi., and then struggles up a very steep, ledgy pitch—probably the most difficult scramble on this section. It continues up with several more scrambles and good outlooks, makes a final long, steep scramble in the open, enters the woods, and soon reaches the jumbled, ledgy summit of Mt. Webster at 3.3 mi.

The trail then descends north, and in 0.1 mi., the Mt. Webster branch of Webster–Jackson Trail from US 302 at the top of Crawford Notch enters left. Webster Cliff Trail swings east along the ridge with a few ups and downs and occasional sharp scrambles, crossing several wet gullies. The final ascent up the ledgy cone of Mt. Jackson is quite steep, with several scrambles, reaching the summit at 4.7 mi., where the Mt. Jackson branch of Webster–Jackson Trail enters left.

Webster Cliff Trail leaves the summit of Mt. Jackson toward Mt. Pierce, following a line of cairns running north, and descends very steeply over the ledges at the north end of the cone into the scrub, where the grade eases. At 5.1 mi., the trail enters and winds through open alpine meadows with views of Mt. Washington and Mt. Jackson; then it turns sharply left and drops into the woods. The trail continues over a hump along the ridge toward Mt. Pierce and then ascends gradually to the jct. at 6.3 mi. with Mizpah Cutoff, which leads left (west) to Crawford Path. At 6.4 mi., Mizpah Spring Hut (where a side path on the right leads 100 yd. south to Nauman Tentsite) is reached, and Mt. Clinton Trail to the Dry River valley diverges right (southeast), heading diagonally down the hut clearing. Continuing past the front of the hut, Webster Cliff Trail soon ascends a steep, rough section with two ladders and reaches an open ledge with good views south and west at 6.6 mi. The grade lessens, and after a sharp right turn in a ledgy area, the trail reaches the summit of the southwest knob of Mt. Pierce, which offers a view of the summit of Mt. Washington. The trail descends into a sag and then ascends easily through scrub to the summit of

Mt. Pierce at 7.2 mi., where the trail comes into the open. Webster Cliff Trail descends moderately to the northeast over open alpine terrain, where hikers should take care to stay on the defined footway, and ends in about 150 yd. at its jct. with Crawford Path.

MIZPAH CUTOFF (MAP 1: G8)
From Crawford Path (3,490 ft.) to:

Mizpah Spring Hut (3,793 ft.)	0.7 mi.	350 ft. (rev. 50 ft.)	0:30

From Mt. Clinton Rd. parking area (1,884 ft.) to:

Mizpah Spring Hut (3,793 ft.) via Crawford Connector, Crawford Path, Mizpah Cutoff, and Webster Cliff Trail	2.7 mi.	1,950 ft. (rev. 50 ft.)	2:15

AMC This short trail provides a direct route from AMC's Macomber Family Information Center (at Crawford Depot) to Mizpah Spring Hut. Mizpah Cutoff diverges right (east) from Crawford Path 1.9 mi. from the Mt. Clinton Rd. parking area, climbs the ridge at a moderate grade, passes through a fairly level area, and descends slightly to join Webster Cliff Trail 100 yd. southwest of Mizpah Spring Hut; turn left to reach the hut.

SAM WILLEY TRAIL (MAP 1: G8)
Cumulative from Willey House site (1,318 ft.) to:

Saco River Trail (1,300 ft.)	0.5 mi.	0 ft.	0:15
Complete loop	1.0 mi.	0 ft.	0:30

NHDP This blue-blazed trail provides a short, easy walk at the base of the Webster Cliffs from the Willey House site on US 302, starting from the parking area (partly plowed in winter) on the east side of the road.

Leaving the parking area, the trail crosses the wooden dam over the Saco River that forms Willey Pond, with a fine view of the Webster Cliffs and Mt. Willard. At a sign, Pond Loop Trail diverges left, providing a 0.2-mi. loop walk beside Willey Pond, with views up to the surrounding mountains. Sam Willey Trail continues 50 yd. ahead, where Pond Loop Trail rejoins from the left (sign). It turns right and follows a graded path south, soon crossing the outwash from a slide. It turns sharply left at 0.2 mi., where a spur path leads 30 yd. right to a view of the Saco River. The main trail comes to a loop jct. at 0.4 mi. Going left (clockwise), the loop reaches the jct. at 0.5 mi., where Saco River Trail continues ahead (south). Sam Willey Trail swings around back to the north along the river, swings right past a fine view of the notch at the edge of a beaver swamp, and soon returns to the loop jct. To return to the Willey House site, turn left.

SACO RIVER TRAIL (MAP 1: G8–H8)
Cumulative from Sam Willey Trail (1,300 ft.) to:

Lower (west) jct. with Webster Cliff Trail (1,300 ft.)	0.7 mi.	50 ft. (rev. 50 ft.)	0:25
Dry River Trail (1,290 ft.)	2.4 mi.	300 ft. (rev. 250 ft.)	1:20

NHDP This blue-blazed trail provides easy walking through attractive forests along the floor of Crawford Notch, linking the Willey House site (via Sam Willey Trail) with Webster Cliff Trail, Maggie's Run, and Dry River Trail.

Leaving the most southerly point of the southern loop section of Sam Willey Trail, 0.5 mi. from the Willey House site, Saco River Trail runs briefly alongside the Saco River and then bears left away from the river and traverses several minor ups and downs. At 0.5 mi., the trail dips to the edge of an open swamp, where there is a view of Mt. Willey. It then swings left and ascends slightly, and at 0.7 mi., it meets Webster Cliff Trail (AT, white-blazed) at a sign (0.2 mi. from its trailhead on US 302) and turns left onto Webster Cliff Trail. The two trails coincide, climbing steadily eastward. At 0.8 mi., Saco River Trail (blue blazes, no sign in 2021) turns right off Webster Cliff Trail and descends easily to the floor of the valley. At 1.2 mi., Saco River Trail crosses several channels of Webster Brook (often dry) and continues south through open hardwoods; in places, the footway must be followed with extra care. At 1.6 mi., the trail skirts a beaver swamp and then ascends gently, although with some rocky footing, through an old-growth hardwood forest. It passes a connecting trail from Maggie's Run (Section Three) on the right at 2.0 mi., and ends at Dry River Trail, 0.5 mi. from that trail's trailhead on US 302 and directly across from the jct. with Dry River Connection, 0.4 mi. from Dry River Campground.

SACO LAKE TRAIL (MAP 1: G8)
From north jct. with US 302 (1,904 ft.) to:

South jct. with US 302 (1,886 ft.)	0.3 mi.	0 ft. (rev. 25 ft.)	0:10

AMC This short trail makes a loop around the east shore of Saco Lake, beginning and ending on the east side of US 302, with trailheads 0.2 mi. apart. Its north end starts 50 yd. north of the entrance to AMC's Highland Center at Crawford Notch. Parking is available by the northwest corner of the lake, 90 yd. south of the north trailhead. The trail passes a side path left to a pet cemetery at 0.1 mi. and then runs along the shore to a short side path on the left (sign) that climbs steeply to a ledge with a metal railing. This ledge, called Idlewild, offers a vista of Saco Lake and the Willey Range (use caution). Saco Lake Trail continues along the shore, crosses an area of rocky rubble, and ends after crossing the dam at the south end of the lake. The best winter parking is at Highland Center or at the Webster–Jackson trailhead.

DRY RIVER VALLEY
DRY RIVER TRAIL (MAP 1: H8–F9)
Cumulative from US 302 (1,198 ft.) to:

Dry River Connection and Saco River Trail (1,290 ft.)	0.5 mi.	100 ft.	0:20
Suspension bridge (1,560 ft.)	1.7 mi.	500 ft. (rev. 100 ft.)	1:05
Mt. Clinton Trail (1,900 ft.)	2.9 mi.	900 ft. (rev. 100 ft.)	1:55
Isolation Trail (2,600 ft.)	4.9 mi.	1,650 ft. (rev. 50 ft.)	3:20
Mt. Eisenhower Trail (2,675 ft.)	5.2 mi.	1,750 ft.	3:35
Dry River Shelter #3 (3,121 ft.)	6.3 mi.	2,200 ft.	4:20
Lakes of the Clouds Hut and Crawford Path (5,014 ft.)	9.5 mi.	4,300 ft. (rev. 200 ft.)	6:55

WMNF *Note*: In August 2011 and October 2017, intense rainstorms caused extensive damage on Dry River Trail, with major washouts in multiple locations. Several rough relocations around these washouts must be followed with care, and in two locations steep, open, gravelly banks must be traversed with caution. Expect a more primitive trail with a narrower, rougher tread requiring some route finding. Cairns mark the route at relocations and across washed-out, rocky areas. Dry River Trail is not recommended for inexperienced hikers. The washouts and subsequent relocations have opened numerous views of the river; its bed was extensively widened by the storms. Perhaps no other trail in the White Mountains better demonstrates the power of raging water. The remote upper section of the trail in Oakes Gulf is subject to frequent blowdowns.

Dry River Trail is the main route from US 302 up the valley of Dry River and through Oakes Gulf to Lakes of the Clouds Hut, providing access to Mt. Washington, the Southern Presidentials, and the upper portion of Montalban Ridge. This trail is almost entirely within the Presidential Range–Dry River Wilderness. Dry River Shelters #1 and #2 have been removed; Dry River Shelter #3 will be removed whenever major maintenance is required. This trail is, in general, much rougher than most similar valley trails elsewhere in the White Mountains and is more difficult and time-consuming than the statistics would suggest. The first 5.0 mi. follow fairly close to the route of an old logging railroad, although the river and its tributaries have eradicated much of the roadbed, and the relocations that were cut in the 1970s to eliminate several potentially hazardous river crossings have bypassed much of the remaining grade. When water levels are high, the few Dry River crossings that remain on this trail—and on the trails that diverge from it—are at best difficult and at worst very dangerous. At such times, it is prudent not to descend into this valley if major stream crossings lie between you and your destination.

Dry River Trail leaves the east side of US 302 (sign; roadside parking, but very limited in winter) 0.3 mi. north of the entrance to Dry River Campground and 2.6 mi. south of the Willey House site. From the highway, the trail follows a wide woods road northeast for 0.5 mi. to its jct. on the right with the bed of the old logging railroad (sign: "Dry River Connection"), which reaches this point from Dry River Campground in 0.4 mi. At this jct., Saco River Trail enters on the left. From here, Dry River Trail follows the partly washed-out railroad bed and enters the Presidential Range–Dry River Wilderness (sign) at 0.7 mi. Here the 2017 storm opened a large ledgy area on the river (right), with cascades and a pool. The trail soon bears right across a brook bed, briefly returns to the railroad grade, and then bears left at 0.9 mi. at a cairn in a rocky area, passing to the left of flood debris and staying on the west side of the river where the railroad formerly crossed it. The trail crosses a deep washout, climbs over a low bluff, rejoins the roadbed, and leaves it again on a rough relocation across a washout (use caution). It then climbs steeply on a narrow sidehill up a higher bluff to a restricted but beautiful outlook up the Dry River valley to Mt. Washington, Mt. Monroe, and the headwall of Oakes Gulf. At 1.7 mi., after a short, steep, and rough descent, the trail crosses Dry River on a suspension bridge, turns left along the river, and soon turns right and climbs by a short, steep switchback. It continues up the east bank with several ups and downs and then follows portions of the old railroad grade alternating with two rough up-and-down relocations to the right; at the end of the second relocation, the trail angles left across two brook beds to regain the grade. At 2.9 mi., Dry River Trail turns sharply right off the railroad grade, where Mt. Clinton Trail diverges left to cross the river and to ascend to Mizpah Spring Hut. Dry River Trail continues up the valley on a rougher section with several ups and downs. At 3.2 mi. it ascends to cross a steep, open gravel slope with loose footing and then descends sharply on the far side and crosses a brook; use great caution here. After traversing an area of rocky debris, the trail continues roughly along the riverbank. It crosses a second brook and then briefly runs between the brook and the river. At 3.6 mi. it crosses a third brook, wide and rocky. Dry River Trail then follows another relocation to the right above a washout, and at 4.2 mi. it veers sharply away from the river, turns left, and climbs at easy to moderate grades at a higher level. At 4.9 mi., the trail reaches Isolation Brook, turns right and follows the brook bank for 60 yd., turns left to cross the brook, and then turns right again (in reverse, turn left across the brook at a cairn). In another 60 yd., Isolation Trail diverges right, quickly crossing the brook.

Dry River Trail bears left and continues along the high east bank of Dry River. At 5.2 mi., Mt. Eisenhower Trail diverges sharply left and descends the steep bank to cross the river and to climb to Crawford Path. Dry River Trail continues roughly along the east bank, passing at 5.4 mi. an unsigned, muddy, and rough side path on the left that leads 45 yd. down to the pool at the foot of Dry River Falls, a very attractive spot. The top of the falls, with an interesting pothole just above, can also be reached by an obscure path 100 yd. farther along the main trail. At 5.6 mi., after climbing over a small ridge, the trail crosses the river to the west side; the crossing is normally fairly easy but could be a serious problem at high water. The trail continues up the valley, crossing an open washed-out slope with loose footing at 5.8 mi. (use caution). At 6.3 mi., after an obscure section with wet footing, the trail reaches Dry River Shelter #3. It continues ahead to the right of the shelter and in another 70 yd. crosses a major tributary of Dry River (take care to avoid false paths in this area) and a small brook beyond, and continues along the bank of Dry River, gradually rising higher above the water.

At 7.4 mi., Dry River Trail begins to swing away from the river and gradually climbs north into Oakes Gulf, with wet and rough footing at times; this area is subject to frequent blowdowns. After the trail crosses a small ridge and descends sharply on the other side, views begin to appear, although the trail remains well sheltered in the scrub. It climbs steadily up the headwall, with one ledge scramble, and at 8.6 mi. there is a good outlook perch just to the right. The trail soon climbs out of the scrub, turns left, and crosses a small brook at a right angle. At 9.0 mi., it turns sharply right (northeast) from the gully it once ascended, where signs forbid public entry into the area formerly crossed by the trail. (The closed area is the habitat of the dwarf cinquefoil, an endangered plant species.) The trail continues to climb with excellent views down the gulf, passes the Presidential Range–Dry River Wilderness boundary sign in a patch of scrub, and reaches the height-of-land on the southwest ridge of Mt. Washington at 9.3 mi. Dry River Trail swings left (west) and descends to the larger of the two Lakes of the Clouds, follows its south edge, and ends at Crawford Path, at Lakes of the Clouds Hut.

MT. CLINTON TRAIL (MAP 1: G8)
Cumulative from Dry River Trail (1,900 ft.) to:

Dry River Cutoff (3,425 ft.)	2.5 mi.	1,550 ft.	2:00
Mizpah Spring Hut (3,793 ft.)	3.0 mi.	1,900 ft.	2:25

WMNF This trail connects the lower part of the Dry River valley to Mizpah Spring Hut and the southern part of the Southern Presidentials. It lies almost entirely within the Presidential Range–Dry River Wilderness. The trail is lightly used, and parts of it, especially below Dry River Cutoff, are rough and wet and may be overgrown. It requires considerable care to follow, especially at the many stream crossings, and is not recommended for inexperienced hikers. (*Caution*: The crossing of Dry River on Mt. Clinton Trail near its jct. with Dry River Trail can vary from an easy skip over the stones to a waist-high ford in a torrent, and at times there may be no safe way across. In high-water conditions, it is prudent not to descend from Mizpah Spring Hut by Mt. Clinton Trail because the only safe course to reach Dry River Trail might be a very rough bushwhack south along the riverbank for about 1.2 mi.)

Mt. Clinton Trail diverges left from Dry River Trail where the latter trail turns right, 2.9 mi. from US 302. Mt. Clinton Trail continues ahead on a remnant of railroad grade and in 25 yd. turns left at a cairn and makes the potentially hazardous crossing of Dry River. The crossing here is not straight across; after the water crossing, follow cairns upstream to the right (north) for 120 yd. through the outwash in the middle of the riverbed (which is quite wide here), aiming for a tall cairn on the opposite bank. Hikers may need to deviate from the route depending on water levels. The trail then turns left, scrambles up a low, washed-out bank marked by a cairn, enters the woods, and follows an obscure, winding path 60 yd. to the right to meet the original trail route, where it turns left. Mt. Clinton Trail then follows a short stretch of old railroad grade upstream and swings left up the bank of a major tributary, following an old logging road at a moderate grade much of the way. At 0.4 mi., it passes through a large cut blowdown and bears right. At 0.5 mi., the trail crosses the tributary brook for the first of seven times and then scrambles up a washed-out area on the other bank and bears left onto an old logging road. It recrosses the brook, crosses a tributary, and crosses the main brook a third time. At 1.2 mi., the trail turns sharply left off the road and descends to the main brook, makes the fourth crossing at a ledgy spot with a small cascade and pool, and regains the road on the other side via a short but steep scramble, soon skirting to the left of a wet area. The trail stays close to the brook, crossing two more tributaries as well as the main brook twice more, to the seventh crossing of the main brook at 1.8 mi. It soon climbs more steadily, and above an eroded section where a small brook has taken over the footway (with one slippery, wet ledge slab where the road has been worn down to bare granite), walking on the old road becomes more pleasant. Dry River Cutoff enters on the right at 2.5 mi. From here, Mt. Clinton Trail crosses two small streams, ascends past a large boulder and through a large blow-down area to the Presidential Range–Dry River Wilderness boundary at 2.9 mi., and soon enters the clearing of Mizpah Spring Hut, where it ends at a jct. with Webster Cliff Trail.

MT. EISENHOWER TRAIL (MAP 1: G8)
Cumulative from Dry River Trail (2,675 ft.) to:

Dry River Cutoff (2,700 ft.)	0.3 mi.	150 ft. (rev. 100 ft.)	0:10
Crawford Path (4,465 ft.)	2.4 mi.	1,900 ft.	2:10

WMNF This lightly used trail connects the middle part of the Dry River valley to Crawford Path just east of the Eisenhower–Franklin col and lies almost entirely within the Presidential Range–Dry River Wilderness. The trail's grades are mostly easy to moderate with good footing, and it runs above treeline for only a short distance at the ridge crest.

Mt. Eisenhower Trail diverges left from Dry River Trail 5.2 mi. from US 302 and descends rather steeply on a former route of Dry River Trail through an area with many side paths; take care to stay on the main trail. The trail turns right, crosses Dry River (may be difficult or impassable at high water), and follows the bank downstream. At 0.2 mi., the trail joins its former route and bears right up a rather steep logging road. Dry River Cutoff diverges left at 0.3 mi. Soon the grade on Mt. Eisenhower Trail eases as it leads generally north, keeping a bit to the west of the crest of the long ridge that runs south from a point midway between Mts. Franklin and Eisenhower. At 1.6 mi., the trail turns sharply right, then left, and ascends more steeply for a while. At 2.1 mi., it finally gains the crest of the ridge and winds up through scrub, passing the Presidential Range–Dry River Wilderness boundary sign. Mt. Eisenhower Trail breaks into the open, affording fine views, and runs nearly level to Crawford Path in the Eisenhower–Franklin col, 0.2 mi. north of Crawford Path's northern jct. with Mt. Eisenhower Loop.

DRY RIVER CUTOFF (MAP 1: G8)
From Mt. Eisenhower Trail (2,700 ft.) to:

Mt. Clinton Trail (3,425 ft.)	1.5 mi.	800 ft. (rev. 50 ft.)	1:10

AMC This trail connects the middle part of the Dry River valley to Mizpah Spring Hut and the southern section of the Southern Presidentials. Grades are mostly easy with some moderate sections. The trail is entirely within the Presidential Range–Dry River Wilderness. It is lightly used, wet, and overgrown in places, and it requires care to follow.

Dry River Cutoff diverges left from Mt. Eisenhower Trail 0.3 mi. from the latter trail's jct. with Dry River Trail. In 0.1 mi., Dry River Cutoff crosses a substantial brook after a slight descent, turns sharply left and climbs the bank, crosses a tributary, and then swings back and climbs above the bank of the tributary. The trail crosses the tributary at 0.5 mi. and again at 0.8 mi. (the crossing here is obscured by tree growth). It swings left and climbs to the height-of-land on the southeast ridge of Mt. Pierce at 1.1 mi. Dry River Cutoff then runs almost on the level, with wet and obscure footing in places, and descends slightly to its jct. with Mt. Clinton Trail at 1.5 mi. Mizpah Spring Hut is 0.5 mi. to the right from this jct. via Mt. Clinton Trail.

MONTALBAN RIDGE
DAVIS PATH (MAPS 1 & 3: H8–F9)
Cumulative from parking area near US 302 (993 ft.) to:

Mt. Crawford spur path (2,900 ft.)	2.2 mi.	1,900 ft.	2:05
Mt. Parker Trail (3,040 ft.)	3.7 mi.	2,250 ft. (rev. 200 ft.)	3:00
Stairs Col Trail (3,030 ft.)	4.0 mi.	2,300 ft. (rev. 50 ft.)	3:10
Giant Stairs spur path (3,450 ft.)	4.4 mi.	2,700 ft.	3:35
Mt. Davis spur path (3,600 ft.)	8.5 mi.	3,650 ft. (rev. 800 ft.)	6:05
Mt. Isolation spur path (3,950 ft.)	9.7 mi.	4,100 ft. (rev. 100 ft.)	6:55
Isolation Trail, east branch (3,850 ft.)	10.6 mi.	4,200 ft. (rev. 200 ft.)	7:25
Isolation Trail, west branch (4,140 ft.)	10.9 mi.	4,500 ft.	7:40
Glen Boulder Trail (5,175 ft.)	12.5 mi.	5,650 ft. (rev. 100 ft.)	9:05
Boott Spur Trail (5,450 ft.)	13.0 mi.	5,900 ft.	9:25
Lawn Cutoff (5,475 ft.)	13.6 mi.	6,000 ft. (rev. 100 ft.)	9:50
Crawford Path (5,625 ft.)	14.4 mi.	6,200 ft. (rev. 50 ft.)	10:20
Mt. Washington summit (6,288 ft.) via Crawford Path	15.0 mi.	6,850 ft.	10:55
From parking area near US 302 (993 ft.) to:			
Lakes of the Clouds Hut (5,012 ft.) via Camel Trail	14.6 mi.	6,000 ft. (rev. 450 ft.)	10:20

AMC Davis Path, completed by Nathaniel T. P. Davis in 1845, was the third (and longest) bridle path constructed to the summit of Mt. Washington. The path was in use until about 1854 but became impassable soon afterward; it went entirely out of existence until it was reopened as a foot trail by AMC in 1910. At that time, the path was so overgrown that some sections could be located only by one of the original laborers, then a very old man, who relied on his memory of where the path had been built. The sections leading up the dauntingly steep southern slopes of Mt. Crawford and Stairs Mtn. give some idea of the magnitude of building a trail passable to horses along this ridge. The resolution that enabled Davis to push forward with this apparently hopeless task was the inspiration for the naming of Mt. Resolution. Davis Path is almost entirely within the Presidential Range–Dry River Wilderness. The section of the trail between Stairs Mtn. and Mt. Isolation is lightly used, rough and muddy in places, and may be overgrown, requiring care to follow. Drinking water is scarce along this ridge in dry seasons; to find water, you may have to go some distance down one of the trails that descend off the ridge.

Davis Path leaves the east side of US 302 (on the west side of the Saco River) at a large paved parking lot (plowed in winter) just north of Notchland Inn, 5.6 mi. south of the Willey House site in Crawford Notch State Park and 6.3 mi. north of the jct. with Bear Notch Rd. in Bartlett. It starts between a trail sign and a kiosk for the Cohos Trail, for which this trailhead is the southern terminus.

The path follows a gravel road (Crawford Valley Way; not open to public vehicle travel) along the bank of the river about 200 yd. upstream (north) to a suspension footbridge (Bemis Bridge). Beyond the east end of the bridge, the trail passes through private land, continuing straight east across an overgrown field to the left of a house. Then it turns left through a brushy area and crosses a small brook on a log bridge. Davis Path (here marked by blue blazes) then swings right and enters the woods and the WMNF. It soon joins and follows a logging road along the bed of a small brook (normally dry in summer), entering the Presidential Range–Dry River Wilderness at 0.4 mi. where the blue blazes end. The trail crosses the brook bed—where there may be running water upstream—crosses a tributary, and begins to climb away from the main brook. At 0.9 mi., the trail turns sharply right, soon enters the old and carefully graded bridle path, and begins a long, steady ascent of the steep and rugged ridge between Mt. Crawford and Mt. Hope by zigzags, with many rock steps. Attaining the crest and the first ledgy outlook at 1.9 mi., Davis Path follows this ridge north, rising over bare ledges (marked with small cairns and faded white blazes) with more outlooks, particularly to Mt. Carrigain and the Tripyramids; follow the trail with care in this ledgy section. At 2.2 mi. from US 302, at the foot of a large, sloping ledge, a side path (sign: "Mt. Crawford") diverges left and climbs 0.3 mi. and 200 ft. (15 min.) to the bare, peaked summit of Mt. Crawford, where the reward is a magnificent view of Crawford Notch, the Dry River valley, and the surrounding ridges and peaks.

From this jct., Davis Path turns northeast, descends slightly to the col between the peak of Mt. Crawford and its ledgy, domelike east knob (sometimes called Crawford Dome), and resumes the ascent. The trail soon passes over a ledgy shoulder of Crawford Dome, with good views back to the impressively precipitous face of the small peak of Mt. Crawford, and dips to the Crawford–Resolution col. Leaving this col, the trail runs north, rises slightly, and keeps close to the same level along the steep west side of Mt. Resolution.

At 3.7 mi., Mt. Parker Trail diverges right (east) and in 0.5 mi. leads to open ledges near the summit of Mt. Resolution; it continues to Mt. Parker and then Mt. Langdon Trail and the village of Bartlett. Fine views can be obtained from open ledges by ascending this trail for a little more than 0.1 mi. from the Davis Path jct. The spur path that diverged left at this jct., opposite Mt. Parker Trail, and descended to the Resolution Shelter is no longer maintained, and the shelter has been removed. It may be possible to find water on a branch of Sleeper Brook by following the unmaintained spur path down for about 120 yd. to the former shelter site; in dry seasons it may be necessary to go farther down the brook.

At 4.0 mi., Davis Path runs just west of Stairs Col—the small, wild pass between Mt. Resolution and Stairs Mtn. Here, Stairs Col Trail to the Rocky Branch valley diverges right. Davis Path now veers northwest, passing west of the precipitous Giant Stairs, ascending gradually along a steep mountainside and then zigzagging boldly northeast—with occasional steep scrambles on ledges—toward the flat top of Stairs Mtn. As the trail turns sharply left shortly before reaching the top of the slope, a branch path leads right a few steps to the "Down-look," a good viewpoint at the brink of a cliff. (On the descent, where the main trail turns sharply right, take care not to follow this branch inadvertently because it ends very abruptly at the dropoff.) At the top of the climb, 4.4 mi. from US 302, a branch path (sign: "Stairs Mt.") leads right (southeast) at easy grades for 0.2 mi., passing just south of the true summit of Stairs Mtn., to the flat, ledgy top of Giant Stairs and an inspiring view to the east and south.

Davis Path turns left and descends moderately along the north ridge of Stairs Mtn. for 1.0 mi.; it then turns right and runs east in a sag for about 0.1 mi. Turning north again and crossing a small brook (watch for this left turn), the trail passes over a small rise and descends into another sag. It then begins to ascend the long north and south ridge of Mt. Davis, keeping mostly to the west slopes, with several ups and downs. Grades are mostly easy along this wild, little-used section, but the footing is rough in places, and hikers may encounter blowdowns, mud, and overgrown sections.

At 6.1 mi., the trail passes a small spring on the right, and at 6.5 mi., as the trail ascends to the next knob on the ridge, it crosses a small brook. At 7.3 mi., Davis Path passes through a small, sharp col, climbs steeply out of it, and becomes almost level. At 8.5 mi., a side path (sign: "Mt. Davis") diverges right (east) and climbs steeply 0.2 mi. and 200 ft. (10 min.) to the bare south summit of Mt. Davis, which commands perhaps the finest view on Montalban Ridge and one of the best in the mountains. Davis Path now descends to the col between Mt. Davis and Mt. Isolation, where it crosses a small brook before ascending moderately up the south side of Mt. Isolation. At 9.7 mi., a spur path (sign: "Mt. Isolation") diverges left at a ledgy spot, leading steeply in 125 yd. (swinging left to the high point at the top) to the open summit of Mt. Isolation, which provides magnificent views in most directions.

Davis Path descends moderately for 0.2 mi. and then runs north along the ridge at easy grades, traversing several muddy sections with deteriorating bog bridges. At 10.5 mi., the trail leads past the site of the former Isolation Shelter, and at 10.6 mi., the east branch of Isolation Trail enters on the right from the Rocky Branch valley. Water can be obtained by going down Isolation Trail to the right (east); decent-looking water (which is nevertheless unsafe to drink without treatment) may be a considerable distance down. Davis Path now climbs steadily, and at 10.9 mi., as it reaches the top of the ridge and the grade decreases, the west branch of Isolation Trail diverges and descends left into the Dry River valley. Davis Path passes over a hump, runs through a sag at 11.5 mi., and then ascends steadily to treeline at 12.1 mi. From here, the trail is above treeline and completely exposed to the weather. At 12.5 mi., Glen Boulder Trail joins on the right just below a small crag; at 13.0 mi., Davis Path passes just west of the summit of Boott Spur, and Boott Spur Trail from AMC's Pinkham Notch Visitor Center enters on the right (east).

Turning northwest, Davis Path leads along the almost-level ridges of Boott Spur and crosses Bigelow Lawn. At 13.6 mi., Lawn Cutoff diverges right to Tuckerman Junction, and 200 yd. farther on, Camel Trail diverges left (west) to Lakes of the Clouds Hut. At 14.0 mi., Davis Path begins to follow the original location of Crawford Path and crosses Tuckerman Crossover; in another 0.3 mi., Davis Path is joined on the right by Southside Trail. At 14.4 mi., Davis Path ends at the present Crawford Path, which climbs to the summit of Mt. Washington in another 0.6 mi.

STAIRS COL TRAIL (MAP 1: H9)
From Rocky Branch Trail (1,420 ft.) to:

Davis Path (3,030 ft.)	1.8 mi.	1,650 ft. (rev. 50 ft.)	1:45

AMC This trail connects the Rocky Branch valley with Stairs Col on Davis Path, providing, in particular, the easiest route to Giant Stairs (although now considerably longer with the closure of the upper section of Jericho Rd.). Very little water is to be found along Davis Path, but water is usually available in small streams along the upper part of Stairs Col Trail. This trail is almost entirely within the Presidential Range–Dry River Wilderness.

Stairs Col Trail leaves Rocky Branch Trail opposite and 20 yd. north of the side path to Rocky Branch Shelter #1 and follows an old railroad siding for 50 yd. The trail then turns sharply left, crosses a swampy area, and climbs briefly to a logging road, where it enters the Presidential Range–Dry River Wilderness. From here nearly to Stairs Col, the trail follows old logging roads along the ravine of Lower Stairs Brook, becoming quite steep at 1.3 mi. and crossing the headwaters of the brook at about 1.5 mi., where the trail enters a birch glade. The trail becomes gradual as it approaches Stairs Col, with an impressive view up to the cliffs of Stairs Mtn. It crosses the small, ferny pass and continues down the west slope a short distance to meet Davis Path at 1.8 mi. For Giant Stairs, turn right at this jct.

ROCKY BRANCH TRAIL (MAP 3: G10–H9)
Cumulative from parking lot off NH 16 (1,228 ft.) to:

Height-of-land (3,100 ft.)	2.8 mi.	1,900 ft. (rev. 50 ft.)	2:20
Isolation Trail (2,800 ft.)	3.7 mi.	1,900 ft. (rev. 300 ft.)	2:50
Stairs Col Trail (1,420 ft.)	7.9 mi.	2,000 ft. (rev. 1,500 ft.)	4:55
End of Jericho Rd. (1,105 ft.)	9.9 mi.	2,000 ft. (rev. 300 ft.)	5:55
Parking area on Jericho Rd. (875 ft.)	11.7 mi.	2,000 ft. (rev. 250 ft.)	6:50

WMNF *Note*: In 2011, Tropical Storm Irene caused extensive damage on the southern section of Rocky Branch Trail, with major washouts in multiple locations. The section between Isolation Trail and Stairs Col Trail was closed by the USFS in fall 2011 and reopened in fall 2015 with numerous relocations, some of which require care to follow. In 2017, an October storm caused additional damage to the trail and also severely damaged the upper portion of Jericho Rd., which is now permanently closed to vehicle access 2.5 mi. from US 302. In the section between the Isolation Trail and Stairs Col Trail jcts., expect a more primitive trail with a narrower, rougher tread requiring some route finding. This section is not recommended for inexperienced hikers.

Rocky Branch Trail provides access to the Saco River's Rocky Branch valley, which lies between the two longest subsidiary ridges of Mt. Washington: Montalban Ridge to the west and Rocky Branch Ridge to the east. In the upper part of the valley, the forest has largely recovered from fires that swept the slopes from 1912 to 1914. (*Caution*: Four river crossings between the jcts. with Isolation Trail and Stairs Col Trail, one just east of the Isolation Trail jct. and one just north of the end of Jericho Rd., are wide, difficult, and possibly dangerous at high water.)

The northeast terminus of this trail is located at a paved parking lot (plowed in winter) at the end of a short spur road on the west side of NH 16, 5.4 mi. north of the red covered bridge on NH 16A in Jackson and just north of the highway bridge over Ellis River; this is 4.1 mi. south of AMC's Pinkham Notch Visitor Center. The Jericho (south) trailhead is reached by following Jericho Rd.—called Rocky Branch Rd. (FR 27) by the USFS—which leaves US 302 just east of the bridge over Rocky Branch, 1.0 mi. west of the jct. of US 302 and NH 16 in Glen. The road is paved for 1.6 mi. and then is a good gravel road up to the trailhead parking area and gate at 2.5 mi. Beyond this point the road was severely damaged by the October 2017 storm and has been permanently closed to vehicle travel by the USFS. Hikers approaching from the south must walk 1.8 mi. up Jericho Rd. beyond the gate to reach the beginning of the trail proper, where there is a potentially difficult crossing of Rocky Branch.

At the northeast terminus, on NH 16 below Pinkham Notch, the yellow-blazed trail leaves the north end of the parking lot (avoid a gravel road that branches left just below the parking lot) and climbs moderately by switchbacks on an old logging road. At about 0.5 mi., Avalanche Brook Ski Trail enters from the left; it leaves on the right at 0.7 mi. At 1.3 mi., Rocky Branch Trail swings left, away from the bank of a small brook, and continues to ascend steadily. It turns sharply left at 1.8 mi. and follows an old, very straight road on a slight downhill grade. After about 0.5 mi. on this road, the trail swings gradually right and climbs moderately, following a brook part of the way, and reaches the Presidential Range–Dry River Wilderness boundary just east of the ridgetop, where the yellow blazes end. Passing the almost imperceptible height-of-land at 2.8 mi., the trail follows a short bypass to the left of a wet area and runs almost level before descending easily, with wet, rocky footing and small brooks running in and out of the trail.

At 3.5 mi., the trail begins to swing left, crosses a small brook, descends gradually to Rocky Branch, and follows it downstream for a short distance before crossing it at 3.7 mi. This crossing may be very difficult. (The trail can be hard to follow from this crossing for travelers going toward NH 16, because the route is poorly marked and there are well-beaten side paths to campsites. Heading for NH 16, the main trail first parallels the river going upstream and then swings gradually away from the river on a well-defined old road.) On the west bank of the river at this crossing is the jct. with Isolation Trail, which turns right (north), following the riverbank upstream on the old railroad grade.

Rocky Branch Trail turns left downstream, also following the old railroad grade from this jct., and passes the former site of Rocky Branch Shelter #2 in 60 yd. (This shelter has been removed and the site is a revegetation area; the USFS plans to replace the shelter with tent pads in the future.) The trail crosses a muddy spot and a rocky tributary below a cascade and runs generally south along the west bank, at times on the old railroad grade, crossing the top of a washed-out bank at 4.2 mi. It continues down the grade, crossing three tributaries (the second crossing is steep); shortly after the third tributary crossing, at 5.0 mi., the trail skirts the lower edge of a washed-out bank on the river, requiring care to follow. It then follows several relocated sections off and back onto the grade, crossing another tributary. At 6.1 mi., the trail makes the first of four crossings of Rocky Branch. The 2017 storm shifted the main flow of the river to the east, so the first two crossings are now dry overflow channels at lower water levels, but they may be difficult in high water. The third and fourth crossings are difficult at high water and can only be avoided by a rough and strenuous bushwhack along the west bank. Hikers must take care to follow the trail at the crossings (some of which are marked by cairns), particularly at the first one, where the trail angles to the right through a rocky area after crossing the usually dry channel and then swings left across another dry brook bed, between piles of uprooted trees, before turning right into the woods. The second crossing is at 6.2 mi., and the third at 6.4 mi. After the fourth crossing at 6.8 mi., the trail climbs by switchbacks on a relocation to a high bank, runs along the top of the bank, and then descends back near the river. It leaves the Presidential Range–Dry River Wilderness and swings right across Upper Stairs Brook at 7.1 mi. It continues off and then on the railroad grade, passes to the right of a large logjam, and reaches a jct. at 7.9 mi. with Stairs Col Trail on the right. In another 20 yd. along Rocky Branch Trail, a spur path on the left leads 60 yd. to WMNF Rocky Branch Shelter #1; from the front of the shelter, a path leads 75 yd. ahead to the river, passing a spur on the right leading to three tent platforms. Rocky Branch Trail continues south along the railroad grade, loops out to the right on a relocation, and crosses Lower Stairs Brook at 8.5 mi. At 8.8 mi., it makes a bypass on the uphill (right) side of a boggy section of the grade, crosses another brook, rejoins the grade, and at 9.5 mi. enters a gravel logging road. It follows this road for another 0.4 mi. to the end of Jericho Rd., making a potentially difficult crossing of Rocky Branch and then crossing Otis Brook just before reaching the end of Jericho Rd at 9.9 mi. (The USFS plans to remove the bridges over these streams in the near future; in 2024 the bridge over Rocky Branch was severely damaged and dangerous to cross.) From here, hikers must continue on foot 1.8 mi. along Jericho Rd., descending gradually, to the parking area and gate.

In the reverse direction, where the logging road swings to the left 0.4 mi. from the crossing of Rocky Branch at the end of Jericho Rd., Rocky Branch Trail continues straight ahead into the woods at a kiosk on the old railroad grade, which looks like an old grassy road.

ISOLATION TRAIL (MAP 1: G9–G8)
Cumulative from Rocky Branch Trail (2,800 ft.) to:

Fourth crossing of Rocky Branch (3,423 ft.)	1.7 mi.	600 ft.	1:10
Davis Path, south jct. (3,850 ft.)	2.6 mi.	1,050 ft.	1:50
Davis Path, north jct. (4,140 ft.)	2.9 mi.	1,350 ft.	2:10
Isolation Brook (3,275 ft.)	4.3 mi.	1,400 ft. (rev. 900 ft.)	2:50
Dry River Trail (2,600 ft.)	5.3 mi.	1,400 ft. (rev. 700 ft.)	3:20

Cumulative from Rocky Branch Trail parking area on NH 16 (1,228 ft.) to:

Isolation Trail (2,800 ft.) via Rocky Branch Trail	3.7 mi.	1,900 ft. (rev. 350 ft.)	2:50
Davis Path, south jct. (3,850 ft.)	6.3 mi.	2,950 ft.	4:40
Mt. Isolation summit (4,004 ft.) via Davis Path	7.3 mi.	3,200 ft. (rev. 100 ft.)	5:15

WMNF *Note*: In August 2011 and October 2017, intense rainstorms caused extensive damage on the lower, western section of Isolation Trail. Expect a more primitive trail with a narrower, rougher tread requiring some route finding.

This trail links the Dry River valley (Dry River Trail), Montalban Ridge (Davis Path), and the Rocky Branch valley (Rocky Branch Trail), crossing the ridge crest north of Mt. Isolation. Isolation Trail is entirely within the Presidential Range–Dry River Wilderness. The section west of Davis Path is lightly used, and parts may be rough, wet, and overgrown, although experienced hikers should be able to follow it fairly easily. This section was well cleared in 2023. East of Davis Path, Isolation Trail receives much more use but is still wet and rough in places and not marked well. The four crossings of Rocky Branch are difficult in high water; some of the crossings are marked by cairns. Isolation Trail diverges from Rocky Branch Trail just north of the former site of Rocky Branch Shelter #2 (now a revegetation area) on the west bank of the river, at the point where Rocky Branch Trail crosses the river, 3.7 mi. from its northeast terminus on NH 16. Isolation Trail follows the river north along the west bank on what is left of the old railroad grade, crosses a tributary, and then crosses the river at 0.4 mi. and another tributary in another 0.1 mi. At 0.7 mi., the trail turns sharply right off the railroad grade, climbs briefly, and then follows a logging road that at first runs high above the river. The trail crosses the river three more times; the next two crossings, at 1.4 mi., are only 70 yd. apart. If the water is high, they can be bypassed by following a beaten path along the east side. The last crossing comes at 1.7 mi., after which the trail swings away from the main stream and climbs easily along a tributary, crossing and recrossing it, with very wet and rocky footing. Isolation Trail swings right and reaches Davis Path at 2.6 mi. after passing through an area of confusing side paths among campsites where the main trail must be followed with care. The spur path to the summit of Mt. Isolation is reached by following Davis Path left (south) for 0.9 mi.

Now turning right and coinciding with Davis Path, Isolation Trail climbs steadily north for 0.3 mi. until it approaches the ridge crest. Here, where the grade decreases, Isolation Trail turns left off Davis Path. It runs at easy grades with minor ups and downs for 0.2 mi. and then descends moderately southwest along the crest of a ridge into the Dry River valley. The trail descends fairly steeply to the left (south) off the ridge, and at 4.3 mi., reaches Isolation Brook, a branch of Dry River. The trail follows the northwest bank of the brook on an old logging road that has been disrupted by several small slides from the 2011 and 2017 storms, where care is required to follow the footway on muddy side slopes. The trail continues down at moderate grades, crossing several small brooks, and then crosses over and back through a washed-out area of Isolation Brook (follow cairns with care); 15 yd. beyond the second crossing of the brook, Isolation Trail ends at Dry River Trail, 4.9 mi. from US 302.

MT. LANGDON TRAIL (MAP 3: H9)
Cumulative from road on north bank of Saco River (683 ft.) to:

Mt. Parker Trail (1,894 ft.)	2.5 mi.	1,450 ft. (rev. 250 ft.)	2:00
Mt. Langdon Shelter (1,774 ft.)	2.9 mi.	1,450 ft. (rev. 150 ft.)	2:10
High point on Mt. Langdon (2,380 ft.) via Mt. Stanton Trail	3.7 mi.	2,050 ft.	2:55

SSOC This trail runs to the Mt. Langdon Shelter site from the road on the north side of the Saco River near the village of Bartlett, meeting both Mt. Parker Trail and Mt. Stanton Trail, and thus gives access to both the higher and lower sections of Montalban Ridge. Despite its name, Mt. Langdon Trail does not get particularly close to the summit of Mt. Langdon, which is crossed by Mt. Stanton Trail. Most of Mt. Langdon Trail is either within or close to the boundary of the Presidential Range–Dry River Wilderness; Mt. Langdon Shelter (removed in 2022) was just outside the Wilderness Area. The WMNF plans to establish primitive tentsites at the location. The first 1.0 mi. of this trail is on private land.

From the four corners at the jct. of US 302 and Bear Notch Rd. in Bartlett, follow River St. (the road that leads north) across a bridge over the Saco River to a T intersection at 0.4 mi. and bear left a short distance to the small trailhead parking area (sign) on the right. Additional parking is available in a riverside parking lot across from the trailhead; these parking areas are partly plowed in winter. A third option is a parking lot (plowed in winter) at the jct. of River St. and Yates Farm Rd., diagonally across from the trailhead.

Mt. Langdon Trail follows a brushy logging road north; just beyond the trailhead on the right is the grave site of Dr. Leonard Eudy, who died from smallpox in 1877 after saving dozens of Bartlett residents from the disease. At a three-way jct. in 75 yd., the yellow-blazed trail continues straight on the middle road and climbs north at easy to moderate grades through an area of recent logging, where there are intersections with several diverging logging roads. In general, Mt. Langdon Trail follows the main road straight ahead (north), and directional arrows and some blazes are found at the major intersections, but care must be taken to follow the correct route. At 0.3 mi., the path to Cave Mtn. (marked by a small sign) diverges left. At 0.8 mi., Mt. Langdon Trail veers slightly right at an intersection of several roads, and at 0.9 mi., it bears left off the main road. The trail enters the Presidential Range–Dry River Wilderness just before crossing a brook at 1.0 mi. After recrossing the brook, the trail climbs more steadily, with gravelly footing, bearing sharply right twice.

Mt. Langdon Trail crosses Oak Ridge at 2.2 mi. after passing through an unusual stand of red oak. It then descends, sharply at times, to the Oak Ridge–Mt. Parker col, where it bears right (east) at a jct. at 2.5 mi.; here, Mt. Parker Trail continues ahead (north). Mt. Langdon Trail then descends gradually to the WMNF Mt. Langdon Shelter site (shelter removed in 2022), where this trail and Mt. Stanton Trail both end. Some care is required to follow the trail near the shelter site. Water may be found in a brook 60 yd. from the shelter site on Mt. Stanton Trail, although in dry weather hikers may need to follow the brook bed downhill for a distance.

MT. PARKER TRAIL (MAP 3: H9)
Cumulative from Mt. Langdon Trail (1,894 ft.) to:

Summit of Mt. Parker (3,013 ft.)	1.3 mi.	1,100 ft.	1:10
Branch trail to open southerly knob (3,200 ft.)	3.1 mi.	1,650 ft. (rev. 350 ft.)	2:25
High point on Mt. Resolution (3,400 ft.)	3.6 mi.	1,850 ft.	2:45
Davis Path (3,040 ft.)	4.1 mi.	1,850 ft. (rev. 350 ft.)	3:00

SSOC This pleasant, rugged, lightly used trail passes several excellent viewpoints and provides access from the village of Bartlett to Mt. Parker, Mt. Resolution, the Stairs Col area, and the upper Montalban Ridge. The trail runs almost entirely within or close to the boundary of the Presidential Range–Dry River Wilderness. Parts of the trail may require care to follow due to blowdown and encroaching brush, although experienced hikers should have little problem. No reliable water is available on this trail.

Mt. Parker Trail begins in the Oak Ridge–Mt. Parker col 2.5 mi. from Bartlett, continuing straight ahead to the north where Mt. Langdon Trail turns right (east). Mt. Parker Trail climbs moderately with many switchbacks through brushy beech and oak woods, descends briefly to the right, and then swings left and continues its winding ascent to the open summit of Mt. Parker at 1.3 mi., where there are excellent views, especially north up the Rocky Branch valley to Mt. Washington.

The trail descends and follows the long ridge between Mt. Parker and Mt. Resolution, passing over three bumps and remaining in spruce woods nearly all the way. This section in particular is lightly used and may be obscured in places by spruce growth and blowdowns. The trail then runs along the west and south slopes of the remainder of the ridge (swinging inside the Presidential Range–Dry River Wilderness for the rest of its length) until reaching the southeast corner of Mt. Resolution. Here, the trail turns sharply right and zigzags up to the flat, scrubby col between the main summit ridge and a southerly knob at 3.1 mi. An unmarked and overgrown branch path leads left 0.1 mi. to the top of this knob, which is a large, flat, open ledge with excellent views; the beginning of this obscure side path is along a flat section of the trail. After climbing moderately, Mt. Parker Trail winds along the flat top of Mt. Resolution, reaching an open ledge with excellent views at 3.6 mi. One summit knob is just above this ledge; another knob of almost equal elevation (considered to be the true summit of Mt. Resolution) is about 0.1 mi. northeast and affords excellent views north, but no path leads to this knob through the dense scrub. From the ledge, Mt. Parker Trail descends into a gully where it crosses a small, sluggish brook (unreliable water), heads down (northwest) over fine open ledges, and finally drops steeply to Davis Path; the former branch path to Resolution Shelter that left Davis Path opposite Mt. Parker Trail has been abandoned, and the shelter has been removed.

MT. STANTON TRAIL (MAP 3: H10–H9)
Cumulative from trailhead off Covered Bridge Lane (642 ft.) to:

White's Ledge (1,380 ft.)	1.1 mi.	750 ft.	0:55
High point on Mt. Stanton (1,710 ft.)	1.5 mi.	1,050 ft.	1:15
High point on Mt. Pickering (1,920 ft.)	2.2 mi.	1,550 ft. (rev. 250 ft.)	1:55
Fourth Crippie (1,888 ft.)	3.3 mi.	1,900 ft. (rev. 400 ft.)	2:35
High point on Mt. Langdon (2,380 ft.)	4.5 mi.	2,600 ft. (rev. 200 ft.)	3:35
Mt. Langdon Trail (1,774 ft.)	5.3 mi.	2,600 ft. (rev. 600 ft.)	3:55

SSOC This trail passes over the low eastern summits of Montalban Ridge and affords many views from scattered ledges. To reach the east trailhead (the west trailhead is at the jct. with Mt. Langdon Trail), leave the north side of US 302, 1.8 mi. west of its jct. with NH 16 in Glen and 0.1 mi. east of the bridge over the Saco River. Follow a paved road (Covered Bridge Lane) west, bearing left at 0.2 mi. The road swings right (north), and at 0.9 mi., the trailhead (sign) is on the left where the road swings right again to head east as Hemlock Drive. Park on the roadside (limited in winter), taking care not to block any driveways.

The yellow-blazed trail follows the left edge of a driveway for 80 yd. and enters the woods. It swings right, entering the WMNF and passing around a house, and climbs, turning left onto the older route of the trail at 0.3 mi. At 0.4 mi., Mt. Stanton Trail turns sharply left where the red-blazed WMNF boundary continues straight ahead. The trail climbs moderately, levels briefly, and then ascends a steep, gravelly section with poor footing. At the top of this pitch, the trail turns left and ascends at an easier grade, soon passing the first of several outlooks from White's Ledge and reaching the crest of the ledge at 1.1 mi. The trail climbs steeply again, with gravelly, slippery footing, after passing a large boulder on the right. At 1.4 mi., the trail turns sharply right on a ledge, offering a good viewpoint just to the left, and climbing becomes easier. At 1.5 mi., the trail passes about 15 yd. to the right of the true summit of Mt. Stanton. The summit area is covered with a fine stand of red pines and provides good views from nearby scattered ledges.

The trail descends past a north outlook to the Stanton–Pickering col, then ascends steadily, crosses a ledgy ridge, and descends slightly. It then climbs steeply and passes 30 yd. to the right of the true summit of Mt. Pickering at 2.2 mi. The trail then leads to ledges on a slightly lower knob that offer excellent views north. The trail descends to a minor col and then crosses several interesting small humps, sometimes called the Crippies (the origin of this peculiar name is one of the mysteries of White Mountain nomenclature). These humps have scattered outlook ledges. The first Crippie is reached at 2.6 mi.; the best views are from several ledges on the fourth and last Crippie, which is crossed at 3.3 mi.

After crossing the last Crippie, Mt. Stanton Trail may be less well cleared and harder to follow. It descends somewhat along the north side of the ridge toward Mt. Langdon and then climbs northwest moderately on a sidehill with a few steep and rough pitches, passing a restricted outlook to Carter Dome, Carter Notch, and Wildcat Mtn. The trail swings left (south), and at 4.5 mi., it passes about 35 yd. to the right of the summit of Mt. Langdon, which is wooded and viewless. It then descends easily to a gravel slope, turns right, and continues downward to a brook that is crossed 60 yd. east of the site of Mt. Langdon Shelter (removed in 2022), where Mt. Stanton Trail ends.

CAVE MTN. PATH (MAP 3: H9)
Cumulative from Mt. Langdon Trail (840 ft.) to:

Cave (1,200 ft.)	0.3 mi.	350 ft.	0:20
Outlook (1,300 ft.)	0.4 mi.	450 ft.	0:25

Cave Mtn. (located on private property) is remarkable for the shallow cave on its south slope. Cave Mtn. Path is reached from the village of Bartlett by following Mt. Langdon Trail for 0.3 mi. to a well-worn branch path that diverges left (watch for it carefully; marked by a small wooden sign: "Cave Mt"). Cave Mtn. Path follows an old road through a logged area and skirts the east side of Cave Mtn. After 0.3 mi., this trail passes a large prow-shaped boulder, swings right, and leads up an extremely steep and eroded gravel slope with very poor and slippery footing (especially difficult on the descent) to the cave. A rough path with occasional faded red blazes to the right of the cave leads to the top of the cliff and, after a short scramble, a restricted view of mountains to the south.

JACKSON AREA
WINNIWETA FALLS TRAIL (MAP 3: G10)
From NH 16 (976 ft.) to:

Winniweta Falls (1,300 ft.)	0.9 mi.	350 ft.	0:40

WMNF This trail provides access to an attractive waterfall. Its trailhead (sign; limited parking, especially in winter) is located on the west side of NH 16, 3.2 mi. north of the red covered bridge on NH 16A in Jackson and 6.3 mi. south of AMC's Pinkham Notch Visitor Center. Hikers using this trail must ford the wide bed of Ellis River, which is often a rather shallow stream, but can require wading in even moderate flow and may be dangerous or impassable at high water. In winter, the crossing is even more treacherous because there is often considerable running water under a seemingly stable pack of snow and ice. This trail makes use of several cross-country ski trails maintained by Jackson Ski Touring Foundation. During winter, hikers should avoid walking on ski tracks and should yield to skiers, who have the right of way.

After reaching the far bank of Ellis River, Winniweta Falls Trail bears right and skirts the north side of an overgrown field, crossing Ellis River Ski Trail at 0.2 mi. After crossing another ski trail, Winniweta Falls Trail bears left onto and follows Winniweta Falls Ski Trail (sign), climbing easily as it approaches the north bank of Miles Brook on an old logging road. The trail temporarily steers away from the brook, passing through several muddy sections. After a moderate ascent, the trail again nears the bank of Miles Brook, and a short, unsigned path leads 20 yd. left to the top of the falls. To reach the base of the falls, head into the woods just below the unsigned path and carefully continue steeply downhill 75 yd. to the edge of the stream. The ski trail, meanwhile, continues uphill along the logging road and ends at Hall Trail (X-C) at 1.7 mi. from NH 16.

IRON MTN. TRAIL (MAP 3: H10)
Cumulative from Hayes Farm (1,906 ft.) to:

Summit of Iron Mtn. (2,723 ft.)	1.3 mi.	800 ft.	1:05
South cliffs (2,430 ft.)	2.0 mi.	850 ft. (rev. 350 ft.)	1:25

WMNF The summit of Iron Mtn. (once home to a fire tower) is wooded, with restricted views, but outlooks on the north side and the fine south cliffs provide very attractive views for relatively little effort. Somewhat down the slope to the east of the cliffs are the abandoned iron mines for which the mountain is known. A prominent easterly ridge, on which there was once a trail, descends over the open summit of Green Hill to the cliff called Duck's Head, named for its shape when seen from a point on NH 16 just north of the Jackson covered bridge. Iron Mtn. Trail is reached by leaving the west side of NH 16 in Jackson, next to the golf course and 0.3 mi. north of the red covered bridge (NH 16A) that leads to Jackson village, and following Green Hill Rd. (sign) to the west. At 1.2 mi., the pavement and maintenance ends (from here, the road is called Iron Mtn. Rd.; no formal parking), and at 1.4 mi., the road (FR 119) bears left at a fork through a gate (no parking here) where FR 325 (sign: "Forest Service Rd.") bears right. The road now becomes fairly steep, a bit rough, and very narrow (be prepared to back up for other cars to get by), passing several private cabins; above the fork, the road is not passable in mud season and is not plowed in winter. Parking is extremely limited at the fork. At 2.6 mi. from NH 16, where the road ahead soon becomes very poor, park in a designated area (sign: "Parking")—generously provided by the landowner—on the right just before reaching the house of the former Hayes Farm (now a summer residence). Alternate parking is available in a signed lot ("Overflow Parking") 0.2 mi. before (east of) the main parking area. Hikers should park in either of the two lots and not along the narrow road.

Iron Mtn. Trail starts at a sign ("Trail") on the left, 10 yd. up the road. The trail climbs a wooden staircase and crosses a field with fine views, traverses a smaller field, passes through a band of trees (trail signs seen along the trail are not official and do not show reliable distances), and emerges at the base of a brushy slope at an overgrown logging road. Iron Mtn. Trail bears left onto the road and then immediately bears right off it at 0.15 mi. Now on a newly built section constructed by USFS and WMTC in 2021 (which replaces the closed steep and severely eroded original route), the yellow-blazed trail ascends gradually, swinging out to the west via long and short switchbacks with excellent footing. At 0.8 mi. it turns sharply left (east) through more switchbacks, then turns right, and rejoins the original route at 1.1 mi. Yellow blazes end here. The trail soon passes a side path to a ledge on the right leading 20 yd. to an excellent outlook up the Rocky Branch valley to Mt. Washington, with the Southern Presidentials visible over Montalban Ridge, and climbs to the wooded summit at 1.3 mi. The trail passes to the left of the remnants of the old fire tower, runs across the summit ridge (route is marked with cairns), and then descends about 300 ft. off the south side of the mountain, easily at first, then steep and rough, with one drop down a short rockslide, after which grades ease. It continues down over several small wooded humps to a fork at 1.9 mi. (cairns) where a signed but unmaintained side path (marked with sporadic small cairns) diverges left and descends 0.2 mi. and 250 ft. to the old mines (tailings, water-filled shaft, tunnel). Iron Mtn. Trail bears right at the fork and ascends slightly onto open ledges (route is marked with small cairns), turns right, turns left, and reaches the open top of the south cliffs at 2.0 mi. These cliffs are the most scenic spot on the mountain and offer wide views to the south and west; swing right to reach the best viewpoint. Hikers should use caution here in wet or icy conditions as the ledges slope downward toward the cliffs. Hikers also should make a note of where they entered onto the ledges because there are numerous beaten paths in the area. On the return, Iron Mtn. Trail leaves the northeast corner of the ledge area behind the cliffs and soon makes a right turn.

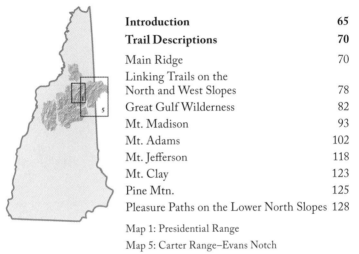

is useful for people who want to explore some of the attractive, less crowded paths in this section. RMC maintains a considerable number of trails on the northern peaks; some of these paths are very lightly used and are wilder and rougher than many trails in the WMNF. Adventurous hikers will find them a delightful alternative to the heavily used principal routes in the range. This network of paths also provides opportunities for less strenuous, varied walks to the many waterfalls and other interesting places on the lower slopes of the range.

Caution: The peaks and higher ridges of this range are nearly as exposed to the elements as Mt. Washington and should be treated with the same degree of respect and caution. Severe winter-like storms can occur at any time of the year, and many lives have been lost in this area from failure to observe the basic principles of safety. In addition, all of the major peaks are strenuous climbs by even the easiest routes. The distances quoted may not seem long to a novice, but only one route to a major peak, Caps Ridge Trail to Mt. Jefferson, involves less than 3,000 ft. of climbing, and that trail is challenging. Although Caps Ridge Trail is relatively short, it is also quite steep, with numerous scrambles on ledges that a person unfamiliar with mountain trails might find daunting. Most other routes to the summits involve 4,000 to 4,500 ft. of climbing, due to lower-elevation trailheads, thus making these ascents roughly equivalent in strenuousness to the ascent of Mt. Washington. Another consideration is the very rough, rocky footing on the upper slopes, which can slow travel times considerably. The substantial amount of effort required to climb these peaks, together with the threat of sudden and violent storms, should make the need to avoid overextending oneself quite apparent.

The Northern Presidentials were observed by Thomas Gorges and Richard Vines from the summit of Mt. Washington in 1642, but the explorers evidently considered these peaks to be part of Mt. Washington, for after their trip, they wrote, with considerable geographic confusion, "The mountain runs E. and W. 30 mi., but the peak is above all the rest." In the early summer of 1820, a party led by Ethan Allen Crawford visited Mt. Washington, and from that summit named Mts. Jefferson, Adams, and Madison, but did not explore them. Later that summer, two members of a second party spent part of a day on the Northern Presidentials and were probably the first persons of European extraction to visit these summits. Dr. J. W. Robbins, who spent much time collecting botanical and other specimens on the Northern Presidentials, made a more thorough exploration in 1829.

The first trail on the northern peaks was probably Stillings Path, which was cut around 1852, primarily for transporting building materials from

Randolph to the summit of Mt. Washington, and did not cross any of the summits. In 1860 or 1861, a partial trail was made over the peaks to Mt. Washington; some sections still exist as parts of current trails. Lowe's Path on Mt. Adams was cut between 1875 and 1876; the branch path through King Ravine was made in 1876; and Osgood Path on Mt. Madison was opened in 1878. Numerous trails were constructed between 1878 and 1902, but this network was greatly damaged by timber cutting, which began in 1903 and continued for several years. Many trails were temporarily obliterated. The more important ones were restored by the newly formed RMC after the most intensive period of lumbering ceased.

In Randolph Valley, where the Link crosses Cold Brook just below scenic Cold Brook Fall, Memorial Bridge stands in honor of J. Rayner Edmands, Eugene B. Cook, and other pioneer path makers who helped construct the superb trail network in the Presidential Range, including Thomas Starr King, James Gordon, Charles E. Lowe, Laban M. Watson, William H. Peek, Hubbard Hunt, William G. Nowell, and William Sargent.

In this section, the AT follows Gulfside Trail from its jct. with Trinity Heights Connector near the summit of Mt. Washington to Madison Spring Hut. The AT then follows Osgood Trail over Mt. Madison and down into the Great Gulf, proceeding to Mt. Washington Auto Rd. via Osgood Cutoff, Great Gulf Trail (for a very short distance), and Madison Gulf Trail.

ROAD ACCESS

The highest points from which to climb the Northern Presidentials, not including the summit of Mt. Washington, are Jefferson Notch Rd. at Caps Ridge Trail (3,008 ft.); the parking lot on Cog Railway Base Rd., 1.1 mi. east of Jefferson Notch Rd., for Jewell Trail (2,495 ft.); AMC's Pinkham Notch Visitor Center (2,028 ft.); and Pinkham B Rd. (Dolly Copp Rd.) at Pine Link (1,648 ft.). Other important parking areas are the Great Gulf trailhead located on NH 16, 1.9 mi. south of Dolly Copp Campground and 1.5 mi. north of Mt. Washington Auto Rd.; Randolph East, on Pinkham B Rd. (Dolly Copp Rd.), 0.2 mi. south of its jct. with US 2; Appalachia, on US 2, 0.8 mi. west of Pinkham B Rd. (a stop for the AMC Hiker Shuttle); Lowe's Store on US 2, 2.0 mi. west of Appalachia (nominal fee charged by owner; the store was closed in 2024, but parking was still available except in winter); and Bowman, on US 2, 0.9 mi. west of Lowe's Store. Several trailheads in the region, such as Randolph East, Appalachia, and Bowman, owe their names and locations to their former status as stations on the Boston & Maine railroad line. The tracks were removed in 1997, and the railroad grade is now

Presidential Rail Trail and is available for hiking. Pinkham B Rd. (Dolly Copp Rd.)—partly paved, partly gravel, and rough in places—runs 4.3 mi. from US 2, 0.8 mi. east of Appalachia at the foot of the long rise leading up to Randolph Hill, to NH 16, 4.5 mi. south of US 2 in Gorham, where it serves as the access road for Dolly Copp Campground. Gravel-surfaced Jefferson Notch Rd. runs 8.9 mi. between Cog Railway Base Rd. and Valley Rd. in Jefferson; see the Caps Ridge Trail description for more information. Both Pinkham B Rd. and Jefferson Notch Rd. are closed in winter.

HUTS
Madison Spring Hut (AMC)

For more than 130 years, AMC's White Mountain hut system has offered hikers bunks for the night in spectacular locations, with home-cooked dinners and breakfasts, cold running water, and composting or waterless toilets. In 1888, at Madison Spring (4,795 ft.), a little north of the Adams–Madison col, AMC built a stone hut. The present hut, rebuilt and improved after a fire in 1940 and reconstructed in 2010 and 2011, accommodates 52 guests in three bunkrooms. Lodging, with meals included, is available for a fee; reservations are highly recommended (603-466-2727; outdoors.org /destinations). Limited drinks, snacks, and gear are available for purchase by day visitors. The hut is open to the public from early June to mid-September. It is 6.0 mi. from the summit of Mt. Washington via Gulfside Trail and 6.8 mi. from Lakes of the Clouds Hut via Gulfside Trail, Westside Trail, and Crawford Path. In bad weather, the best approach (or exit) is via Valley Way, which is sheltered to within a short distance of the hut. Nearby points of interest include Star Lake and the Parapet, a crag overlooking Madison Gulf. Pets are not permitted in the hut.

CAMPING
Great Gulf Wilderness

No camping is allowed within 200 ft. of any trail except at designated Wilderness Tentsites, of which several are marked by tentsite symbols along Great Gulf Trail between a high gravelly bank called the Bluff and the jct. with Sphinx Trail. Wood or charcoal fires are not permitted anywhere in the Great Gulf Wilderness. Camping is prohibited within 0.25 mi. of Great Gulf Trail south of its jct. with Sphinx Trail, including Spaulding Lake and its vicinity. Camping and fires are also prohibited above treeline (where trees are less than 8 ft. tall), except in winter, when camping is permitted above treeline in places where snow cover is at least 2 ft. deep and not on any frozen body of water. All former shelters have been removed.

Forest Protection Areas

The WMNF has established several FPAs, where camping and wood or charcoal fires are prohibited throughout the year. See p. xxvii for general FPA regulations.

In the area covered by Section Two, no camping is permitted within 200 ft. of certain trails. In 2024, designated trails included Valley Way from its jct. with Scar Trail up to Madison Spring Hut.

No camping is permitted in the WMNF within 0.25 mi. of certain roads (camping on private roadside land is illegal except by permission of the land-owner). In 2024, these roads included NH 16, Cog Railway Base Rd. (FR 173), Jefferson Notch Rd. (FR 220) from Cog Railway Base Rd. (FR 173) to the Caps Ridge Trail trailhead, and Pinkham B Rd. (Dolly Copp Rd.).

Established Trailside Campsites

The Log Cabin (RMC), first built in 1889 and rebuilt in 1985, is located at a spring at 3,274 ft. elevation, beside Lowe's Path at the jct. with Cabin–Cascades Trail. The cabin is partly enclosed and has room for about ten guests. A fee is charged. No stove is available, and no wood fires are permitted in the area. Guests are requested to leave the cabin clean and are required to carry out all trash.

The Perch (RMC) is an open log shelter (rebuilt in 2010) located at 4,305 ft. on Perch Path between Randolph Path and Israel Ridge Path, but much closer to the former. It accommodates eight, and four tent platforms are also available at the site. The caretaker at Gray Knob (see below) often visits to collect the overnight fee. Wood fires are not allowed in the area, and guests must carry out all trash.

Crag Camp (RMC) is situated at the edge of King Ravine on Spur Trail at 4,245 ft. This enclosed cabin has room for about twenty guests. A fee is charged throughout the year. During July and August, it is maintained by a caretaker. Hikers are required to limit groups to ten people. Wood fires are not allowed in the area, and guests must carry out all trash.

Gray Knob (RMC) is an enclosed, winterized cabin on Gray Knob Trail at its jct. with Hincks Trail, near Lowe's Path, at 4,355 ft. The cabin has a caretaker year-round, and a fee is charged throughout the year. Gray Knob has room for about fifteen guests and is supplied with cooking utensils. Hikers are required to limit groups to ten people. Wood fires are not allowed in the area, and guests must carry out all trash.

These RMC shelters are all in FPAs, and no camping is allowed within 0.25 mi. of them, except in the shelters and on the tent platforms themselves. Fees should be mailed to RMC (P.O. Box 279, Gorham, NH 03581) if not collected by caretakers. Any infraction of rules or acts of vandalism should be reported to the same address.

Osgood Tentsite (WMNF; 2,519 ft.), consisting of five tent platforms, is located near the jct. of Osgood Trail and Osgood Cutoff (which is on the AT).

Valley Way Tentsite (WMNF; 4,114 ft.), consisting of two tent pads and a designated overflow camping area, is located on a spur path off Valley Way, 3.2 mi. from the Appalachia parking area.

Wilderness Tentsites (WMNF): A number of designated tentsites are located along trails in the Great Gulf Wilderness. These are marked with small wooden posts. They are not shown on the maps in this guide and are not indicated in the text because the USFS may relocate some of these sites periodically. Fires are not permitted.

TRAIL DESCRIPTIONS

MAIN RIDGE

GULFSIDE TRAIL (MAP 1: F9)
Cumulative from Madison Spring Hut (4,795 ft.) to:

Air Line, east jct. (5,125 ft.)	0.3 mi.	300 ft.	0:20
Thunderstorm Junction (5,490 ft.)	0.9 mi.	700 ft.	0:50
Israel Ridge Path, north jct. (5,475 ft.)	1.0 mi.	700 ft.	0:50
Israel Ridge Path, south jct. (5,250 ft.)	1.5 mi.	750 ft.	1:10
Edmands Col (4,933 ft.)	2.2 mi.	750 ft.	1:30
Mt. Jefferson Loop, north end (5,200 ft.)	2.4 mi.	1,000 ft.	1:40
Six Husbands Trail (5,325 ft.)	2.7 mi.	1,150 ft.	1:55
Mt. Jefferson Loop, south end (5,375 ft.)	3.1 mi.	1,200 ft.	2:10
The Cornice (5,275 ft.)	3.2 mi.	1,200 ft.	2:10
Sphinx Trail (4,975 ft.)	3.7 mi.	1,200 ft.	2:25
Mt. Clay Loop, north end (5,025 ft.)	3.8 mi.	1,250 ft.	2:30
Jewell Trail (5,400 ft.)	4.6 mi.	1,600 ft.	3:05
Mt. Clay Loop, south end (5,400 ft.)	4.9 mi.	1,650 ft.	3:15
Westside Trail (5,500 ft.)	5.0 mi.	1,750 ft.	3:25
Great Gulf Trail (5,925 ft.)	5.5 mi.	2,200 ft.	3:50
Trinity Heights Connector (6,100 ft.)	5.7 mi.	2,350 ft.	4:00
Crawford Path (6,150 ft.)	5.8 mi.	2,400 ft.	4:05
Mt. Washington summit (6,288 ft.) via Crawford Path	6.0 mi.	2,550 ft.	4:15
From Madison Spring Hut (4,795 ft.) to:			
Lakes of the Clouds Hut (5,014 ft.) via Gulfside Trail, Westside Trail, and Crawford Path	6.8 mi.	1,950 ft.	4:20

GULFSIDE TRAIL, IN REVERSE (RMC/WMNF; MAP 1: F9)
Cumulative from the summit of Mt. Washington (6,288 ft.) to:

Crawford Path jct. (6,150 ft.)	0.2 mi.	0 ft.	0:05
Trinity Heights Connector (6,100 ft.)	0.3 mi.	0 ft.	0:10
Great Gulf Trail (5,925 ft.)	0.5 mi.	0 ft.	0:15
Westside Trail (5,500 ft.)	1.0 mi.	0 ft.	0:30
Mt. Clay Loop, south end (5,400 ft.)	1.1 mi.	0 ft.	0:35
Jewell Trail (5,400 ft.)	1.4 mi.	50 ft.	0:45
Mt. Clay Loop, north end (5,025 ft.)	2.2 mi.	50 ft.	1:05
Sphinx Trail (4,975 ft.)	2.3 mi.	50 ft.	1:10
The Cornice (5,275 ft.)	2.8 mi.	350 ft.	1:35
Mt. Jefferson Loop, south end (5,375 ft.)	2.9 mi.	450 ft.	1:40
Six Husbands Trail (5,325 ft.)	3.3 mi.	450 ft.	1:55
Mt. Jefferson Loop, north end (5,200 ft.)	3.6 mi.	450 ft.	2:00
Edmands Col (4,933 ft.)	3.8 mi.	450 ft.	2:10
Israel Ridge Path, south jct. (5,250 ft.)	4.5 mi.	750 ft.	2:40
Israel Ridge Path, north jct. (5,475 ft.)	5.0 mi.	1,050 ft.	3:00
Thunderstorm Junction (5,490 ft.)	5.1 mi.	1,050 ft.	3:05
Air Line, east jct. (5,125 ft.)	5.7 mi.	1,050 ft.	3:20
Madison Spring Hut (4,795 ft.)	6.0 mi.	1,050 ft.	3:30
From Lakes of the Clouds Hut (5,014 ft.) to:			
Madison Spring Hut (4,795 ft.) via Crawford Path, Westside Trail, and Gulfside Trail	6.8 mi.	1,750 ft.	4:15

RMC/WMNF This trail, the main route along the Northern Presidential ridge crest, leads from Madison Spring Hut to the summit of Mt. Washington. The trail threads its way through the principal cols, avoiding the summits of the Northern Presidentials, and offers extensive, ever-changing views. Elevations range from about 4,800 ft. close to the hut to 6,288 ft. on the summit of Mt. Washington. Gulfside Trail was named by J. Rayner Edmands, who, starting in 1892, located and constructed the greater part of the trail, sometimes following trails that had existed before. All but about 0.8 mi. of the trail was once a graded path, and parts were paved with carefully placed stones—a work cut short by Edmands's death in 1910. Gulfside Trail is part of the AT, except for a very short segment at the south end. For its entire distance, the trail forms the northwestern boundary of the Great Gulf Wilderness, although the trail itself is not within the Wilderness. It is well marked with large cairns, many topped with a yellow-painted stone, and while care must be used, it can often be followed even in dense fog.

Always carry a compass and study the map before starting so you will be aware of your alternatives if a storm strikes suddenly. The trail is continuously exposed to the weather; dangerously high winds and low temperatures may occur with little warning at any season of the year. If such storms threaten serious trouble on Gulfside Trail, do not attempt to ascend the summit cone of Mt. Washington, where conditions are usually far worse. If you are not close to either of the huts (Madison Spring or Lakes of the Clouds), descend below treeline to shelter in the woods, by trail if possible, or without trail if necessary. A night of discomfort in the woods is better than potentially fatal exposure to the weather on the heights. Slopes on the Great Gulf side (east and southeast) are more sheltered from the wind but are generally much steeper, with numerous dangerous cliffs, and are much farther from highways than slopes on the west side. It is particularly important not to head toward Edmands Col in deteriorating conditions; there is no easy trail out of this secluded mountain pass (which often acts as a natural wind tunnel) in bad weather, and hikers have sometimes been trapped in this desolate and isolated place by a storm. The emergency refuge shelter once located here was removed in 1982 after years of misuse and abuse (including illegal camping) by thoughtless visitors. To enjoy a safe trip through this spectacular but often dangerous area, there is no substitute for studying the map carefully, checking the weather forecast, and fully understanding the hazards and options before setting out on the ridge.

The trail is described in the southbound direction (toward Mt. Washington). Distances, elevation gains, and times are also given for the reverse (northbound) direction.

Part I. Madison Spring Hut–Edmands Col

The trail begins on the northwest side of Madison Spring Hut and runs 35 yd. northwest to a jct. where Valley Way diverges right. Here Gulfside Trail swings left and leads southwest through a patch of scrub. The trail then aims to the right (north) of Mt. Quincy Adams and ascends its steep, open north slope. At the top of this slope, at 0.3 mi., on the high plateau between King Ravine and Mt. Quincy Adams, Gulfside Trail is joined from the right by Air Line, which in turn was just joined by King Ravine Trail. Here, you have striking views back to Mt. Madison and into King Ravine at the Gateway, a short distance down on the right. Gulfside Trail and Air Line coincide for 70 yd., and then Air Line branches left toward the summit of Mt. Adams. Much of Gulfside Trail for about the next 0.5 mi. is paved with carefully placed stones. It rises moderately southwest, then becomes steeper, and at 0.9 mi. from Madison Spring Hut, reaches a grassy lawn in the saddle (5,490 ft.) between Mt. Adams and Mt. Sam Adams. Here, several trails intersect at a spot called Thunderstorm

Junction, marked by a large and prominent cairn. The RMC has made recent improvements in this area to better define the trails. Entering Gulf-side Trail on the right, 8 yd. before reaching the cairn, is Great Gully Trail, coming up across the slope from the southwest corner of King Ravine. At the cairn, Gulfside Trail is crossed by Lowe's Path, ascending on the right (northwest) from Lowe's Store on US 2 to the summit of Mt. Adams. About 100 yd. down Lowe's Path, Spur Trail branches right for Crag Camp. The summit of Mt. Adams is 0.3 mi. from the jct. (left, southeast) via Lowe's Path; a round trip to the summit requires about 30 min.

Continuing southwest from Thunderstorm Junction and beginning to descend, Gulfside Trail passes a jct. on the left with Israel Ridge Path, which ascends a short distance to Lowe's Path and then to the summit of Mt. Adams. For 0.5 mi., Gulfside Trail and Israel Ridge Path coincide, passing Peabody Spring (unreliable) just to the right in a small, grassy flat; more reliable water lies a short distance beyond, at the base of a conspicu-ous boulder just to the left of the path. Soon the trail climbs easily across a small ridge, where Israel Ridge Path diverges right at 1.5 mi. from Madi-son Spring Hut. Just north of this jct. in wet weather is a small pool called Storm Lake. Gulfside Trail bears a bit left toward the edge of Jefferson Ravine and, always leading toward Mt. Jefferson, descends southwest along the narrow ridge that divides Jefferson Ravine from Castle Ravine, near the edge of the southeast cliffs, from which are fine views into the Great Gulf. (*Note*: This part of Gulfside Trail was never graded.) At the end of this descent, the trail reaches Edmands Col at 2.2 mi. from Madison Spring Hut, with 3.8 mi. to go to Mt. Washington.

At Edmands Col (4,938 ft.) is a bronze tablet in memory of J. Rayner Edmands, who made most of the graded paths on the northern peaks. Gulfside Spring is 50 yd. south of the col on Edmands Col Cutoff, and Spaulding Spring (reliable) is 0.1 mi. north along Randolph Path, near its jct. with Castle Ravine Trail and a trail called the Cornice. The emergency shelter once located at this col has been dismantled, and none of the trails leaving this area are entirely satisfactory escape routes in bad weather. From the col, Edmands Col Cutoff leads south, entering scrub almost immediately, affording the quickest route to this rough form of shelter in dangerous weather. It continues about 0.5 mi. to Six Husbands Trail lead-ing down into the Great Gulf, but it is very rough, and Six Husbands Trail is very difficult to descend, making it a far-less-than-ideal escape route unless the severity of the weather leaves no other choice. Randolph Path leads north into the Randolph Valley, running above treeline with great exposure to northwest winds for more than 0.5 mi. Nevertheless, this is probably the fastest, safest route to civilization, unless high winds make it too dangerous to cross through Edmands Col. Branching from Randolph Path, 0.1 mi. north of the col, are the Cornice, a very rough trail leading west entirely above treeline to Castle Trail, and Castle Ravine Trail, which descends steeply over loose talus and may be hard to follow.

Part II. Edmands Col–Sphinx Col

South of Edmands Col, Gulfside Trail ascends steeply over rough rocks, with Jefferson Ravine on the left. The trail passes flat-topped Dingmaul Rock, which offers a good view down the ravine, with Mt. Adams on the left. This rock is named for a legendary alpine beast to which the rock is reputed to bear a remarkable resemblance—the more remarkable because there has never been a verified sighting of the beast. In another 0.1 mi., Mt. Jefferson Loop branches right and leads 0.4 mi. to the summit of Mt. Jefferson (5,714 ft.). The views from the summit are excellent, and Mt. Jefferson Loop is only slightly longer than the parallel section of Gulfside Trail, although it requires about 300 ft. of extra climbing and about 10 min. more hiking time.

Gulfside Trail now rises less steeply. It crosses Six Husbands Trail and soon reaches its greatest height, about 5,400 ft., on Mt. Jefferson. Curving southwest and descending a little, the trail crosses Monticello Lawn, a comparatively smooth, grassy plateau. Here, at 3.1 mi., Mt. Jefferson Loop rejoins Gulfside Trail about 0.3 mi. from the summit. A short distance beyond the edge of the lawn, the Cornice enters right from Caps Ridge Trail. Gulfside Trail descends to the south, and from one point, the rock formation known as the Sphinx can be seen down the slope to the left. A few yd. north of the low point in Sphinx Col, Sphinx Trail branches left (east) into the Great Gulf through a grassy passage between ledges. Sphinx Col is 3.7 mi. from Madison Spring Hut, with 2.3 mi. remaining to the summit of Mt. Washington. In bad weather, a fairly quick descent to sheltering scrub can be made via Sphinx Trail, although once treeline is reached, this trail becomes rather steep and difficult.

Part III. Sphinx Col–Mt. Washington (MAP 1: F9)

From Sphinx Col, Gulfside Trail leads toward Mt. Washington. In 220 yd., Mt. Clay Loop diverges left to climb over the summits of Mt. Clay, offering impressive views into the Great Gulf. Mt. Clay Loop adds about

300 ft. of climbing and 10 min. of time; the distance is about the same. Gulfside Trail is slightly easier and passes close to a spring but misses the best views. It bears right from the jct. with Mt. Clay Loop, runs south, and climbs moderately, angling up the west side of Mt. Clay. About 0.3 mi. above Sphinx Col, a loop leads to potential water a few steps down to the right. The side path continues about 30 yd. farther to Greenough Spring (more reliable) and then rejoins Gulfside Trail about 100 yd. above its exit point. Gulfside Trail continues its moderate ascent, and Jewell Trail from Cog Railway Base Rd. enters from the right at 4.6 mi. Gulfside Trail swings southeast and soon descends slightly to a point near the Clay–Washington col (5,389 ft.), where Mt. Clay Loop rejoins the trail from the left.

The path continues southeast, rising gradually on Mt. Washington. About 0.1 mi. above the col, Westside Trail branches right, crosses under the Cog Railway, and leads to Crawford Path and Lakes of the Clouds Hut. Gulfside Trail continues southeast between the Cog Railway on the right and the edge of the gulf on the left, with magnificent views into the gulf and across to the northern peaks. If the path is lost, the railway can be followed to the summit. At the extreme south corner of the gulf, Great Gulf Trail joins Gulfside Trail from the left, 5.5 mi. from Madison Spring Hut. Here, Gulfside Trail turns sharply right, crosses the railroad, and continues south to the plateau just west of the summit, where it passes a jct. with Trinity Heights Connector, a link in the AT, which branches left and climbs for 0.2 mi. to the true summit of Mt. Washington. In another 0.1 mi., Gulfside Trail meets Crawford Path. Now coinciding with Crawford Path, Gulfside Trail turns left (southeast) and passes through the old corral (outlined by rock walls) in which saddle horses from the Glen House were kept. The combined trails swing left (northeast) and lead between the Yankee Building and the Tip Top House on the left and the Stage Office and Cog Railway track on the right. Follow the sign: "Crawford Path to Summit." The summit, also marked by a sign, is an outcropping between the Tip Top House and the Sherman Adams summit building.

Descending from the summit of Mt. Washington and coinciding with Crawford Path, Gulfside Trail is on the right (west) side of the Cog Railway track. The combined trails lead southwest between the buildings and then swing to the right (northwest) at a sign for Crawford Path and a large cairn (avoid random side paths toward the south). After passing through the old corral, the two trails reach a jct. where Gulfside Trail turns sharply right (north) as Crawford Path turns left.

MT. JEFFERSON LOOP (MAP 1: F9)
Cumulative from north jct. with Gulfside Trail (5,200 ft.) to:

Mt. Jefferson summit (5,713 ft.)	0.4 mi.	500 ft.	0:25
South jct. with Gulfside Trail (5,375 ft.)	0.7 mi.	500 ft. (rev. 350 ft.)	0:35

AMC This trail provides access to the summit of Mt. Jefferson from Gulfside Trail. It diverges right (southwest) from Gulfside Trail 0.2 mi. south of Edmands Col and climbs steeply up the slope. Just below the summit, Six Husbands Trail enters on the left, and in 125 yd. Castle Trail enters on the right; in a few more yd. the jct. with Caps Ridge Trail is reached at the base of the summit crag, near a large cairn. The true summit is 40 yd. right (west) on Caps Ridge Trail; a short scramble up to the right reaches the high point. Mt. Jefferson Loop then turns left and descends moderately to the south, with reasonably good footing, to rejoin Gulfside Trail on Monticello Lawn.

Descending from the trail jct. near the summit crag, northbound Mt. Jefferson Loop leads northeast, and southbound Mt. Jefferson Loop leads south.

MT. CLAY LOOP (MAP 1: F9)
Cumulative from north jct. with Gulfside Trail (5,025 ft.) to:

Mt. Clay summit (5,531 ft.)	0.5 mi.	500 ft.	0:30
South jct. with Gulfside Trail (5,400 ft.)	1.2 mi.	600 ft. (rev. 250 ft.)	0:55

AMC This trail traverses the summit ridge of Mt. Clay roughly parallel to Gulfside Trail, providing access to superb views into the Great Gulf from Mt. Clay's east cliffs. The entire trail (except for its end points) is within the Great Gulf Wilderness.

Mt. Clay Loop diverges left (southeast) from Gulfside Trail 220 yd. south of Sphinx Col and ascends a steep, rough slope to the ragged ridge crest. After crossing the summit and passing over several slightly lower knobs, Mt. Clay Loop descends easily to the flat col between Mt. Clay and Mt. Washington, where the loop rejoins Gulfside Trail.

EDMANDS COL CUTOFF (MAP 1: F9)
From Edmands Col (4,933 ft.) to:

Six Husbands Trail (4,925 ft.)	0.5 mi.	100 ft. (rev. 100 ft.)	0:20

RMC This important link, connecting Gulfside Trail and Randolph Path at Edmands Col with Six Husbands Trail, makes possible a quick escape from Edmands Col into plentiful sheltering scrub on the lee side of Mt. Jefferson. Footing on this trail is very rough and rocky. It is almost entirely within the Great Gulf Wilderness.

Leaving Edmands Col, the trail passes Gulfside Spring in 50 yd. and then begins a rough scramble over rockslides and through scrub, marked by cairns. The trail is generally level but has many small rises and falls over minor ridges and gullies, with good views to the Great Gulf and out to the east. Edmands Col Cutoff ends at Six Husbands Trail 0.3 mi. below that trail's jct. with Gulfside Trail.

THE CORNICE (MAP 1: F9)
Cumulative from Randolph Path (4,900 ft.) to:

Castle Trail (5,100 ft.)	0.6 mi.	250 ft. (rev. 50 ft.)	0:25
Caps Ridge Trail (5,025 ft.)	1.3 mi.	300 ft. (rev. 150 ft.)	0:50
Gulfside Trail (5,275 ft.)	1.8 mi.	550 ft.	1:10

RMC This trail circles the west slope of Mt. Jefferson, running completely above treeline, with many interesting views. The Cornice starts near Edmands Col, crosses Castle Trail and Caps Ridge Trail, and returns to Gulfside at Monticello Lawn, linking the trails on the west and northwest slopes of Mt. Jefferson. The Cornice's southern segment, which has relatively good footing, provides an excellent shortcut from Caps Ridge Trail to Gulfside Trail on Monticello Lawn, south of Mt. Jefferson. The section leading from Edmands Col to Caps Ridge Trail is extremely rough, however, with a large amount of tedious and strenuous rock-hopping, which is very hard on knees and ankles. This section of the trail, therefore, may take considerably more time than the estimates above. As a route between Edmands Col and Caps Ridge Trail, the Cornice saves a little climbing compared with the route over the summit of Mt. Jefferson, but the Cornice is much longer, requires more exertion, and is just as exposed to the elements. This makes its value questionable as a route to avoid Mt. Jefferson's summit in bad weather.

The Cornice diverges west from Randolph Path near Spaulding Spring, 0.1 mi. north of Gulfside Trail in Edmands Col, where Castle Ravine Trail also diverges from Randolph Path. The Cornice crosses a small, grassy depression where there may be no perceptible footway until it climbs the rocky bank on the other side. The trail then ascends moderately over large rocks, passing above a rock formation that resembles a petrified cousin of the Loch Ness monster, and circles around the north and west sides of Mt. Jefferson, crossing Castle Trail above Upper Castle. The Cornice continues across the rocky slope with minor ups and downs, intersects Caps Ridge Trail above the Upper Cap, and turns left (east) up Caps Ridge Trail for about 20 yd. before diverging right (east) and climbing gradually, with improved footing, to Gulfside Trail just below Monticello Lawn.

LINKING TRAILS ON THE NORTH AND WEST SLOPES

RANDOLPH PATH (MAP 1: E9–F9)

Cumulative from Randolph East parking area (1,239 ft.) to:

Valley Way (1,953 ft.)	1.5 mi.	750 ft.	1:05
Air Line (2,000 ft.)	1.6 mi.	800 ft.	1:10
Short Line, north jct. (2,275 ft.)	1.9 mi.	1,050 ft.	1:30
King Ravine Trail and Amphibrach (2,925 ft.)	3.1 mi.	1,700 ft.	2:25
Lowe's Path (3,600 ft.)	3.9 mi.	2,400 ft.	3:10
Perch Path (4,325 ft.)	4.9 mi.	3,100 ft.	4:00
Israel Ridge Path, north jct. (4,825 ft.)	5.4 mi.	3,600 ft.	4:30
Edmands Col and Gulfside Trail (4,933 ft.)	6.1 mi.	3,700 ft.	4:55
Mt. Washington summit (6,288 ft.) via Gulfside Trail and Crawford Path	9.9 mi.	5,500 ft. (rev. 450 ft.)	7:40

RMC This graded path extends southwest from Pinkham B Rd. (Dolly Copp Rd.) near the village of Randolph, ascending diagonally up the slopes of Mt. Madison and Mt. Adams to Gulfside Trail in Edmands Col, between Mt. Adams and Mt. Jefferson. In addition to providing a route from Randolph to Edmands Col, Randolph Path crosses numerous other trails along the way and thus constitutes an important link between them. Some sections are heavily used and well beaten, but others see very little traffic and, although well cleared and marked, have a less obvious footway. J. Rayner Edmands made Randolph Path from 1893 to 1899. Parts of it were reconstructed in 1978 as a memorial to Christopher Goetze, an active RMC member and former editor of *Appalachia*, AMC's mountaineering and conservation journal.

The blue-blazed trail begins at the parking area (sometimes plowed in winter; roadside parking usually available) known as Randolph East, on Pinkham B Rd., 0.2 mi. south of US 2. Pinkham B Rd. leaves US 2 0.8 mi. east of the Appalachia parking area and 1.0 mi. west of the jct. with Randolph Hill Rd. Coinciding with Howker Ridge Trail, Randolph Path quickly crosses Presidential Rail Trail and 30 yd. beyond turns right (southwest), where Howker Ridge Trail diverges left (southeast). Randolph Path runs to the south of a power-line clearing for about 0.2 mi. and then swings southwest and ascends to a brushy logged area, where it bears right (follow signs and blazes carefully). Entering mature woods, the trail ascends moderately to cross Sylvan Way at 0.7 mi., and at 1.4 mi., Randolph Path reaches Snyder Brook, where Inlook Trail and Brookside join on the left. Brookside and Randolph Path cross the brook together on large stepping-stones (the former bridge at this crossing was washed out in 2005 and will not be replaced) before Brookside diverges right and leads down to Valley Way. After a short climb, Randolph Path crosses Valley Way and soon joins Air Line, coincides with it for 20 yd., and then leaves it on the right.

At 1.9 mi., Short Line enters right; by this shortcut route, it is 1.3 mi. to US 2 at Appalachia. Short Line coincides with Randolph Path for 0.4 mi. and then branches left for King Ravine. Randolph Path descends slightly and crosses Cold Brook on Sanders Bridge; Cliffway diverges right just beyond. At 3.1 mi., Randolph Path crosses King Ravine Trail at its jct. with the Amphibrach. This 5-way intersection is called the Pentadoi. Randolph Path continues across Spur Brook on ledges just below some interesting pools and cascades, and a bit beyond the brook, Spur Trail diverges left. Randolph Path climbs around the nose of a minor ridge and becomes steeper and rougher. Soon, Log Cabin Cutoff diverges right and runs, nearly level but with rough footing, 0.2 mi. to the Log Cabin.

At 3.9 mi. from Randolph East, Randolph Path crosses Lowe's Path, and the grade moderates as Randolph Path angles southward up the steep west side of Nowell Ridge, although the footing is rocky. At 4.7 mi., good outlooks begin to appear, providing particularly notable views of the Castles (striking rock formations on Mt. Jefferson's Castellated Ridge) nearby and Mt. Lafayette in the distance to the southwest. At 4.9 mi., Perch Path crosses, leading left (north) to Gray Knob Trail and right (south) to the Perch and to Israel Ridge Path; a small brook runs across Perch Path about 60 yd. south of Randolph Path. Above this jct., Randolph Path rises due south through high scrub. At 5.4 mi., Gray Knob Trail from Crag Camp and Gray Knob enters left at about the point where Randolph Path rises out of the high scrub. In another 70 yd., Israel Ridge Path enters right (north), ascending from US 2, and the trails coincide for about 150 yd.; then Israel Ridge Path branches left for Mt. Adams in an area where views to Mt. Jefferson and the Castles are particularly fine. From this point, Randolph Path is nearly level to its end at Edmands Col, curving around the head of Castle Ravine and offering continuous excellent views; despite the easy grade, the footing is often rough. The trail is above treeline, much exposed to the weather, and its treadway is visible for a long distance ahead. Near Edmands Col is Spaulding Spring (reliable water), located in a small, grassy valley on the right, where two trails enter Randolph Path from the right at nearly the same point: Castle Ravine Trail from US 2 comes up through the length of this little valley from the north, and the Cornice, leading to the Caps and the Castles, runs west across the valley. In 0.1 mi. more, Randolph Path joins Gulfside Trail in Edmands Col.

THE LINK (MAP 1: E9–F8)
Cumulative from Appalachia parking area (1,305 ft.) to:

Memorial Bridge (1,425 ft.)	0.7 mi.	100 ft.	0:25
Cliffway (2,170 ft.)	2.0 mi.	850 ft.	1:25
Lowe's Path (2,475 ft.)	2.7 mi.	1,150 ft.	1:55
Israel Ridge Path (2,800 ft.)	4.0 mi.	1,500 ft.	2:45
Castle Ravine Trail, lower jct. (3,125 ft.)	5.1 mi.	1,900 ft. (rev. 100 ft.)	3:30
Castle Trail (4,025 ft.)	6.0 mi.	2,800 ft.	4:25
Caps Ridge Trail (3,800 ft.)	7.6 mi.	2,950 ft. (rev. 350 ft.)	5:15

RMC This path links the Appalachia parking area (plowed in winter) with the trails ascending Mt. Adams and Mt. Jefferson, connecting to the Amphibrach, Cliffway, Lowe's Path, Israel Ridge Path, Castle Ravine, and Emerald, Castle, and Caps Ridge trails. The Link is graded as far as Cascade Brook. The section between Caps Ridge and Castle trails, although very rough, makes possible a circuit of the Caps and the Castles from Jefferson Notch Rd. Although some parts of the Link are heavily traveled, much of it is very lightly used and, although well cleared and marked with yellow blazes, may have little evident footway.

The Link diverges right from Air Line 100 yd. south of Appalachia, just after entering the woods beyond a power-line clearing, and runs west, fairly close to the edge of this clearing. The trail crosses a small brook, passes under maple sap lines, and bears left twice where logging roads enter from the right. At 0.6 mi., Beechwood Way diverges left, and, just east of Cold Brook, Sylvan Way enters left. The Link crosses Cold Brook at 0.7 mi. on Memorial Bridge, with a fine view upstream to Cold Brook Fall, which can be reached in less than 100 yd. by Sylvan Way or by a spur from the Amphibrach. Memorial Bridge honors the pioneer path makers of the northern peaks.

Just west of the brook, the Amphibrach diverges left and the Link continues straight ahead. The Link then follows old logging roads southwest, crossing several small brooks, with gradually increasing grades and occasional wet footing. At 2.0 mi., Cliffway leads left (east) to White Cliff, a viewpoint on Nowell Ridge, and the Link swings to the south and climbs at easy grades, crossing Lowe's Path at 2.7 mi. The Link crosses the north branch of Mystic Stream at 3.1 mi. and the main Mystic Stream, in a region of small cascades, at 3.3 mi. The trail soon curves left, rounds the western buttress of Nowell Ridge, and becomes rougher, running southeast nearly level and entering Cascade Ravine on the mountainside high above the stream. At 4.0 mi., the Link joins Israel Ridge Path coming up on the right from US 2; the two trails coincide for 50 yd. before Israel Ridge Path diverges left for Mt. Adams, passing Cabin–Cascades Trail in about 60 yd.

The Link continues straight from this jct., descending sharply for 60 yd. to Cascade Brook and crossing it behind a large, flat ledge at the top of the First Cascade, which offers a view of Mt. Bowman. (This crossing may be difficult at high water.) The trail climbs steeply above the brook, swings right, and crosses a sidehill slope and an old landslide with very rough footing (follow markings carefully). The grade eases and the footing gradually improves as the trail rounds the tip of Israel Ridge and runs generally south into Castle Ravine, with minor ups and downs.

At 5.1 mi., the Link joins Castle Ravine Trail, and the two trails pass the jct. with Emerald Trail on the left and cross Castle Brook. Just beyond the crossing, at 5.4 mi., the Link diverges sharply right from Castle Ravine Trail and ascends steeply west, with difficult footing, angling up the very rough southwest wall of Castle Ravine. At 6.0 mi., the Link crosses Castle Trail below the first Castle at about 4,025 ft. and then runs south, generally descending gradually, with occasional minor ascents, over a very rough footway with countless treacherous roots, rocks, and hollows that are tricky and tedious to negotiate. At 6.5 mi., the trail crosses an old slide with a limited view west; in another 125 yd., it crosses a steep brook widened into a slide by the 2011 storm (use caution), with good views northwest, and at 7.0 mi., it crosses a fair-sized brook flowing over mossy ledges. After a section with improved footing, at 7.6 mi., the Link turns sharply left uphill and in 50 yd. reaches Caps Ridge Trail 1.1 mi. above Jefferson Notch Rd., about 100 yd. above a ledge with several potholes that provides a fine view up to Mt. Jefferson.

PRESIDENTIAL RAIL TRAIL (MAP 1: E9–E8)
Noncumulative segments from Randolph East (1,239 ft.) to:

Appalachia (1,305 ft.)	0.9 mi.	85 ft.	0:30
Appalachia (1,305 ft.) to Lowe's Path (1,450 ft.)	2.2 mi.	140 ft.	1:10
Lowe's Path (1,450 ft.) to Bowman trailhead (1,496 ft.)	0.9 mi.	50 ft.	0:30

FPRT This multiuse trail follows the roadbed of the former railroad right of way (tracks removed in 1997) that runs for 18.3 mi. from Gorham to Waumbek Junction near Cherry Pond. Presidential Rail Trail is open to a variety of nonmotorized uses, including walking, snowshoeing, cross-country skiing, bicycling, and dogsled traveling; it is open to motorized uses in winter. On its own, the trail has limited interest for hikers, but—running roughly parallel to US 2—it is useful as a connecting link between the trails on the northern edge of the Presidential Range. The trail provides an easy and also pleasant and safe (compared with the alternative of walking along high-speed US 2) pedestrian route between the Randolph East and

Appalachia trailheads, Lowe's Path, and the Bowman trailhead—even at night. Although this trail also is encountered near Cherry Pond (Section Twelve), only the small part that is useful to Northern Presidential hikers is covered here. It is assumed that hikers will use only segments as needed rather than the Northern Presidential section as a whole, so segment distances and times—rather than cumulative ones—are given. For more information on Presidential Rail Trail, visit friendsofthepresidentialrailtrail.org.

GREAT GULF WILDERNESS
GREAT GULF TRAIL (MAP 1: F10–F9)
Cumulative from parking area on NH 16 (1,347 ft.) to:

Osgood Trail (1,850 ft.)	1.8 mi.	500 ft.	1:10
Osgood Cutoff (2,300 ft.)	2.7 mi.	950 ft.	1:50
Madison Gulf Trail, south jct. (2,300 ft.)	2.8 mi.	1,000 ft. (rev. 50 ft.)	1:55
Six Husbands and Wamsutta trails (3,100 ft.)	4.5 mi.	1,800 ft.	3:10
Sphinx Trail (3,625 ft.)	5.6 mi.	2,350 ft.	4:00
Spaulding Lake (4,228 ft.)	6.5 mi.	2,950 ft.	4:45
Gulfside Trail jct. (5,925 ft.)	7.4 mi.	4,650 ft.	6:05
Mt. Washington summit (6,288 ft.) via Gulfside Trail and Trinity Heights Connector	7.8 mi.	5,000 ft.	6:25

WMNF This trail begins at the Great Gulf Wilderness parking area (Recreation Pass required; restrooms; plowed in winter) on the west side of NH 16, 1.9 mi. south of its jct. with Pinkham B Rd. (Dolly Copp Rd.) near Dolly Copp Campground and 1.5 mi. north of Mt. Washington Auto Rd. The trail follows the West Branch of Peabody River through the Great Gulf, climbs the headwall, and ends at a jct. with Gulfside Trail 0.5 mi. below the summit of Mt. Washington. Some of the brook crossings may be difficult or dangerous in moderate to high water conditions, and brooks can rise quickly during heavy rains in this deep, steep-walled valley. Care is required to follow the trail at some of the crossings in the upper valley. Above the Bluff, the trail is generally rough and rocky, and ascent on the headwall is very steep and rough. Except for the first 1.6 mi., this trail is in the Great Gulf Wilderness; camping is prohibited within 0.25 mi. of the trail above the jct. with Sphinx Trail, and below that point, camping is limited to designated trailside sites or sites at least 200 ft. away from the trail.

Leaving the parking lot, the trail leads north on an old road, turns left, and descends slightly to cross Peabody River on a suspension bridge. The trail then ascends to a jct. with Great Gulf Link Trail from Dolly Copp Campground on the right at 0.3 mi. Great Gulf Trail turns sharply left here and follows a logging road along the northwest bank of the West Branch of Peabody River, at first close to the stream and later some distance away from it. At 0.6 mi., the trail bears left off the road (which continues ahead as a ski trail), crosses a small brook, passes a ledgy cascade and pool, and turns left at 1.0 mi. as the ski trail rejoins from the right. At 1.6 mi., Hayes Copp Ski Trail diverges right; Great Gulf Trail soon crosses into the Great Gulf Wilderness; and Osgood Trail diverges right at 1.8 mi. Osgood Campsite is 0.8 mi. from here via Osgood Trail.

Great Gulf Trail follows the West Branch, mostly staying back in the woods, and passes a scenic spot on the river at 2.4 mi. The trail then climbs rather steeply to the high, gravelly bank called the Bluff, where there is a good view of the gulf and the mountains around it, especially from the top of a boulder on the right. The trail follows the edge of the Bluff; then at 2.7 mi., Osgood Cutoff (part of the AT) continues straight ahead, and Great Gulf Trail descends sharply left. For a short distance, Great Gulf Trail is also part of the AT. In 50 yd., the trail crosses Parapet Brook (no bridge; difficult in high water) and then climbs to the crest of the little ridge that separates Parapet Brook from the West Branch, where Madison Gulf Trail enters right, coming down from the vicinity of Madison Spring Hut through Madison Gulf. The two trails coincide for a short distance, descending to cross the West Branch on a suspension bridge and ascending the steep bank on the south side. Here, Madison Gulf Trail branches left, continuing the AT in that direction, and Great Gulf Trail leaves the AT and turns right, becoming rougher and rockier and leading up the south bank of the river past Clam Rock, a huge boulder on the left, at 3.1 mi.

At 3.9 mi., Great Gulf Trail crosses Chandler Brook, and on the far bank, Chandler Brook Trail diverges left and ascends to Mt. Washington Auto Rd. Great Gulf Trail continues close to the river, passing in sight of the mouth of the stream that issues from Jefferson Ravine on the north, to meet Six Husbands Trail (right) and Wamsutta Trail (left) at 4.5 mi. Great Gulf Trail continues up the valley, with glimpses of Jefferson's Knees, and at 5.2 mi., it climbs wet, slippery ledges beside an impressive cascade (use caution) and continues past numerous other attractive cascades for the next 0.2 mi., crossing a tributary brook partway along this section. After crossing to the northwest bank of the West Branch (may be difficult in high water), the trail soon crosses the brook that descends from Sphinx Col and, at 5.6 mi., reaches the jct. where Sphinx Trail, leading to Gulfside Trail, diverges right. Camping is prohibited within 0.25 mi. of Great Gulf Trail above this jct. Great Gulf Trail soon crosses to the southeast bank of the

West Branch and passes more waterfalls, including Weetamoo Falls, the finest in the gulf. Open points along the trail afford remarkable views up to Mt. Adams and Mt. Madison. The trail crosses an eastern tributary and, after a rocky ascent, reaches the tiny tarn called Spaulding Lake (4,228 ft.), with the impressive headwall rising ahead. This point is 6.5 mi. from NH 16 and 1.3 mi. by trail from the summit of Mt. Washington.

Great Gulf Trail continues on the rocky east side of the lake, passes through a section that may be overgrown, and soon begins to ascend the very steep and rough headwall. In this section, up onto the lower part of the headwall, there is often water running down the trail; avoid false beaten paths leading into the scrub. The trail runs south and then southeast, with magnificent views of the gulf and surrounding mountains, rising 1,600 ft. in about 0.8 mi. over fragments of stone, many of which are loose. Use extra caution in an area well up on the headwall where the trail crosses a rock slide caused by the 2011 storm; footing may be especially unstable here. Below and above the slide, the route is partially marked by cairns and faded yellow blazes, but in places it may be difficult to follow. Great Gulf Trail generally curves a little to the left until within a few yd. of the top of the headwall; then, bearing slightly right, the trail emerges from the gulf and ends at Gulfside Trail near the Cog Railway. It is 0.4 mi. from here to the summit of Mt. Washington by Gulfside Trail and Trinity Heights Connector.

GREAT GULF LINK TRAIL (MAP 1: F10)
From Dolly Copp Campground (1,243 ft.) to:

Great Gulf Trail (1,375 ft.)	0.9 mi.	150 ft.	0:30

WMNF This trail was formerly a segment of Great Gulf Trail. Great Gulf Link Trail leaves Dolly Copp Campground at a sign at the south end of the main camp road (a dead end) 0.2 mi. south of the trailhead for Daniel Webster–Scout Trail and 1.0 mi. south of Pinkham B Rd. (Dolly Copp Rd.). Parking is available near the trail entrance. The road into the campground is closed in winter; plowed parking is available on Pinkham B Rd. at its jct. with the campground road, 0.4 mi. from NH 16. The trail enters the woods and turns left (arrow) in 0.1 mi. onto an old logging road that has cross-country ski markers in both directions. It follows the logging road south along the west bank of Peabody River, passing some interesting pools. Great Gulf Link Trail ends at a jct. with Great Gulf Trail, which comes in on the left from the parking lot on NH 16 and continues straight ahead into the gulf.

MADISON GULF TRAIL (MAP 1: F9)
Cumulative from Mt. Washington Auto Rd. (2,675 ft.) to:

Great Gulf Trail, south jct. (2,300 ft.)	2.1 mi.	250 ft. (rev. 650 ft.)	1:10
Foot of Madison Gulf headwall at Sylvan Cascade (3,900 ft.)	3.9 mi.	1,850 ft.	2:55
Parapet Trail (4,850 ft.)	4.5 mi.	2,800 ft.	3:40
Madison Spring Hut (4,795 ft.) via Parapet and Star Lake trails	4.8 mi.	2,850 ft. (rev. 100 ft.)	3:50
From Pinkham Notch Visitor Center (2,028 ft.) to:			
Madison Spring Hut (4,795 ft.) via Old Jackson Road and Madison Gulf, Parapet, and Star Lake trails	6.7 mi.	3,550 ft. (rev. 800 ft.)	5:10

AMC This trail begins on Mt. Washington Auto Rd. a little more than 2.0 mi. from the Glen House site, opposite Old Jackson Road. Madison Gulf Trail first crosses a low ridge and then descends gently to the West Branch of Peabody River, where the trail meets Great Gulf Trail. Madison Gulf Trail ascends along Parapet Brook through Madison Gulf to the Parapet, where the trail ends 0.3 mi. from Madison Spring Hut. Madison Gulf Trail is almost entirely within the Great Gulf Wilderness. From the Auto Rd. to its departure from Great Gulf Trail, Madison Gulf Trail is part of the AT, but because the trail is in a Wilderness Area, paint blazes (including the familiar white AT blazes) are not used. Care is needed to follow the trail at several stream crossings where it follows Parapet Brook on the approach to the headwall.

Caution: The section of this trail on the headwall of Madison Gulf is one of the most difficult in the White Mountains, going over several ledge outcroppings, boulder-strewn areas, and a rock chimney. The steep slabs may be slippery when wet, and several ledges require scrambling and the use of handholds. Stream crossings may be very difficult in wet weather. The trail is not recommended for the descent, for hikers with heavy packs, or for use in wet weather. Allow extra time and do not start up the headwall late in the day. The ascent of the headwall may require several hours more than the estimated time; parties frequently fail to reach the hut before dark due to slowness on the headwall.

Madison Gulf Trail is well protected from storms and has plenty of water. Combined with Old Jackson Road, this is the shortest route (6.7 mi.) from Pinkham Notch Visitor Center to Madison Spring Hut via the Great Gulf but not usually the easiest; there are several reasonable alternate routes, although none of them is without drawbacks. The route via Osgood

Cutoff and Osgood Trail, 7.5 mi. long, is steep in parts but has no difficult brook crossings or tricky scrambles; however, the route is very exposed to weather in the upper part, even if the rough but more sheltered Parapet Trail is used to bypass Mt. Madison's summit. The route via Buttress Trail is 8.4 mi. long; it has two significant and potentially dangerous brook crossings and somewhat more weather exposure than Madison Gulf Trail, although substantially less than the Osgood–Parapet route. In any event, parties traveling to Madison Spring Hut from the Great Gulf side cannot avoid the 0.3-mi. walk to the hut across the windswept col between Mt. Madison and Mt. Adams except by going over the summit of Mt. Madison, where conditions may well be much worse. Therefore, choice of route comes down to a trade-off among the factors of distance, weather exposure, brook crossings, and rock scrambles; hikers must consider which factors they feel better prepared to deal with, taking current and expected conditions into account. In adverse conditions, hikers who are not prepared for this level of challenge would be well advised to change their plans rather than attempt any of the direct routes between Pinkham Notch Visitor Center and Madison Spring Hut; even in favorable conditions, Madison Gulf Trail must be approached with caution.

Madison Gulf Trail leaves the Auto Rd. above the 2-mi. mark, opposite the Old Jackson Road jct., and enters the Great Gulf Wilderness. After a climb of 0.2 mi., a side path branches right in a little pass west of Low's Bald Spot and climbs 0.1 mi., with a bit of ledge scrambling, to this little ledgy knob, an excellent viewpoint. Madison Gulf Trail bears left and ascends over a ledge with a limited view and then descends, first rapidly for a short distance and later easily, crossing many small brooks. The trail ascends briefly, curves into the valley of the West Branch of Peabody River, and then descends gently until it meets Great Gulf Trail (which runs straight ahead, north, into the gulf) on the south bank at 2.1 mi. Here, Madison Gulf Trail turns sharply right (east) as the two trails run together, descending the steep bank to the West Branch, crossing a suspension bridge to the north bank, and climbing to the crest of the little ridge that divides Parapet Brook from the West Branch. Here, Great Gulf Trail continues straight ahead, leading to NH 16 or to Osgood Trail (via Osgood Cutoff) for Mt. Madison and Madison Spring Hut. Madison Gulf Trail (which here leaves the AT) turns left (north) up the narrow ridge, passing a view of Mt. Adams, and continues between the two streams until it enters its former route near the bank of Parapet Brook at 2.5 mi. At 2.7 mi., the trail crosses one channel of the divided brook, runs between the two channels for 0.1 mi., and then crosses the other to the northeast bank. The trail follows the brook bank for a little way before turning right, away from the brook, then left, and, becoming rougher, ascending along the valley wall at a moderate grade. It comes back to the brook at the mouth of the branch stream from Osgood Ridge, which it crosses. From here, the trail follows Parapet Brook rather closely and, at 3.4 mi., crosses the brook for the first of three times in less than 0.5 mi., ascending to the lower floor of the gulf where the trail reaches Sylvan Cascade, a fine waterfall, at 3.9 mi.

Madison Gulf Trail then ascends to the upper floor of the gulf, where it crosses several small brooks (follow with care at these crossings). From the floor, the trail rises gradually to Mossy Slide, a small cascade at the foot of the headwall, and then ascends very rapidly alongside a stream, which becomes partly hidden among the rocks as the trail rises. The trail then reaches the headwall of the gulf and climbs very steeply, with some difficult scrambles on the ledges. This section has several fine views. As Madison Gulf Trail emerges on the rocks at treeline, it bears right and the grade moderates, and soon the trail ends at Parapet Trail. For the Parapet (0.1 mi.) and Madison Spring Hut (0.3 mi.), turn left; for Osgood Trail via Parapet Trail, turn right.

CHANDLER BROOK TRAIL (MAP 1: F9)
From Great Gulf Trail (2,800 ft.) to:

Mt. Washington Auto Rd. (4,125 ft.)	0.9 mi.	1,350 ft.	1:10

AMC This steep and rough trail passes many cascades as it climbs from Great Gulf Trail to Mt. Washington Auto Rd., just above the 4-mi. post. Chandler Brook Trail lies on a very steep slope, so its brook crossings can quickly become difficult in rainy weather. The rocks are slippery when wet. Chandler Brook Trail is almost entirely within the Great Gulf Wilderness.

The trail diverges south from Great Gulf Trail 3.9 mi. from NH 16, just above that trail's crossing of Chandler Brook, and rises moderately. It crosses two small brooks and then becomes steep as it approaches the first of three crossings of Chandler Brook at 0.3 mi. The second crossing, at 0.4 mi., presents waterfalls and an impressive view of Mt. Adams. From the last crossing, the trail runs southeast, rising very steeply over a jumbled mass of stones with a fine vista across the Great Gulf, and keeps west of interesting rock formations. The trail enters the Auto Rd. near a ledge of white quartz at the Horn, 0.3 mi. above the 4-mi. post. About 125 yd. left down the road are a parking area and adjacent ledges with wide views. (Descending, look for this white ledge, which is close to the Auto Rd. The trail is marked by cairns here and is visible from the road.)

WAMSUTTA TRAIL (MAP 1: F9)
Cumulative from Great Gulf Trail (3,100 ft.) to:

Outlook on promontory (4,350 ft.)	0.9 mi.	1,250 ft.	1:05
Mt. Washington Auto Rd. (5,305 ft.)	1.7 mi.	2,200 ft.	1:55

AMC This steep and rough trail, with one particularly difficult scramble, begins on Great Gulf Trail and ascends to Mt. Washington Auto Rd. just above the 6-mi. marker and opposite Alpine Garden Trail, with which Wamsutta Trail provides routes to Tuckerman Junction, Lakes of the Clouds Hut, and other points to the south. Wamsutta Trail is almost entirely within the Great Gulf Wilderness. The trail was named for Wamsutta, the first of six successive husbands of Weetamoo, a queen of the Pocasset tribe, for whom a beautiful waterfall in the Great Gulf is named.

Leaving Great Gulf Trail opposite Six Husbands Trail, 4.5 mi. from NH 16, Wamsutta Trail crosses a small stream and ascends gradually. Soon it climbs the very steep and rough northerly spur of Chandler Ridge, with one difficult scramble up a chimney. Higher up, in an area with several more scrambles, are impressive views across the floor of the gulf to Mts. Jefferson, Adams, and Madison. The trail continues to ascend, steeply and then more gradually, to a small, open promontory on the crest of the spur, which offers another good view, at 0.9 mi. The trail then ascends gradually through woods, passing a spring on the right. Continuing along the ridge crest at a moderate grade, the trail emerges at treeline and climbs to a point near the top end of the winter shortcut route of the Auto Rd. After turning right along this road, the trail ends in another 100 yd. at the main route of the Auto Rd., just above the 6-mi. post.

SPHINX TRAIL (MAP 1: F9)
From Great Gulf Trail (3,625 ft.) to:

Gulfside Trail (4,975 ft.)	1.1 mi.	1,350 ft.	1:15

AMC This steep and rough trail runs from Great Gulf Trail below Spaulding Lake to Gulfside Trail in Sphinx Col, between Mt. Jefferson and Mt. Clay. The trail's name is derived from the profile of a rock formation seen from just below the meadow where water is found. This trail is particularly important because it affords the quickest escape route for anyone overtaken by a storm in the vicinity of Sphinx Col. For the descent, the trail diverges east from Gulfside Trail 40 yd. north of the lowest point in the col, running through a grassy, rock-walled corridor, and descends to Great Gulf Trail. Once below the col, hikers are quickly protected from west and northwest winds. For a considerable part of its length, this trail climbs very steeply; there is a long section of slippery rocks in a brook bed, very tedious particularly on the descent, and some of the scrambles on the ledges in the upper part are challenging. The trail can be difficult to follow at the brook crossings. This trail is almost entirely within the Great Gulf Wilderness.

Sphinx Trail branches northwest from Great Gulf Trail 5.6 mi. from NH 16, just beyond the crossing of the brook that flows down from Sphinx Col, through the minor ravine between Mts. Clay and Jefferson. The trail soon turns due west and ascends close to the brook, first gradually and then very steeply, crossing the brook four times (follow with care) and passing several attractive cascades and pools. Above the second brook crossing, the trail crosses the base of a landslide caused by Tropical Storm Irene in 2011. Just before the third crossing, the trail runs along the steep edge of a flumelike formation. For about 100 yd. above the fourth crossing, the trail runs directly in the brook bed, where the rocks are extremely slippery. At 0.6 mi., at the foot of a broken ledge with several small streams cascading over it, the trail turns left, away from the brook, and angles up across two more small brooks, with a couple of short, tricky scrambles. It climbs a small, fairly difficult chimney, where views out from the scrubby slope start to appear, and then scrambles up ledges with several rock pitches of some difficulty. About 100 yd. above the chimney, after a slight descent, the trail crosses a small meadow where there is usually water visible under a rock just downhill to the north. Sphinx Trail then climbs steeply up a rocky cleft, ascends easily over the crest of a small, rocky ridge, and descends into a slight sag. It finally ascends to the ridge crest and traverses a grassy passage at the base of a rock wall to Gulfside Trail, just north of Sphinx Col.

SIX HUSBANDS TRAIL (MAP 1: F9)
Cumulative from Great Gulf Trail (3,100 ft.) to:

Buttress Trail (3,350 ft.)	0.5 mi.	250 ft.	0:25
Edmands Col Cutoff (4,925 ft.)	1.7 mi.	1,850 ft.	1:45
Gulfside Trail (5,325 ft.)	2.0 mi.	2,250 ft.	2:10
Mt. Jefferson Loop (5,625 ft.)	2.3 mi.	2,550 ft.	2:25

AMC This steep, rough, and challenging trail provides magnificent views of the inner part of the Great Gulf. The name honors the six successive husbands of Weetamoo, queen of the Pocasset tribe. Six Husbands Trail diverges from Great Gulf Trail 4.5 mi. from NH 16, opposite Wamsutta Trail, crosses the West Branch of Peabody River, climbs up the north knee of Mt. Jefferson, crosses Gulfside Trail, and ends at Mt. Jefferson Loop a short distance northeast of the summit. Six Husbands Trail is very steep and difficult and is not recommended for descent except to escape danger-ous weather conditions above treeline. Up to the Gulfside Trail jct., Six Husbands Trail is entirely within the Great Gulf Wilderness.

Leaving Great Gulf Trail, Six Husbands Trail descends directly across the West Branch, avoiding side paths along the stream. In times of high water, this crossing may be very difficult, but there may be a better crossing upstream. The trail climbs easily northward across a low ridge to join Jefferson Brook, which flows from Jefferson Ravine, and ascends along its southwest bank. At 0.5 mi., Buttress Trail branches right and crosses the brook. Six Husbands Trail swings left away from the brook (last sure water) and runs through an area containing many large boulders. Soon the trail begins to attack the very steep main buttress, the north knee of Mt. Jefferson, passing by one boulder cave and through another. At 1.0 mi., the trail ascends a steep ledge on a pair of ladders and then climbs under an over-hanging ledge on a second pair of ladders. At the top of these ladders is a tricky traverse of a sloping ledge under the overhang, with a dropoff to the left, that is especially difficult with a large pack and might be dangerous if wet or icy. The trail climbs another ladder just above and soon reaches a promontory with a fine view before beginning a steep and difficult climb with several more scrambles up the crest of a rocky ridge.

At 1.3 mi., Six Husbands Trail reaches the top of the knee approximately at treeline—with magnificent views—and the grade moderates. The trail winds up through scrub and across bare stretches, where it is marked by cairns. At 1.7 mi., Edmands Col Cutoff branches right, leading in 0.5 mi. to Edmands Col, and Six Husbands Trail becomes steeper as it begins to climb the cone of Mt. Jefferson. Soon, the trail passes over a talus slope that is usually covered by a great drift of snow well into July and is conspicuous for a considerable distance from viewpoints to the east. Marked by cairns, Six Husbands Trail crosses Gulfside Trail and climbs moderately west toward the summit of Mt. Jefferson, swinging right at the end and joining Mt. Jefferson Loop 0.1 mi. below the summit.

BUTTRESS TRAIL (MAP 1: F9)
Cumulative from Six Husbands Trail (3,350 ft.) to:

Star Lake Trail (4,900 ft.)	1.9 mi.	1,600 ft. (rev. 50 ft.)	1:45
Madison Spring Hut (4,800 ft.) via Star Lake Trail	2.2 mi.	1,600 ft. (rev. 100 ft.)	1:55

AMC This trail leads from Six Husbands Trail to Star Lake Trail, near Madison Spring Hut, and is the most direct route from the upper part of the Great Gulf to Madison Spring Hut. Buttress Trail is mostly well sheltered until it nears the hut, and grades are moderate; although the footing is rough in the upper section, overall this trail is easier than most other Great Gulf trails. In bad weather, for hikers with heavy packs, or for descending, this is probably the best route from the lower part of the Great Gulf to the hut, despite the somewhat greater distance. (See Madison Gulf Trail, the principal alternative, for a discussion of other options.) Buttress Trail is almost entirely within the Great Gulf Wilderness.

The trail diverges north from Six Husbands Trail 0.5 mi. from Great Gulf Trail and immediately crosses Jefferson Brook (last sure water), which flows out of Jefferson Ravine. On the far side of the brook, Buttress Trail bears left through a wet area on bog bridges; avoid several beaten paths that diverge right into a camping area.

After 0.1 mi., the trail bears right (east) and, rising moderately, climbs diagonally across a steep slope of large, loose, angular rock fragments (take care not to dislodge the loose rocks). At the top of this talus slope is a spectacular view up the Great Gulf and to the steep buttress of Mt. Jefferson's north knee, rising nearby across a small valley. The trail continues east, ascending steadily along a steep, wooded incline. At 0.5 mi., it reaches a ridge corner, swings left (north), and runs at easy grades across a gently sloping upland covered with trees, passing to the right of a spring (reliable water) at 1.0 mi. At 1.2 mi., Buttress Trail passes through a cave formed by a large boulder across the path, reaches the foot of a steep ledge, swings left, and climbs it. At 1.4 mi., the trail swings right after passing between two ledges; the ledge on the right provides a fine view. The trail now ascends less steeply (but with rough footing) on open rocks above the scrub line, with an excellent view across Madison Gulf to Mt. Madison. It crosses a minor ridge and descends moderately. After passing under an overhanging rock, the trail reenters high scrub that provides shelter almost all the way to the jct. with Star Lake Trail, which is reached in the gap between the Parapet and Mt. Quincy Adams, just southwest of Star Lake and 0.3 mi. from Madison Spring Hut.

OSGOOD TRAIL (MAP 1: F10–F9)
Cumulative from Great Gulf Trail (1,850 ft.) to:

Osgood Cutoff (2,486 ft.)	0.8 mi.	650 ft.	0:45
Osgood Junction (4,822 ft.)	2.8 mi.	2,950 ft.	2:55
Mt. Madison summit (5,363 ft.)	3.3 mi.	3,500 ft.	3:25
Madison Spring Hut (4,795 ft.)	3.8 mi.	3,500 ft. (rev. 550 ft.)	3:40

From Great Gulf Trail parking area on NH 16 (1,347 ft.) via Great Gulf and Osgood trails to:			
Mt. Madison summit (5,363 ft.)	5.1 mi.	4,000 ft.	4:35

AMC This trail runs from Great Gulf Trail, 1.8 mi. from the Great Gulf Wilderness parking area on NH 16, up the southeast ridge of Mt. Madison to the summit, and then down to Madison Spring Hut. The upper 1.7 mi. is very exposed to the weather and has very rough footing. Built by Benjamin F. Osgood in 1878, this is the oldest trail now in use to the summit of Mt. Madison. Above Osgood Cutoff, Osgood Trail is part of the AT. Osgood Trail begins in the Great Gulf Wilderness, but for most of its length is just outside the boundary; in fact, it constitutes the northern section of the Wilderness Area's eastern boundary.

Osgood Trail leaves Great Gulf Trail and ascends at an easy to moderate grade. At 0.3 mi., it crosses a small brook, follows it, recrosses it, and bears away from it to the left. At 0.8 mi., Osgood Cutoff comes in from the left, and a spur path leads right over a small brook (last sure water) and continues about 100 yd. to Osgood Tentsite.

At 1.4 mi., Osgood Trail begins to climb a very steep and rough section. At about 1.6 mi., it gradually but steadily becomes less steep; the grade is easy by the time the trail emerges on the crest of Osgood Ridge, at treeline, at 2.1 mi. Ahead, on the crest of the ridge, ten or twelve small, rocky peaks curve to the left in a crescent toward the summit of Mt. Madison; the trail, marked by cairns, follows this ridge crest with rough footing and magnificent views. At 2.8 mi. from Great Gulf Trail, Osgood Trail reaches Osgood Junction in a small hollow. Here, Daniel Webster–Scout Trail enters on the right—ascending from Dolly Copp Campground—and Parapet Trail diverges left on a level path marked by cairns. Parapet Trail passes around the south side of the cone of Mt. Madison with little change of elevation, making a very rough but comparatively sheltered route to Madison Spring Hut.

From Osgood Junction, Osgood Trail climbs over a prominent crag, turns left (west), crosses a shallow sag, and starts up the east ridge of Mt. Madison's summit cone, where it is soon joined on the right by Howker Ridge Trail at 3.1 mi. Hikers planning to descend on Howker Ridge Trail must take care to distinguish that trail from beaten side paths that lead back to Osgood Trail. Osgood Trail ascends to the summit of Mt. Madison at 3.3 mi., where Watson Path enters on the right. (In the reverse direction, Osgood Trail descends almost due east, and Watson Path descends northeast.) Osgood Trail follows the crest of the ridge west past several large cairns, drops off to the left (south), and continues to descend westward just below the ridge crest and above the steep slopes falling off into Madison Gulf on the left. Soon Osgood Trail crosses to the north side of the ridge and descends steeply, and 30 yd. before the trail reaches the front of Madison Spring Hut, Pine Link joins on the right.

OSGOOD CUTOFF (MAP 1: F9)
From Great Gulf Trail (2,300 ft.) to:

Osgood Trail (2,486 ft.)	0.6 mi.	200 ft.	0:25

AMC This link trail, part of the AT, provides a convenient shortcut from Great Gulf and Madison Gulf trails to Osgood Trail. Osgood Cutoff is entirely within the Great Gulf Wilderness. It leaves Great Gulf Trail on the Bluff, 2.7 mi. from the Great Gulf parking area, continuing straight ahead where Great Gulf Trail turns sharply left to descend to Parapet Brook. Osgood Cutoff climbs moderately for 0.2 mi. and then turns sharply right. From the turn, the trail runs nearly on contour east across several small brooks to its jct. with Osgood Trail; directly across Osgood Trail is the spur path leading to Osgood Tentsite, which has reliable water.

MT. MADISON
DANIEL WEBSTER–SCOUT TRAIL (MAP 1: F10–F9)
Cumulative from Dolly Copp Campground (1,249 ft.) to:

Foot of small buttress (2,800 ft.)	2.0 mi.	1,550 ft.	1:45
Osgood Junction (4,822 ft.)	3.5 mi.	3,550 ft.	3:30
Mt. Madison summit (5,363 ft.) via Osgood Trail	4.0 mi.	4,100 ft.	4:05

WMNF This trail, cut in 1933 by Boy Scouts from the Daniel Webster Council, leads from Dolly Copp Campground to Osgood Trail at Osgood Junction, 0.5 mi. below the summit of Mt. Madison. Daniel Webster–Scout Trail begins on the west side of the main campground road, 0.8 mi. south of the campground entrance on Pinkham B Rd. (Dolly Copp Rd.); the entrance is 0.4 mi. west of NH 16. Parking is available on the left (east) side of the road, 0.1 mi. south of the trail entrance. The road into the campground is closed in winter; plowed parking is available on Pinkham B Rd. at its jct. with the campground road. Grades are moderate for much of Daniel Webster–Scout Trail's length, and footing is somewhat rocky but not unusually rough; however, the upper section is very steep, with rough footing on talus, and is very exposed to the weather.

The blue-blazed trail starts out through a section of open woods with some very large trees, crosses Hayes Copp Ski Trail (here a grassy logging road) at 0.2 mi., and swings northwest almost to the bank of Culhane Brook, passing numerous small logging cuts and crossing several old skid roads. Veering left (southwest) away from the brook just before reaching it, Daniel Webster–Scout Trail climbs moderately up the east slope of Mt. Madison, mostly angling upward and avoiding a more direct assault on the steeper parts of the mountainside. At 2.0 mi., the trail reaches the base of a small buttress, where the forest changes rather abruptly from hardwoods to evergreens. The trail winds steeply up to the top of the buttress, switchbacks upward a bit farther, and then resumes its steady ascent, angling northwest across the slope, becoming steeper and rockier. At 2.9 mi., the trail begins a very steep and rough climb west, nearly straight up the slope, with ever-increasing amounts of talus and decreasing amounts of scrub, where views begin to appear and improve. At 3.2 mi., the trail reaches treeline and moderates somewhat, although it is still steep. (Descending, the trail enters the scrub at a lower left corner of a large, steep talus slope.) On the open talus, the route is somewhat poorly marked with small cairns and both blue and yellow blazes, which must be followed with great care. As Daniel Webster–Scout Trail approaches the ridge crest, it turns left and directly ascends for the last 100 yd. to Osgood Junction and Osgood Trail.

PARAPET TRAIL (MAP 1: F9)
Cumulative from Osgood Junction (4,822 ft.) to:

Madison Gulf Trail (4,850 ft.)	0.8 mi.	150 ft. (rev. 100 ft.)	0:30
Star Lake Trail (4,900 ft.)	1.0 mi.	200 ft.	0:35
Madison Spring Hut (4,795 ft.) via Star Lake Trail	1.2 mi.	200 ft. (rev. 100 ft.)	0:40

AMC This trail, marked with cairns and blue blazes, runs at a nearly constant elevation around the south side of the cone of Mt. Madison, from the Osgood and Daniel Webster–Scout trails at Osgood Junction to Star Lake Trail between the Parapet and Madison Spring Hut. Although above timberline and extremely rough, particularly in its eastern half, Parapet Trail is mostly sheltered from the northwest winds in bad weather. However, the rocks can be very slippery, the trail may be hard to follow if visibility is poor, and the extra effort of rock-hopping more than expends the energy saved by avoiding the climb of about 500 ft. over the summit of Mt. Madison. Therefore, this route is probably only useful as a bad-weather route if strong northwest or west winds are a major part of the problem.

From Osgood Junction, Parapet Trail leads west and rises very slightly, marked by cairns across the open rocks (at the start, take care to distinguish these cairns from those ascending the ridge crest on the right, which belong to Osgood Trail). Parapet Trail traverses a large area of open talus, swings left, and descends briefly into scrub. The trail continues along the steep slope with minor ups and downs, often in the open, with several minor scrambles. It passes to the right of a crag with excellent views and descends slightly to a jct. at 0.8 mi., where Madison Gulf Trail enters left at the bottom of a little gully. Parapet Trail ascends a ledge and then makes a sharp right turn at 0.9 mi., where a spur path leads left 30 yd. onto the Parapet, a ledge that commands excellent views over the Great Gulf and Madison Gulf to the mountains beyond. Parapet Trail then runs north, passing above Star Lake, and joins Star Lake Trail 0.2 mi. south of Madison Spring Hut.

PINE LINK (MAP 1: E10–F9)
Cumulative from Pinkham B Rd. (Dolly Copp Rd.) (1,648 ft.) to:

Howker Ridge Trail, lower jct. (3,850 ft.)	2.4 mi.	2,300 ft. (rev. 100 ft.)	2:20
Watson Path (4,950 ft.)	3.5 mi.	3,400 ft.	3:25
Madison Spring Hut (4,795 ft.)	4.0 mi.	3,400 ft. (rev. 150 ft.)	3:40

AMC Pine Link ascends the slopes of Mt. Madison from the highest point of Pinkham B Rd. (Dolly Copp Rd.), almost directly opposite the private road to the Horton Center on Pine Mtn., 2.4 mi. from US 2 at the foot of the big hill west of Gorham and 1.9 mi. from NH 16 near Dolly Copp Campground. Pinkham B Rd. is not plowed in winter. Pine Link features an interesting variety of views from its outlook ledges and from the section above treeline on Mt. Madison's northwest slope. Combined with the upper part of Howker Ridge Trail, Pine Link provides a very scenic loop. It is not unusually steep, but the footing is often rough and demands an unusual amount of attention and energy compared with most trails of similar steepness. The section above treeline is continually exposed to the full force of northwest winds for about 0.7 mi., might be difficult to follow if visibility is poor, and requires a considerable amount of fairly strenuous rock-hopping. The result is that the trail generally proves more challenging than its statistics might indicate.

Blue-blazed Pine Link first ascends the northwest slope of a spur of Howker Ridge, climbing by a series of short, steep pitches interspersed with level sections. At 1.0 mi., it crosses a flat, swampy area, ascends another steep pitch, and then climbs to the ridge crest of the spur and follows it southwest. At 1.7 mi., Pine Link passes an overgrown outlook with restricted views from the south side of the trail, the result of a 1968 fire. At 1.9 mi., just before the trail descends into a sag, a spur path leads left 20 yd. to a bare crag that offers fine views up to Mt. Madison and out to the Carter Range. At 2.4 mi., after a fairly long section of trail that has a brook running in and out of it, Pine Link turns right and joins Howker Ridge Trail in a shady little glen. Turning left at this jct., Pine Link coincides with Howker Ridge Trail. The two trails pass over a ledgy minor knob (a "howk") that offers a good view and then descend from the ledge down a steep cleft to a wet sag. After passing a small cave on the right, Pine Link branches right from Howker Ridge Trail at 2.7 mi., at the foot of the most prominent Howk. An excellent viewpoint at the top of this crag is only about 0.1 mi. above the jct. along Howker Ridge Trail and well worth a side trip. From the jct., Pine Link runs nearly level across a wet area before rising moderately then rather steeply on the slope above Bumpus Basin, crossing several small brooks and sections of slippery rocks. Climbing out of the scrub at 3.3 mi., the trail runs above treeline at easier grades, with fine views but great exposure to the weather. After crossing Watson Path at 3.5 mi. (0.3 mi. below the summit of Mt. Madison), Pine Link descends gradually, frequently crossing jumbles of large rocks that require strenuous rock-hopping. The footing improves in the last 0.1 mi., where the trail crosses two small meadows with little evident footway and ends at Osgood Trail 30 yd. from the front of Madison Spring Hut.

HOWKER RIDGE TRAIL (MAP 1: E9–F9)
Cumulative from Pinkham B Rd. (Dolly Copp Rd.) (1,239 ft.) to:

Hitchcock Fall (1,875 ft.)	1.0 mi.	650 ft.	0:50
First Howk (3,450 ft.)	2.3 mi.	2,200 ft.	2:15
Pine Link, lower jct. (3,850 ft.)	3.1 mi.	2,800 ft. (rev. 200 ft.)	2:55
Osgood Trail (5,100 ft.)	4.2 mi.	4,200 ft. (rev. 100 ft.)	4:10
Mt. Madison summit (5,363 ft.) via Osgood Trail	4.4 mi.	4,450 ft.	4:25

RMC This wild, rough, very scenic trail was built by Eugene B. Cook and William H. Peek, although the lower part no longer follows the original route. The trail leads from Pinkham B Rd. (Dolly Copp Rd.) at the Randolph East parking area (sometimes plowed in winter; roadside parking usually available), 0.2 mi. south of US 2, to Osgood Trail, 0.2 mi. below the summit of Mt. Madison. Pinkham B Rd. leaves US 2 0.8 mi. east of the Appalachia parking area and 1.0 mi. west of the jct. with Randolph Hill Rd. This is an interesting trail with a great variety of attractive scenery and woods, passing cascades in the lower part and offering excellent outlooks at different elevations higher up. Howker Ridge is the long, curving northeast ridge of Mt. Madison that partly encloses the deep, bowl-shaped valley called Bumpus Basin. Howker Ridge Trail follows the crest of the ridge, on which are four little peaks called the Howks; there are several ups and downs along this crest. The ridge gets its name from a family named Howker who once had a farm at its base.

Coinciding with Randolph Path, blue-blazed Howker Ridge Trail quickly crosses Presidential Rail Trail and 30 yd. beyond diverges left (southeast) on a series of plank walkways where Randolph Path turns right (southwest). Howker Ridge Trail ascends gradually through partly logged areas, crossing several overgrown skid roads. At 0.4 mi., the trail reaches the bank of Bumpus Brook, where a side path leads to ledges and cascades. The main trail follows the brook, passing Stairs Fall (on a side stream) at 0.5 mi. It quickly enters the WMNF (sign) and passes a rocky gorge called the Devil's Kitchen, as well as other interesting pools and cascades. At 0.7 mi., at Coosauk Fall (sign; mostly dry), Sylvan Way enters on the right, and in less than 0.1 mi., Kelton Trail diverges right. At 1.0 mi., Howker Ridge Trail descends to make a somewhat difficult crossing of Bumpus Brook at the foot of Hitchcock Fall and then climbs steeply up the slope on the other side, following a relocation. The trail soon levels off, descends slightly, and reaches a jct. with a spur path (sign) that leads right 40 yd. to the Bear Pit, a natural cleft in the ledge that forms a trap-like box. Howker Ridge Trail climbs steeply through conifer woods and then moderates, reaching a rocky shoulder and descending into a slight sag. Then it resumes climbing and passes over a ledgy ridge crest called Blueberry Ledge—now far too overgrown to produce many blueberries—before continuing up the ridge. The trail keeps ascending, steeply at first and then moderately, with occasional restricted views north, as it approaches the crest of the first Howk, a long, narrow, densely wooded ridge capped by a number of small knobs. Following the ridge at easy grades, the trail crosses the ledgy, viewless summit of the first Howk at 2.3 mi., passes a limited outlook ahead to Mt. Madison, and then descends steeply for a short distance. After crossing through a long, fairly level sag, the trail climbs seriously again, and at 3.0 mi., it passes over the ledgy summit of the second Howk, which offers fine views up to Mt. Madison and out to the Crescent and Pliny ranges to the north and northwest. Descending rather steeply back into the woods, with one ledgy scramble, the trail passes through a shady glen where Pine Link enters on the left; water is down this trail in less than 100 yd.

From this jct., the two trails coincide for 0.3 mi., ascending over one of a group of several small, ledgy knobs that constitute the third Howk, affording another good view. Descending a steep cleft to a wet sag, the trails pass a small cave to the right and then ascend to a jct. where Pine

Link branches right. Bearing slightly left, Howker Ridge Trail climbs steeply up ledges to the open summit of the highest, most prominent Howk (4,315 ft.) at 3.5 mi., which affords fine views in all directions. The trail descends back into the scrub, climbs over another minor crag, and passes through one last patch of high scrub before breaking out above treeline for good. The ensuing section of trail is very exposed to northwest winds and may be difficult to follow in poor visibility; however, if the trail is lost, and conditions do not dictate a retreat below the treeline, it is easy enough to reach Osgood Trail simply by climbing to the ridge crest, as Osgood Trail follows that crest closely. From treeline, Howker Ridge Trail climbs steeply up the rocks, generally angling to the southwest and aiming for the notch between the most prominent visible crag and the lower crag to its left. As the trail approaches the ridge crest, it bears more to the right, heading for the most prominent visible crag, and then bends slightly left and enters Osgood Trail about 100 yd. above a small sag and 0.2 mi. below the summit of Mt. Madison.

On the descent, at the jct. of Howker Ridge and Osgood trails, take care to avoid beaten paths that lead back into Osgood Trail. When leaving the jct., keep to the left, descending only slightly, until the RMC sign a short distance down the path is in sight.

KELTON TRAIL (MAP 1: E9)
Cumulative from Howker Ridge Trail (1,700 ft.) to:

Kelton Crag (2,075 ft.)	0.3 mi.	400 ft.	0:25
Inlook Trail (2,732 ft.)	0.9 mi.	1,050 ft.	1:00
Brookside (2,750 ft.)	1.7 mi.	1,100 ft. (rev. 50 ft.)	1:25

RMC This yellow-blazed path runs from Howker Ridge Trail just above Coosauk Fall to Brookside just below Salmacis Fall, from which Watson Path and Valley Way can be quickly reached. Kelton Trail passes two fine viewpoints: the Overlook and the Upper Inlook.

Kelton Trail branches right from Howker Ridge Trail 0.8 mi. from Pinkham B Rd. (Dolly Copp Rd.). It climbs steeply, with some slippery sections, to Kelton Crag and then ascends toward the fingerlike north spur of Gordon Ridge, reaching an upper crag at the edge of a very old burn. Both crags offer restricted views; there is usually water between them, on the right. Kelton Trail then ascends to the Overlook at the edge of the old burn, where good views can be seen north and east a few steps left of the trail. The trail then swings right (west) to the Upper Inlook (viewpoint to the west) at 0.9 mi., where Inlook Trail enters right from Dome Rock.

Kelton Trail then runs south nearly level through dense woods. It crosses Gordon Rill (reliable water) and traverses a section where extensive trail work has made travel across a rough slope easier. At 1.7 mi., the trail descends to cross Snyder Brook, climbs a steep bank, and ends at Brookside 0.1 mi. below the foot of Salmacis Fall.

INLOOK TRAIL (MAP 1: E9)
Cumulative from Randolph Path (1,900 ft.) to:

Dome Rock (2,662 ft.)	0.6 mi.	750 ft.	0:40
Kelton Trail (2,732 ft.)	0.7 mi.	850 ft.	0:45

RMC This path ascends the ridge that leads northwest from the end of the fingerlike north spur of Gordon Ridge, offering excellent views—the best of any lower-elevation trail on the northern slopes—from the brink of the line of cliffs that overlook Snyder Brook and culminate in Dome Rock. The yellow-blazed trail begins at the jct. of Randolph Path and Brookside on the east bank of Snyder Brook. Inlook Trail ascends, steeply at the start, and soon reaches the first of several ledgy "inlooks" up the valley of Snyder Brook to Mt. Madison, Mt. John Quincy Adams, and Mt. Adams. The trail then ascends alternately over open ledges marked with cairns and through the woods, steeply at times. After passing Dome Rock, which offers an excellent view north from the tip of the finger, Inlook Trail swings right, leaving from the back of the ledge (sign), and continues up to the Upper Inlook (good view west) near the crest of the finger, where it ends at its jct. with Kelton Trail.

BROOKSIDE (MAP 1: E9)
From Valley Way (1,900 ft.) to:

Watson Path (3,250 ft.)	1.6 mi.	1,350 ft.	1:30

RMC This yellow-blazed trail follows Snyder Brook, offering views of many cascades and pools. The upper part is fairly steep and rough. The trail begins at its jct. with Valley Way, at the point where Valley Way leaves the edge of the brook 0.9 mi. from the Appalachia parking area, and climbs along the brook to Watson Path, a short distance north of Bruin Rock.

Brookside leaves Valley Way about 30 yd. above Valley Way's jct. with Beechwood Way, continuing straight where Valley Way turns uphill to the right. After a short, washed-out section, Randolph Path joins on the right, and the two trails cross Snyder Brook together on large stepping-stones (the former bridge at this crossing was washed out in 2005 and will not be replaced). Here, Randolph Path turns left; Inlook Trail leaves straight ahead; and Brookside turns right (south), continuing up the bank of the brook. At 0.3 mi., Brookside recrosses the brook and climbs along the west bank at a moderate grade with good footing, rising well above the brook through a fine birch forest, with glimpses through the trees to cliffs on the valley wall on the other side of the brook. Returning gradually to brook level, Brookside comes to a jct. with Kelton Trail, which enters from the left at 1.2 mi. Above this point, Brookside becomes steeper and rougher and again runs close to the brook, passing Salmacis Fall (limited view north from the top) at 1.3 mi. The trail continues along a wild and beautiful part of the brook, with cascades and mossy rocks in a fine forest. The trail then climbs away from the brook and finally ascends sharply to Watson Path at 1.6 mi., a short distance north of Bruin Rock.

WATSON PATH (MAP 1: E9–F9)
Cumulative from Scar Trail (3,175 ft.) to:

Valley Way (3,175 ft.)	0.2 mi.	0 ft.	0:05
Pine Link (4,950 ft.)	1.4 mi.	1,800 ft.	1:35
Mt. Madison summit (5,363 ft.)	1.7 mi.	2,200 ft.	1:55
From Appalachia parking area (1,305 ft.) to:			
Mt. Madison summit (5,363 ft.) via Valley Way and Watson Path	3.9 mi.	4,050 ft.	4:00

RMC The original Watson Path, completed by Laban M. Watson in 1882, led from the Ravine House to the summit of Mt. Madison. The present path begins at Scar Trail, leads across Valley Way to Bruin Rock, and then follows the original route to the summit. This is an interesting route to Mt. Madison, but Watson Path is very steep and rough and, on the slopes above treeline, is exposed to the full fury of northwest winds in a storm. The cairns above treeline are not very prominent, and the trail may be hard to follow when visibility is poor. Therefore, in bad weather this is potentially one of the most dangerous routes on the Northern Presidentials.

Branching south from Scar Trail 0.3 mi. from Valley Way, blue-blazed Watson Path runs level, crossing Valley Way at 0.2 mi. (2.4 mi. on that trail from the Appalachia parking area). This first section of Watson Path is seldom used and is rather difficult to follow. After crossing Valley Way, the trail continues at an easy grade (but with one rough scramble around a large boulder), passing the jct. with Brookside on the left just before reaching Bruin Rock—a large, flat-topped boulder on the west bank of Snyder Brook. In another 80 yd., at 0.4 mi., Lower Bruin (trail) branches to the right toward Valley Way, and Watson Path crosses the brook at the foot of

Duck Fall. The trail soon attacks the steep flank of Gordon Ridge on a very rough footway. At 1.0 mi., Watson Path emerges from the scrub onto the grassy, rocky back of the ridge, continues its relentless ascent, and crosses Pine Link at 1.4 mi., where the grade is briefly easier. It then climbs steadily southward to the summit of Mt. Madison over rough and shelving stones, swinging right (southwest) near the top.

Descending from the summit, Watson Path leads northeast, and Osgood Trail descends to the east and to the west.

VALLEY WAY (MAP 1: E9–F9)
Cumulative from Appalachia parking area (1,305 ft.) to:

Randolph Path crossing (1,953 ft.)	0.9 mi.	650 ft.	0:45
Watson Path crossing (3,175 ft.)	2.4 mi.	1,850 ft.	2:10
Upper Bruin jct. (4,150 ft.)	3.3 mi.	2,850 ft.	3:05
Madison Spring Hut (4,795 ft.)	3.8 mi.	3,500 ft.	3:40
Mt. Madison summit (5,363 ft.) via Osgood Trail	4.3 mi.	4,050 ft.	4:10

AMC This is the most direct and easiest route from the Appalachia parking area (plowed in winter) on US 2—2.0 mi. east of the western jct. with Durand Rd. by Lowe's Store and 0.8 mi. west of the jct. with Pinkham B Rd. (Dolly Copp Rd.)—to Madison Spring Hut. The trail is well sheltered almost to the door of the hut. The parking area is a stop of the AMC Hiker Shuttle. In bad weather, this is the safest route to or from the hut. J. Rayner Edmands constructed the trail in his unmistakable style from 1895 to 1897, using parts of earlier trails constructed by Laban Watson and Eugene Cook.

Blue-blazed Valley Way, coinciding with Air Line at the start, begins at Appalachia and crosses Presidential Rail Trail to a fork, where Valley Way leads to the left and Air Line to the right across a power-line clearing. Just into the woods, Maple Walk diverges left, and at 0.2 mi., Sylvan Way crosses. Valley Way soon enters the WMNF, and at 0.5 mi., Fallsway comes in on the left; it soon departs on the left for Tama Fall and Brookbank and then reenters Valley Way at 0.6 mi.—a short but worthwhile loop.

Valley Way leads nearer Snyder Brook and is soon joined from the right by Beechwood Way. About 30 yd. above this jct., Brookside continues straight. Valley Way turns right and climbs 100 yd. to the crossing of Randolph Path at 0.9 mi., and continues to climb at a comfortable grade high above Snyder Brook, crossing several small brooks at their confluence at 1.4 mi. before swinging east, then south. At 2.1 mi., Scar Trail branches right, leading to Air Line via Durand Scar, an excellent outlook on Scar Loop only about 0.2 mi. above Valley Way (well worth the small effort required to visit it). At 2.4

mi., Watson Path crosses, leading left to the summit of Mt. Madison. Valley Way angles up the rather steep slopes of Durand Ridge at a moderate grade considerably above the stream. At 2.8 mi., Lower Bruin enters left, coming up from Bruin Rock and Duck Fall. At 3.2 mi., a side path on the right leads 150 yd. to Valley Way Tentsite. Soon the trail passes a spring to the right. At 3.3 mi., Upper Bruin branches steeply right, leading in 0.2 mi. to Air Line at the lower end of the knife-edged crest of Durand Ridge.

Now Valley Way becomes steep and rough and approaches nearer to Snyder Brook. High up in the scrub, the trail swings to the right, away from the brook, and then swings back toward the stream and emerges from the scrub close to the brook, reaching a jct. with Air Line Cutoff 45 yd. below Madison Spring Hut. Valley Way ends in another 10 yd. at a jct. with Gulfside Trail, which continues another 35 yd. to the hut. From the hut, the summit of Mt. Madison can be reached by ascending 0.5 mi. on Osgood Trail.

Descending, follow Gulfside Trail 35 yd. northwest from the hut to a jct. where Valley Way diverges right (north) as Gulfside Trail bears left (southwest). Bear right in another 10 yd. where Air Line Cutoff diverges left.

MT. ADAMS
LOWER BRUIN (MAP 1: E9)
From Watson Path (3,275 ft.) to:

Valley Way (3,584 ft.)	0.2 mi.	300 ft.	0:15

RMC This short, yellow-blazed trail, a remnant of the original trail to Mt. Adams from Randolph, branches right from Watson Path on the west bank of Snyder Brook, where Watson Path crosses the brook at Duck Fall. Lower Bruin climbs steeply with a fairly difficult scramble, passes through a small clearing, and turns right uphill, moving away from the brook. The trail soon turns left and continues to climb rather steeply then becomes gradual and ends at Valley Way. In the reverse direction, take care to turn left into the small clearing rather than following a beaten path down to the brook.

UPPER BRUIN (MAP 1: F9)
From Valley Way (4,150 ft.) to:

Air Line (4,400 ft.)	0.2 mi.	250 ft.	0:15

RMC This short trail links two popular routes, Valley Way and Air Line. Yellow-blazed Upper Bruin branches to the right from Valley Way 3.3 mi. from Appalachia and climbs moderately, with rocky footing, to Air Line near treeline, 3.1 mi. from Appalachia.

AIR LINE (MAP 1: E9–F9)
Cumulative from Appalachia parking area (1,305 ft.) to:

Randolph Path (2,000 ft.)	0.9 mi.	700 ft.	0:50
Scar Trail (3,700 ft.)	2.4 mi.	2,400 ft.	2:25
Chemin des Dames (4,475 ft.)	3.2 mi.	3,150 ft.	3:10
Air Line Cutoff (4,800 ft.)	3.5 mi.	3,500 ft.	3:30
Gulfside Trail (5,125 ft.)	3.7 mi.	3,800 ft.	3:45
Mt. Adams summit (5,797 ft.)	4.3 mi.	4,500 ft.	4:25
From Appalachia parking area (1,305 ft.) to:			
Madison Spring Hut (4,795 ft.) via Air Line and Air Line Cutoff	3.7 mi.	3,500 ft.	3:35

AMC This trail, completed in 1885, is the shortest route to Mt. Adams from a highway. The trail runs from the Appalachia parking area (plowed in winter) on US 2—2.0 mi. east of the western jct. with Durand Rd. by Lowe's Store and 0.8 mi. west of the jct. with Pinkham B Rd. (Dolly Copp Rd.)—up Durand Ridge to the summit. The middle section is steep and rough, and the sections on the knife-edged crest of Durand Ridge and above treeline are very exposed to weather, but afford magnificent views.

The blue-blazed trail, running in common with Valley Way at first, begins at Appalachia and crosses Presidential Rail Trail to a fork near the edge of a power-line clearing, where Air Line leads right and Valley Way left. In 40 yd., just after Air Line enters the woods, the Link diverges right. Air Line crosses Sylvan Way at 0.2 mi. and Beechwood Way and Beechwood Brook at 0.6 mi. At 0.8 mi. from Appalachia, Short Line diverges right, and at 0.9 mi., Air Line enters Randolph Path, coincides with it for 20 yd., and then diverges left uphill. At 1.6 mi., there may be water in a spring 30 yd. left (east) of the trail. From here, Air Line becomes quite steep and rough for 0.5 mi. then eases up and reaches a site once known as Camp Placid Stream (water unreliable) at 2.4 mi. Here, Scar Trail enters on the left, coming up from Valley Way.

At 3.0 mi., after a moderate climb, Air Line emerges from the scrub, and at 3.1 mi., yellow-blazed Upper Bruin comes up left from Valley Way. Air Line now ascends over the bare, ledgy crest of Durand Ridge, known as the Knife Edge, passing over crags that drop off sharply into King Ravine on the right and descend steeply, but not precipitously, into Snyder Glen on the left. At 3.2 mi., just south of the little peak called Needle Rock, Chemin des Dames comes up from King Ravine. Air Line now climbs steadily up the ridge toward Mt. Adams. From several points along the upper part of this ridge, one can look back down the ridge for a clear demonstration of the difference between the U-shaped glacial cirque of King Ravine on the left (west) and the ordinary V-shaped brook valley of Snyder Glen on the right (east). At 3.5 mi., Air Line Cutoff diverges left (southeast) to Madison Spring Hut, which is visible from this jct. in clear weather.

Air Line Cutoff (AMC). This short branch path provides a direct route 0.2 mi. (10 min.) long, fully sheltered by scrub, from Air Line high on Durand Ridge to Valley Way just below Madison Spring Hut. Water may be obtained on this trail not far from Air Line.

Air Line now departs a little from the edge of the ravine, going left of the jutting crags at the ravine's southeast corner, and rises steeply. In this section, if visibility is poor, be especially careful in following the trail. At 3.7 mi., Air Line passes the Gateway of King Ravine, where King Ravine Trail diverges right and plunges between two crags into that gulf. Here, there is a striking view of Mt. Madison. In 60 yd., Air Line enters Gulfside Trail, turns right, and coincides with it for 70 yd. on the high plateau at the head of the ravine. Then Air Line diverges to the left (southwest), passing northwest of Mt. Quincy Adams. Marked by blue blazes and cairns, it climbs steadily and at times steeply up a rough way over large, angular stones to the summit of Mt. Adams. Here, Air Line meets Lowe's Path and Star Lake Trail.

Descending from the summit, Air Line follows cairns slightly east of north down the rocky cone of the mountain.

SCAR TRAIL AND SCAR LOOP (MAP 1: E9)
Cumulative from Valley Way (2,811 ft.) to:

Durand Scar (3,150 ft.) via Scar Loop	0.2 mi.	350 ft.	0:15
Watson Path (3,175 ft.) via main trail	0.3 mi.	350 ft.	0:20
Upper loop jct. (3,280 ft.) via either main trail or loop	0.4 mi.	450 ft.	0:25
Air Line (3,700 ft.) via either main trail or loop	1.0 mi.	900 ft.	0:55
From Appalachia parking area (1,305 ft.) to:			
Mt. Adams summit (5,797 ft.) via Valley Way, Scar Trail or Scar Loop, and Air Line	5.0 mi.	4,500 ft.	4:45

RMC This yellow-blazed trail runs from Valley Way, 2.1 mi. from Appalachia, to Air Line, 2.4 mi. from Appalachia. Scar Trail provides a route to Mt. Adams that includes the spectacular views from Durand Ridge while avoiding the steepest section of Air Line, and Scar Trail also has an excellent outlook of its own from Durand Scar, reached by Scar Loop.

Scar Trail ascends moderately, then steeply, and divides 0.2 mi. above Valley Way. Scar Loop, an alternative route to the right also blazed in yellow, climbs a natural ramp below a rock face, turns sharply left, and scrambles up a steep ledge (use caution if wet or icy), and quickly reaches

Durand Scar, an open ledge that commands excellent views both up and down the valley of Snyder Brook; those up to Mts. Adams and Madison are especially fine. Scar Loop then ascends steeply, passes an outlook on the left up the Snyder Brook valley toward Mt. Madison, and descends over a ledge to rejoin Scar Trail 0.4 mi. above Valley Way. Scar Loop is best done on the ascent: the steep, narrow footway below Durand Scar can be tricky for a descending hiker.

The main Scar Trail, which is easier but misses the best views, bears left at the lower loop jct. In 0.1 mi., it turns sharply right as Watson Path diverges left. Scar Trail then climbs across a small brook to the upper loop jct., where Scar Loop reenters from the right at 0.4 mi. From here, Scar Trail winds its way west and then south up the mountainside to Air Line, with mostly moderate grades and good footing.

STAR LAKE TRAIL (MAP 1: F9)
Cumulative from Madison Spring Hut (4,795 ft.) to:

Buttress Trail (4,900 ft.)	0.3 mi.	100 ft.	0:10
Mt. Adams summit (5,797 ft.)	1.0 mi.	1,000 ft.	1:00

AMC This trail leads from Madison Spring Hut to the summit of Mt. Adams, angling up the steep southeast side of Mt. John Quincy Adams for much of the way. Star Lake Trail is often more sheltered from the wind than Air Line is, but it is very steep and rough, especially in the upper part, where it rock-hops a great deal of large talus and then tackles some fairly challenging rock scrambles on the steep section just below the summit ridge. Star Lake Trail may also be difficult to follow when descending.

The trail runs south from the hut, rising gently, and at 0.2 mi., Parapet Trail branches to the left, passing east of Star Lake and leading to the Parapet and to Madison Gulf and Osgood trails. Star Lake Trail passes along the west shore of the lake, and beyond the lake at 0.3 mi., Buttress Trail diverges left and descends into the Great Gulf. Star Lake Trail ascends southwest on the steep southeast slope of Mt. Quincy Adams, leaving the scrub and passing a good spring below the trail. The trail becomes progressively steeper and rougher as it angles up the rocky slope, and the rocks become larger and require more strenuous hopping. Approaching the crest of a minor easterly ridge, Star Lake Trail turns right and climbs very steeply, with some fairly difficult scrambles, to the top of the shoulder. Then it ascends moderately along the ridge crest to the summit of Mt. Adams, where it meets Lowe's Path and Air Line.

Descending from the summit, Star Lake Trail leads to the southeast down a shoulder of the mountain and then bears left for the steep descent.

SHORT LINE (MAP 1: E9)
Cumulative from Air Line (1,825 ft.) to:

Randolph Path, lower jct. (2,275 ft.)	0.5 mi.	450 ft.	0:30
Randolph Path, upper jct. (2,500 ft.)	0.9 mi.	700 ft.	0:50
King Ravine Trail (3,150 ft.)	1.9 mi.	1,350 ft.	1:40

RMC This moderate, graded path, leading from Air Line to King Ravine Trail below Mossy Fall, was built from 1899 to 1901 by J. Rayner Edmands. Short Line offers direct access to Randolph Path and to King Ravine from the Appalachia parking area.

Yellow-blazed Short Line branches right from blue-blazed Air Line 0.8 mi. from Appalachia and ascends moderately with good footing. At 0.5 mi., Short Line unites with Randolph Path, coincides with it for 0.4 mi., and then branches left and leads south, with rougher footing, up the valley of Cold Brook toward King Ravine, keeping a short distance east of the stream. At 2.7 mi. from Appalachia, Short Line joins King Ravine Trail just below Mossy Fall.

KING RAVINE TRAIL (MAP 1: E9–F9)
Cumulative from Lowe's Path (2,575 ft.) to:

Randolph Path and the Amphibrach (2,925 ft.)	1.0 mi.	450 ft. (rev. 100 ft.)	0:45
Short Line (3,150 ft.)	1.8 mi.	800 ft. (rev. 100 ft.)	1:20
Chemin des Dames (3,700 ft.)	2.2 mi.	1,350 ft.	1:45
Foot of King Ravine headwall (3,825 ft.)	2.5 mi.	1,450 ft.	2:00
Air Line (5,100 ft.)	3.0 mi.	2,700 ft.	2:50
From Appalachia parking area (1,305 ft.) to:			
Mt. Adams summit (5,797 ft.) via Air Line, Short Line, King Ravine Trail, and Air Line	4.5 mi.	4,500 ft.	4:30

RMC This trail through King Ravine was constructed as a branch of Lowe's Path by Charles E. Lowe in 1876. King Ravine Trail is very steep and rough on the headwall of the ravine, but it is one of the most spectacular trails in the White Mountains, offering an extensive variety of wild and magnificent scenery. This is not a good route to descend due to its steep, rough, slippery footing, and hikers should allow extra time in either direction for the roughness—and for admiring the views. King Ravine Trail is not recommended for hikers with dogs. The trip to the floor of the ravine is well worth the effort, even if you do not choose to ascend the headwall. (*Note*: Snow lingers on the floor and headwall of the ravine late into the spring.) Although King Ravine Trail begins on Lowe's Path, a more direct route to the most scenic part of the trail leads from Appalachia via Air Line and Short Line.

Yellow-blazed King Ravine Trail diverges left from Lowe's Path 1.8 mi. from US 2 and rises over a low swell of Nowell Ridge. The trail then descends gradually, and at 0.8 mi., it crosses Spur Brook below some cascades known as Canyon Fall, swings right (south), and in another 0.2 mi. crosses Randolph Path at its jct. with the Amphibrach; this 5-way intersection is called the Pentadoi. Skirting the east spur of Nowell Ridge, King Ravine Trail enters King Ravine and descends slightly, crosses a western branch of Cold Brook, goes across the lower floor of the ravine, and crosses two branches of the main stream. At 1.8 mi., near the foot of Mossy Fall (last sure water), the trail is joined from the left by Short Line, the usual route of access from the Appalachia parking area. Just above this fall, Cold Brook, already a good-sized stream, gushes from beneath the boulders that have fallen into the ravine.

So far, the path has been fairly gradual, but in the next 0.3 mi., King Ravine Trail becomes much rougher, rising about 500 ft., with several fairly difficult scrambles over large boulders, and gaining the upper floor of the ravine (about 3,700 ft.). The grandeur of the views of the ravine from the jumbled rocks that the trail passes around is ample reward for the trip to this area, even if one does not continue up the headwall. Chemin des Dames, leading very steeply up to Air Line, branches sharply left at 2.2 mi. King Ravine Trail turns sharply right here, emerges into the open, and then divides in another 10 yd., forming two paths: the Subway and the Elevated. The Subway, an alternate route that is more interesting but very difficult, leads to the right from this jct.; this is one of the celebrated features of White Mountain trails—winding through boulder caves over and under rocks ranging up to the size of a small house.

The main path, the Elevated, leads to the left, avoiding many of the boulder caves, and is thus much easier; it also offers some good views of the ravine. The paths rejoin after 220 yd. on the Subway or 140 yd. on the Elevated; soon Great Gully Trail diverges right and King Ravine Trail divides again. The left fork is the main trail, and the right is the rough Ice Caves Loop, about 30 yd. shorter than the main trail, leading through boulder caves near the foot of the headwall; these caves have ice that remains throughout the year. After the forks rejoin at about 0.7 mi. from Short Line jct., the ascent of the headwall begins. Here, King Ravine Trail is very steep and rough, rising about 1,100 ft. in 0.5 mi. over large blocks of rock and loose scree; the route is marked with cairns and paint and must be followed with care. The trail climbs to the Gateway, where it emerges from the ravine between two crags and immediately joins Air Line just below its jct. with Gulfside Trail. From the Gateway is a striking view of Mt. Madison. Madison Spring Hut is in sight and can be reached by taking Gulfside Trail left for 0.3 mi. The summit of Mt. Adams is 0.6 mi. away via Air Line.

CHEMIN DES DAMES (MAP 1: F9)
From King Ravine Trail (3,700 ft.) to:

Air Line jct. (4,475 ft.)	0.4 mi.	800 ft.	0:35

RMC This yellow-blazed trail leads from the floor of King Ravine up its east wall and joins Air Line just above treeline. Chemin des Dames (named for a famous road in France, important during World War I) is the shortest route out of the ravine but is nevertheless very steep and rough, climbing about 800 ft. in 0.4 mi. over gravel and talus, some of which is loose; this is also a difficult trail to descend. Leaving King Ravine Trail just before the point where it divides into the Subway and the Elevated, Chemin des Dames winds through scrub and boulders to the east side of the ravine and then climbs steeply over talus through varying amounts of scrub, permitting plentiful, although not constant, views. About halfway up the steep slope, the trail passes through a boulder cave called Tunnel Rock or the Orange Squeezer. Above this are many fine views out across King Ravine and up to the towering crags of Durand Ridge. High up, Chemin des Dames angles to the right across the top of a small slide and along the base of a rock face, reaching Air Line in a little col.

GREAT GULLY TRAIL (MAP 1: F9)
From King Ravine Trail (3,775 ft.) to:

Gulfside Trail (5,490 ft.)	1.0 mi.	1,700 ft.	1:20

RMC This remarkably wild and beautiful trail provides an alternate route between the floor of King Ravine and Gulfside Trail, reaching the latter near Thunderstorm Junction. Great Gully Trail is extremely steep and rough and, as with the other trails in the ravine, especially difficult to descend. It is well marked but lightly used, and must be followed with some care. It has one particularly difficult scramble and should not be attempted in wet or icy conditions. On this shady north slope, large snowdrifts may cover the trail well into June.

Leaving King Ravine Trail just past the point where the Subway and the Elevated rejoin, blue-blazed Great Gully Trail runs across the floor of the ravine at easy grades and then ascends steadily through scrubby birches in a region damaged by an avalanche, and at 0.3 mi. reaches (but does not cross) the brook that flows down the gully. At the base of an attractive high cascade, the trail turns right, away from the brook, and climbs up rocks to the spine of a narrow ridge and to a promontory with a spectacular view. Great Gully Trail then passes under an overhanging rock on a ledge with a high, sheer drop close by on the left, forcing the faint of heart to crawl on their bellies, possibly dragging their packs behind them. The reward for negotiating this pitch is a fine view of the cascade. Here, the trail turns sharply right and climbs past a sheer dropoff to another viewpoint. It crosses the brook above the cascade at a spot where *Arnica mollis*, an herb of the Aster family sought by Henry David Thoreau on his trips to the mountains, grows in profusion. The trail continues to climb steeply to treeline, with several more scrambles (including one particularly exposed spot with a dropoff on the right). It ascends over a talus slope and then exits left from the rocks (watch for cairns marking this turn). The trail then begins to moderate as it runs almost due south across a grassy area marked by cairns (might be hard to follow in poor visibility) before finally meeting Gulfside Trail 8 yd. north of Thunderstorm Junction. At Thunderstorm Junction, marked by a large cairn, Lowe's Path crosses Gulfside Trail.

THE AMPHIBRACH (MAP 1: E9)
Cumulative from Memorial Bridge (1,425 ft.) to:

Monaway (2,200 ft.)	1.1 mi.	800 ft.	0:55
Randolph Path and King Ravine Trail (2,925 ft.)	1.9 mi.	1,500 ft.	1:40

RMC This moderately graded trail begins on the Link at the west end of Memorial Bridge, 0.7 mi. from the Appalachia parking area, and then runs south near Cold Brook and its tributary Spur Brook to the 5-way jct. with Randolph Path and King Ravine Trail known as the Pentadoi. The Amphibrach takes its unusual name from the marking that was used when the trail was first made, around 1883: three blazes—short, long, and short—arranged vertically. Its moderate grade and relative smoothness make the Amphibrach a good alternate approach to King Ravine or to the various trails on Nowell Ridge. It is one of the kindest trails to the feet in this region. It is blazed in yellow.

From the Link at Memorial Bridge, the Amphibrach follows the course of Cold Brook, ascending west of the stream but generally not in sight of the water. At 20 yd. from the jct., a side path branches left 50 yd. to the foot of Cold Brook Fall. Soon, the Amphibrach enters the WMNF. At 1.1 mi., Monaway crosses, leading right to Cliffway and left to Coldspur Ledges and to cascades at the confluence of Cold and Spur brooks, reached about 80 yd. from this jct.; the last short, steep drop to the view of the ledges requires caution. The Amphibrach soon crosses Spur Brook on the rocks and then bears away to the left (east), ascending the tongue of land between the two brooks and climbing moderately. At 1.5 mi., the Amphibrach crosses Cliffway, which leads right (west) less than 0.2 mi. to picturesque Spur Brook Fall. Becoming a bit rougher, the Amphibrach continues upward to join King Ravine Trail a few steps below the Pentadoi.

CLIFFWAY (MAP 1: E9)
Cumulative from the Link (2,170 ft.) to:

White Cliff (2,484 ft.)	0.7 mi.	300 ft.	0:30
Spur Brook Fall (2,550 ft.)	1.7 mi.	500 ft. (rev. 100 ft.)	1:05
Randolph Path (2,575 ft.)	2.2 mi.	500 ft.	1:20

RMC This path begins on the Link, 2.0 mi. from the Appalachia parking area, and runs across the Amphibrach to Randolph Path, 2.0 mi. from Appalachia via Air Line and Short Line. Cliffway passes several partial views from the cliffs and ledges of the low swell of Nowell Ridge: White Cliff offers a view of the Randolph Valley and the Pliny and Crescent ranges to the north, and Bog Ledge and King Cliff have interesting views of King Ravine. The trail has generally easy grades and is well marked, but it is very lightly used, and care may be required to follow it.

Leaving the Link, yellow-blazed Cliffway climbs gradually southeast, with several turns, to the viewpoint at White Cliff at 0.7 mi., where the trail turns sharply right. Here, two trails diverge from Cliffway. To the left, **Along the Brink** (RMC), just 20 yd. long, descends a few steps to the most open view at White Cliff, at the edge of the dropoff, and then continues along the edge through the woods. Caution is required on this trail, especially when it is wet. Continuing ahead where Cliffway turns sharply right is **Ladderback Trail** (RMC). This short link trail, named for Ladderback Rock, a large boulder in the woods, connects Cliffway to Monaway, permitting a short loop hike that includes the viewpoints at White Cliff, Bog Ledge, and King Cliff. The trail is rough and must be followed with care. It leaves White Cliff, and in a short distance, it turns sharply right and is joined from the left by Along the Brink. Ladderback Trail then descends gradually past Ladderback Rock to Monaway 0.2 mi. from White Cliff.

At 1.0 mi., after ascending a zigzag course, Cliffway crosses Bog Ledge, where there is a cleared view of King Ravine and Mts. Adams and Madison; it then descends sharply for a short distance, turns left, and crosses a boggy area on bog bridges. The trail then turns sharply left again and passes King Cliff, where there is another cleared view of King Ravine. In another 0.1 mi., at 1.3 mi., Cliffway meets Monaway. Monaway continues straight, and Cliffway turns sharply right and drops onto a small, broken ledge that resembles a ruined stairway. Then it runs nearly level across a moist area to Spur Brook at the base of picturesque Spur Brook Fall at 1.7 mi. The trail climbs beside the waterfall, crosses Spur Brook above the fall, runs across the Amphibrach at 1.9 mi. and ends at Randolph Path at 2.2 mi., at the west end of Sanders Bridge over Cold Brook.

MONAWAY (MAP 1: E9)
From the Amphibrach (2,200 ft.) to:

Cliffway (2,550 ft.)	0.4 mi.	350 ft.	0:25

RMC This short yellow-blazed link trail offers the shortest route from the Randolph area to Cliffway at White Cliff or King Cliff. Monaway begins on the Amphibrach just below that trail's crossing of Spur Brook. At this jct., a short segment of Monaway leads downhill (east) about 80 yd. to pleasant Coldspur Ledges at the confluence of Cold and Spur brooks (use caution). The main part of Monaway runs uphill (west) from the Amphibrach at a moderate grade, passes a jct. on the right at 0.3 mi. with Ladderback Trail to White Cliff, swings left (south) at an easier grade, and meets Cliffway about 0.1 mi. east of King Cliff. Turn left here for Spur Brook Fall or turn right for King Cliff, Bog Ledge, and White Cliff.

SPUR TRAIL (MAP 1: E9–F9)
Cumulative from Randolph Path (2,950 ft.) to:

Crag Camp (4,245 ft.)	0.9 mi.	1,300 ft.	1:05
Lowe's Path (5,425 ft.)	2.0 mi.	2,500 ft.	2:15
Mt. Adams summit (5,797 ft.) via Lowe's Path	2.4 mi.	2,850 ft.	2:40

RMC This trail leads from Randolph Path, just above its jct. with King Ravine Trail and the Amphibrach, to Lowe's Path, just below Thunderstorm Junction. Spur Trail ascends the east spur of Nowell Ridge near the west edge of King Ravine, passing Crag Camp (cabin). At several points below treeline are fine outlooks into King Ravine, and above treeline, views into King Ravine and up to Mts. Madison and Adams are continuous and excellent. The lower part of Spur Trail is steep and rough, and the upper part runs completely in the open, very exposed to weather. The RMC rehabilitated sections of this trail in 2011 and 2015.

Yellow-blazed Spur Trail diverges south from Randolph Path about 100 yd. west of its jct. with King Ravine Trail and the Amphibrach, on the west bank of Spur Brook, and climbs rather steeply along Spur Brook past attractive cascades and pools. At 0.2 mi., a branch path leads left 90 yd. to Chandler Fall, where the brook runs down a steep, smooth slab of rock; from the base of the waterfall is a restricted view north. At 0.3 mi., Hincks Trail to Gray Knob Cabin diverges right, and Spur Trail crosses to the east side of the brook, the last water until Crag Camp. The trail climbs steeply up the spur that forms the west wall of King Ravine, ascending several rock staircases and following a short relocation to the right at 0.8 mi., just before reaching a side path that leads left 10 yd. to the Lower Crag, a good outlook to the ravine and Mts. Madison and Adams. At 0.9 mi., Spur Trail reaches the Upper Crag where the trail passes in front of Crag Camp, swings right around the cabin, and soon reaches the jct. on the right with Gray Knob Trail, which leads west 0.4 mi. to Gray Knob Cabin.

Spur Trail bears left at this jct. and continues to climb quite steeply up the ridge, but not as near the edge of the ravine. At 1.1 mi., a side path (sign, hard to see on the descent) leads left 100 yd. to Knight's Castle, a spectacular perch high up on the ravine wall. Here, Spur Trail passes into high scrub, and in another 0.2 mi., it breaks out above treeline, commanding excellent views: those to King Ravine are better in the lower portion, and those to Mts. Madison and Adams are better higher up. The grade moderates as Spur Trail joins Nowell Ridge, ascending well to the east of the crest. Spur Trail finally merges with Lowe's Path 100 yd. below Gulfside Trail at Thunderstorm Junction. Descending, Spur Trail diverges right at a fork where Lowe's Path continues ahead on the left fork.

HINCKS TRAIL (MAP 1: E9–F9)
From Spur Trail (3,450 ft.) to:

Gray Knob Cabin (4,355 ft.)	0.7 mi.	950 ft.	0:50

RMC This short yellow-blazed link trail connects Spur Trail and Randolph Path to Gray Knob Cabin. Hincks Trail is fairly steep and rough. It diverges right from Spur Trail immediately before the crossing of Spur Brook, about 0.3 mi. above Randolph Path. Hincks Trail soon comes to the edge of Spur Brook near a pleasant little cascade over mossy rocks and then winds rather steeply south up the valley, passing through several patches of woods damaged by wind, to Gray Knob.

GRAY KNOB TRAIL (MAP 1: E9–F9)
Cumulative from Spur Trail (4,250 ft.) to:

Lowe's Path (4,400 ft.)	0.5 mi.	150 ft.	0:20
Randolph Path (4,825 ft.)	1.7 mi.	600 ft.	1:10

RMC This yellow-blazed trail connects three of the four RMC camps (Crag Camp, Gray Knob, and the Perch) with one another. It also links the upper parts of Spur Trail and Lowe's, Randolph, and Israel Ridge paths, affording a route from Crag Camp and Gray Knob to Edmands Col without loss of elevation. Grades are mostly easy, but the footing is frequently rough, and south of Lowe's Path, Gray Knob Trail has substantial weather exposure, although some sheltering scrub is usually close by.

Leaving Spur Trail 25 yd. west of Crag Camp, yellow-blazed Gray Knob Trail climbs over a knoll with limited views and at 0.2 mi. passes a side path on the right, leading down 25 yd. to a good piped spring. The trail traverses a rough slope nearly on the level; then, soon after passing a spring (left), it ascends a short pitch to Gray Knob Cabin (left) at 0.4 mi., where Hincks Trail enters on the right. Gray Knob Trail then runs almost level, passing Quay Path, a shortcut on the right that leads 50 yd. to Lowe's Path at a fine outlook ledge called the Quay. Gray Knob Trail crosses Lowe's Path at 0.5 mi. and almost immediately enters scrub of variable height, offering a mixture of shelter and weather exposure with nearly constant views, and begins to climb moderately. At 0.8 mi., Perch Path diverges right. Gray Knob Trail continues to climb moderately up the slope and then levels off and runs nearly on contour to Randolph Path just before its jct. with Israel Ridge Path.

PERCH PATH (MAP 1: F9)
Cumulative from Gray Knob Trail (4,550 ft.) to:

The Perch (4,305 ft.)	0.4 mi.	0 ft. (rev. 250 ft.)	0:10
Israel Ridge Path jct. (4,300 ft.)	0.5 mi.	0 ft.	0:15

RMC This path runs from Gray Knob Trail across Randolph Path and past the Perch (lean-to) to Israel Ridge Path. Perch Path diverges right (south) from Gray Knob Trail 0.3 mi. south of Lowe's Path. It descends moderately, with rough footing and some views, and crosses Randolph Path at 0.3 mi. Perch Path soon crosses a small brook, passes the Perch and its tent platforms on the slope up to the left, and runs nearly level to Israel Ridge Path at a sharp curve.

LOWE'S PATH (MAP 1: E9–F9)
Cumulative from US 2 near Lowe's Store (1,395 ft.) to:

The Link (2,475 ft.)	1.7 mi.	1,100 ft.	1:25
King Ravine Trail (2,575 ft.)	1.8 mi.	1,200 ft.	1:30
Log Cabin (3,274 ft.)	2.4 mi.	1,900 ft.	2:10
Randolph Path (3,600 ft.)	2.7 mi.	2,200 ft.	2:25
Gray Knob Trail (4,400 ft.)	3.2 mi.	3,000 ft.	3:05
Mt. Abigail Adams (5,355 ft.)	4.1 mi.	3,950 ft.	4:00
Gulfside Trail (5,490 ft.)	4.4 mi.	4,150 ft. (rev. 50 ft.)	4:15
Mt. Adams summit (5,797 ft.)	4.7 mi.	4,450 ft.	4:35

RMC This blue-blazed trail, cut from 1875 to 1876 by Charles E. Lowe and Dr. William G. Nowell from Lowe's house in Randolph to the summit of Mt. Adams, is the oldest of the mountain trails that ascend the peaks from the Randolph Valley. The trail begins on the south side of US 2, 150 yd. west of Lowe's Store (closed in 2021), where hikers may park in summer and fall; no parking is available at the trailhead. In winter, parking is not available at Lowe's Store; the best access to Lowe's Path is via the Link from the plowed Appalachia parking area. This trail is perhaps the easiest way to climb Mt. Adams, with mostly moderate grades (although the middle section is steep and rough) and excellent views, but it still has considerable exposure to weather in the section above treeline.

Leaving US 2, Lowe's Path follows a broad woods road for 100 yd. and then diverges right at a sign giving the history of the trail. It crosses a snowmobile trail and Presidential Rail Trail, passes under power lines, and ascends through woods at a moderate grade, heading first southwest and then southeast and crossing several small brooks. At 1.7 mi., the Link crosses, and at 1.8 mi., King Ravine Trail branches left. Lowe's Path continues to ascend, making a switchback out to the left, then becomes steeper and rougher, and at 2.4 mi., it passes just to the right of the Log Cabin. Here, Log Cabin Cutoff, nearly level but rough, runs left 0.2 mi. to Randolph Path, and the very rough Cabin–Cascades Trail to Israel Ridge Path in Cascade Ravine leaves on the right. Water (reliable) is found at the Log Cabin. Lowe's Path now begins to ascend more seriously and crosses Randolph Path at 2.7 mi. At this jct., Randolph Path, angling up to the right, is more obvious than Lowe's Path, which climbs straight ahead up some rocks. Lowe's Path climbs steeply up to the crest of Nowell Ridge and then moderates. (*Caution*: This section is often icy during cold seasons.) At a fine outlook ledge called the Quay, at 3.2 mi., the very short Quay Path diverges left to Gray Knob Trail, and 30 yd. farther, Gray Knob Trail crosses. Gray Knob Cabin is less than 0.1 mi. left (east) by either route.

Soon Lowe's Path breaks out of the scrub, and from here on, the trail is above treeline and completely exposed to wind. Views are very fine. At 4.1 mi., after a steady ascent up Nowell Ridge, the trail passes just to the left of the 5,355-ft. crag formerly known as Adams 4 and in 2010 renamed Mt. Abigail Adams in honor of the wife of President John Adams. The trail descends into a little sag and then rises moderately again, keeping to the left (east) of Mt. Sam Adams. Spur Trail joins on the left, 100 yd. below Thunderstorm Junction (large cairn), the major intersection with Gulfside Trail at 4.4 mi.; Great Gully Trail enters Gulfside Trail 8 yd. to the left (north) of this jct. After crossing Gulfside Trail, Lowe's Path climbs moderately southeast up the jumbled rocks of the cone of Mt. Adams, passing the jct. where Israel Ridge Path enters right at 4.5 mi. Climbing almost due east over the rocks (follow cairns carefully), Lowe's Path reaches the summit of Mt. Adams at 4.7 mi., where the trail meets Air Line and Star Lake Trail.

Descending from the summit, Lowe's Path leads slightly north of west.

CABIN–CASCADES TRAIL (MAP 1: E9–F9)
From Lowe's Path (3,263 ft.) to:

Israel Ridge Path (2,825 ft.)	1.0 mi.	0 ft. (rev. 450 ft.)	0:30

RMC Constructed in 1881 by AMC, Cabin–Cascades Trail leads from the Log Cabin on Lowe's Path to Israel Ridge Path near the cascades on Cascade Brook, descending almost all the way. Cabin–Cascades Trail is generally rough, with one rather steep, very rough section.

The yellow-blazed trail begins at Lowe's Path 2.4 mi. from US 2, opposite the Log Cabin. Cabin–Cascades Trail runs gradually downhill, with minor ups and downs, crossing Mystic Stream at 0.3 mi. At 0.7 mi., the trail enters Cascade Ravine and descends a steep pitch, passing a limited outlook to the Castles and Mt. Bowman rising over Israel Ridge. The trail then begins the final steep, rough descent to Cascade Brook, ending at Israel Ridge Path just above its upper jct. with the Link. The First Cascade can be reached by descending on Israel Ridge Path 60 yd. right to the Link and then following it downward to the left another 60 yd. to the ledges at the top of the cascade. The Second Cascade can be seen by following Israel Ridge Path about 150 yd. upward (left).

ISRAEL RIDGE PATH (MAP 1: E8–F9)
Cumulative from Castle Trail (1,900 ft.) to:

Castle Ravine Trail (2,100 ft.)	0.4 mi.	200 ft.	0:20
The Link (2,800 ft.)	1.2 mi.	900 ft.	1:05
Perch Path (4,300 ft.)	2.4 mi.	2,400 ft.	2:25
Randolph Path, lower jct. (4,825 ft.)	2.8 mi.	2,950 ft.	2:55
Edmands Col (4,938 ft.) via Randolph Path	3.5 mi.	3,050 ft.	3:15
Gulfside Trail (5,250 ft.)	3.3 mi.	3,350 ft.	3:20
Mt. Adams summit (5,797 ft.) via Lowe's Path	4.1 mi.	3,900 ft.	4:00

RMC This blue-blazed trail runs to the summit of Mt. Adams from Castle Trail, 1.3 mi. from US 2 at the Bowman trailhead (1.0 mi. west of Lowe's Store). Beginning in 1892, J. Rayner Edmands constructed Israel Ridge Path as a graded path. Although hurricanes and slides have severely damaged the original trail, and there have been many relocations, the upper section is still one of the finest and most beautiful of the Randolph trails. (*Note*: Some brook crossings are difficult in high water, and parts of the trail are steep and rough.)

From Bowman, follow Castle Trail for 1.3 mi. Here, Israel Ridge Path branches left, and at 0.1 mi., it crosses a rocky brook bed and then the main channel of the Israel River to the east bank. The trail follows the river, with one rough scramble, passing several small cascades, and then turns left up the bank at 0.4 mi., where Castle Ravine Trail diverges right and continues along the river. Israel Ridge Path bears southeast up the slope of Nowell Ridge into Cascade Ravine, climbing on a long sidehill, moderately at first and then becoming steeper and rougher. At 1.2 mi., the Link enters left. The trails coincide for 50 yd., crossing rough ledges, and then the Link diverges right to cross Cascade Brook. The top of the First Cascade can be reached by following the Link 60 yd. downhill to the right. In another 60 yd., Cabin–Cascades Trail enters left from the Log Cabin. Israel Ridge Path now enters virgin growth. From this point to treeline, the forest has never been disturbed by lumbering, although slides and windstorms have done much damage.

The trail ascends steeply on the northeast side of Cascade Brook, climbing one ledge on a pair of ladders. It passes two short side paths leading to open, sloping ledges on the right beside the Second Cascade (with a view to the northwest) and crosses the brook at the head of this cascade at 1.4 mi. (difficult in high water). Then it turns right downstream for a short distance before turning left and climbing. The trail ascends steeply up Israel Ridge (sometimes called Emerald Tongue), which rises between Cascade and

Castle ravines. At 2.2 mi., after a long, mostly moderate sidehill section along the east side of the ridge, with two more ladders up steep ledges, Israel Ridge Path turns sharply left (east) where Emerald Trail diverges right to descend steeply into Castle Ravine. Emerald Bluff, a remarkable outlook to the Castles and Castle Ravine that is well worth a visit, can be reached from this jct. in less than 0.2 mi. by following Emerald Trail and a spur path that diverges right before Emerald Trail begins its steep descent.

Israel Ridge Path angles up a steep slope and then turns right at 2.4 mi., where Perch Path enters left (east), 0.1 mi. from the Perch. Israel Ridge Path ascends steadily south to treeline, where it joins Randolph Path at 2.8 mi. The jct. of Gray Knob Trail with Randolph Path is 70 yd. to the left (north) at this point. For 0.1 mi., Israel Ridge and Randolph paths coincide, and then Israel Ridge Path branches to the left and, curving east, ascends the southwest ridge of Mt. Adams—with fine views of Castle Ravine, the Castellated Ridge, and Mt. Jefferson—and joins Gulfside Trail at 3.3 mi., just south of Storm Lake. Israel Ridge Path coincides with Gulfside Trail for 0.5 mi., running northeast past Peabody Spring to the Adams–Sam Adams col. At 3.8 mi., with the cairn at Thunderstorm Junction in sight ahead, Israel Ridge Path branches right from Gulfside Trail and enters Lowe's Path at 3.9 mi., which leads to the summit of Mt. Adams at 4.1 mi. The cairns between Gulfside Trail and Lowe's Path are not very prominent, so if visibility is poor, it might be better to follow Lowe's Path from Thunderstorm Junction to the summit.

EMERALD TRAIL (MAP 1: F9)
Cumulative from Castle Ravine Trail and the Link (3,225 ft.) to:

Emerald Bluff (4,025 ft.)	0.5 mi.	800 ft.	0:40
Israel Ridge Path (4,050 ft.)	0.6 mi.	850 ft.	0:45

RMC This steep, rough trail connects Israel Ridge Path with Castle Ravine Trail, passing Emerald Bluff, a fine viewpoint to the Castles and Castle Ravine. The short section of Emerald Trail between Israel Ridge Path and Emerald Bluff is uncharacteristically gradual and easy. The path is lightly used and must be followed with some care. Emerald Bluff can be visited from US 2 by a wild, scenic, 7.5-mi. loop hike using Castle Trail, Castle Ravine Trail, Emerald Trail, and Israel Ridge Path.

Yellow-blazed Emerald Trail leaves the combined Castle Ravine Trail and the Link 0.2 mi. southeast of their lower jct. and descends slightly across a channel of Castle Brook. It then climbs a very steep and rough slope, although there are no difficult scrambles. As the trail levels off on the crest of Israel Ridge just south of Emerald Bluff, it turns sharply right.

Here, a side path diverges left and leads 50 yd. to the viewpoint on Emerald Bluff. Emerald Trail continues at easy grades to Israel Ridge Path 0.2 mi. below its jct. with Perch Path.

MT. JEFFERSON
CASTLE RAVINE TRAIL (MAP 1: E8–F9)
Cumulative from Israel Ridge Path (2,100 ft.) to:

The Link, lower jct. (3,125 ft.)	1.5 mi.	1,050 ft.	1:15
Roof Rock (3,600 ft.)	2.1 mi.	1,500 ft.	1:50
Randolph Path (4,900 ft.)	2.8 mi.	2,800 ft.	2:50

RMC This scenic, challenging trail diverges from Israel Ridge Path 1.7 mi. from US 2 at the Bowman trailhead and leads through wild and beautiful Castle Ravine to Randolph Path near Edmands Col. Although Castle Ravine Trail is reasonably well sheltered except for the highest section, parts of it are very rough, especially where it crosses a great deal of unstable talus on the headwall, which makes footing extremely poor for descending or when the rocks are wet. The trail is well marked (yellow blazes below treeline, orange markings above) but lightly used, and must be followed with some care—particularly at the brook crossings, which are marked with "Path" signs and blazes, and on the headwall, where winter avalanches may remove the markings. Some of the brook crossings may be very difficult at moderate to high water, and the ravine walls are very steep, making rapid flooding likely during heavy rain. For all except very experienced hikers, it would be a very difficult escape route from Edmands Col in adverse conditions.

From the Bowman trailhead, follow Castle Trail and then Israel Ridge Path to a point 1.7 mi. from Bowman. Here, Israel Ridge Path turns left up a slope, and Castle Ravine Trail leads straight ahead near the river. It crosses to the west bank (difficult at high water and not easy at other times) and soon reaches a point abreast of the Forks of Israel, where Cascade and Castle brooks unite to form the Israel River. The trail crosses to the east bank of Castle Brook (a crossing with particularly awkward footing), passes a fine cascade, and recrosses to the west bank below another cascade. In general, it follows the route of an old logging road, now almost imperceptible. After entering Castle Ravine, the trail crosses to the east bank and climbs at a moderate grade, with generally good footing, well above the brook. At 1.5 mi., the Link enters from the left, and the two trails coincide on a rougher footway. (About 0.1 mi. beyond this jct., avoid a beaten path that descends right toward the brook.) At 1.7 mi., shortly after a small channel of Castle Brook is crossed, Emerald Trail diverges left (north) for Israel Ridge. After crossing to the southwest side of the main brook in a tract of enchanted, cool, virgin forest beloved of blackflies, the Link diverges right for Castle Trail at 1.8 mi., and Castle Ravine Trail continues up the ravine close to the brook. At one point it turns right upstream into the brook bed (look for a "Path" sign), crosses and follows the bed on the north side for about 30 yd., and then turns right and crosses back to the south side. Near the foot of the headwall, the trail crosses Castle Brook again, where an avalanche swept down from the left in 2010; some woody debris remains on the brook bed. In 50 yd., the trail recrosses the brook where the avalanche has opened a view up to the Castellated Ridge. On the south side of the brook, the trail winds briefly through an area of large rocks where water can often be heard running underground; then it turns left and mounts the steep slope. At 2.1 mi., just after squeezing through a rock crevice, Castle Ravine Trail passes under Roof Rock, a large, flat-bottomed boulder that would provide some shelter in a rainstorm.

The trail rises very steeply southeast with very rough footing and, after a fairly difficult scramble, emerges on a patch of large, jumbled bare rocks, where the winding, strenuous route is marked by cairns and dashes of orange paint. This spot offers good views up to the Castles and down the valley northward to the Pliny Range. Castle Ravine Trail swings right and reenters the scrub at a large cairn, and in 100 yd., after a rough traverse, reemerges from the scrub at the foot of a steep slope of very loose rock (use extreme care, particularly when descending). The trail climbs very steeply to the top of the headwall, marked by cairns and paint blazes on rocks. It then ascends gradually in a grassy valley with little evident treadway and sparsely placed cairns, passing Spaulding Spring on the right and joining Randolph Path (sign) on the rocks to the left of the grassy valley, 0.1 mi. north of Edmands Col. Here, also, the Cornice joins from the right.

Descending, follow Randolph Path north from Edmands Col to the small grassy valley and then descend north along it until the line of cairns is found leading down the headwall.

CASTLE TRAIL (MAP 1: E8–F9)
Cumulative from Bowman trailhead (1,496 ft.) to:

Israel Ridge Path (1,900 ft.)	1.3 mi.	400 ft.	0:50
The Link (4,025 ft.)	3.5 mi.	2,550 ft.	3:00
First Castle (4,450 ft.)	3.8 mi.	2,950 ft.	3:20
Mt. Jefferson summit (5,713 ft.)	5.0 mi.	4,200 ft.	4:35

AMC This trail follows the narrow, serrated ridge that runs northwest from Mt. Jefferson, providing magnificent views in a spectacular setting. The original trail was cut from 1883 to 1884, but much of it has since been relocated. The section that traverses the Castles is rough, with some difficult rock scrambles. In bad weather, Castle Trail can be dangerous due to long and continuous exposure to the northwest winds at and above the Castles.

Blue-blazed Castle Trail begins at the Bowman trailhead on US 2, 3.0 mi. west of the Appalachia parking area and 4.2 mi. east of the jct. of US 2 and NH 115. Park off the highway on the north side of Presidential Rail Trail (the former railroad grade); this parking area was not plowed in 2021; alternate winter parking is at a pull-off on the south side of US 2, 0.3 mi. to the west. Castle Trail (sign) follows the railroad grade to the right (west) for 100 yd. and turns left into the woods just past a gate. The trail crosses a pipeline clearing and then traverses an area of small trees. At 0.3 mi., Castle Trail enters the WMNF, crosses a power-line clearing, and soon reaches the bank of the Israel River. Here, the trail turns sharply left, runs along the bank for 60 yd., and then crosses the river (may be difficult at high water) at 0.4 mi. (The easiest crossing is where the trail first comes to the river; on the far side, a beaten path leads left back to where the trail crosses.) On the far side, the trail turns left and parallels the stream for 100 yd. Then it bears right up a bank and rises at an easy grade through a hardwood forest.

At 1.3 mi., Israel Ridge Path branches left (east) toward the stream. The last sure water is a short distance along this trail. Castle Trail continues to rise above the brook on the northeast flank of Mt. Bowman, and at 1.5 mi., it turns sharply right, going away from the brook. Now climbing the slope at a steeper angle, the trail ascends a long series of rock steps, passes to the right of a very large boulder at 2.2 mi., and becomes much steeper for the next 0.3 mi. At 2.5 mi., it enters a blowdown area near the crest of the ridge connecting Mt. Bowman and the Castellated Ridge and becomes almost level. Soon, the trail ascends easily with excellent footing through open woods with abundant ferns; it gradually steepens again as it climbs the main ridge below the Castles to a densely wooded shoulder with a sharp, ragged crest. Here, the trail winds along the steep slopes near the ridge crest to a little gap at 3.5 mi., where the Link crosses, coming up from Castle Ravine on the left and leading off to Caps Ridge Trail on the right.

The ridge grows very narrow, and Castle Trail becomes steep and rough with some difficult scrambles—the first, a steeply angled slab, is a short distance above the Link jct. After passing over two ledges with good outlooks from both, the trail reaches treeline and climbs to the foot of the first and most impressive Castle, a pair of 20-ft. pillars, at 3.8 mi. The view is very fine, especially into Castle Ravine. The trail leads on past a slightly higher but less impressive Castle and then runs through a small col filled with scrub that would provide reasonable shelter in a storm. It continues to ascend over and around several higher but lesser crags as the Castellated Ridge blends into the main mass of Mt. Jefferson. At 4.5 mi., the Cornice crosses, leading northeast to Randolph Path near Edmands Col and south to Caps Ridge and Gulfside trails. Castle Trail ascends moderately over the rocks and joins Mt. Jefferson Loop in a small, flat area just northeast of the summit crag.

Descending, Castle Trail leads slightly west of north from the jct. with Mt. Jefferson Loop.

ROLLO FALL PATH (MAP 1: E8)
From Bowman trailhead (1,496 ft.) to:

Rollo Fall (1,570 ft.)	0.4 mi.	100 ft.	0:15

RMC Near Bowman is Rollo Fall, an attractive cascade on the Moose River, now within Randolph Community Forest and easily accessed by a signed footpath. From the Bowman trailhead, Rollo Fall Path follows Presidential Rail Trail (sign: "Rollo Fall") to the left (east) for 0.15 mi. and then turns right into the woods onto a footpath (sign: "Rollo Fall"). It passes through the woods and then quickly turns left onto a grassy road (sign: "Path"; in reverse, turn right here). The road climbs slightly, passes under power lines, and turns sharply left onto a gravel footpath at 0.3 mi., which ascends gradually to Rollo Fall at 0.4 mi.

CAPS RIDGE TRAIL (MAP 1: F8–F9)
Cumulative from Jefferson Notch Rd. (3,008 ft.) to:

The Link (3,800 ft.)	1.1 mi.	800 ft.	0:55
Lower Cap (4,422 ft.)	1.5 mi.	1,400 ft.	1:25
Upper Cap (4,830 ft.)	1.9 mi.	1,800 ft.	1:50
The Cornice (5,025 ft.)	2.1 mi.	2,000 ft.	2:05
Mt. Jefferson summit (5,713 ft.)	2.5 mi.	2,700 ft.	2:35
Jct. with Mt. Jefferson Loop (5,700 ft.)	2.6 mi.	2,700 ft.	2:40
Gulfside Trail (5,275 ft.) via Cornice	2.6 mi.	2,250 ft.	2:25
Mt. Washington summit (6,288 ft.) via Cornice, Gulfside Trail, and Trinity Heights Connector	5.3 mi.	3,650 ft. (rev. 350 ft.)	4:30
Cumulative distance for loop over Caps, Mt. Jefferson, and Castles (via Castle Trail, Link, and Caps Ridge Trail)	6.8 mi.	2,850 ft.	4:50

AMC Yellow-blazed Caps Ridge Trail makes a direct ascent of Mt. Jefferson from the height-of-land (3,008 ft.) on the road through Jefferson Notch, the pass between Mt. Jefferson and the Dartmouth Range. (This road is closed in winter.) This is the highest trailhead on a public through-road in the White Mountains, making it possible to ascend Mt. Jefferson with much less elevation gain than on any other trail to a Presidential peak over 5,000 ft., except for a few trails that begin high on Mt. Washington Auto Rd. Caps Ridge Trail is steep and rough, however, with numerous ledges that require rock scrambling and are slippery when wet, and the upper part is very exposed to weather. Therefore, the route is more strenuous than might be anticipated from the relatively small distance and elevation gain. (*Note*: It is not easier to ascend Mt. Washington via Caps Ridge Trail than via Jewell Trail because the descent from Monticello Lawn to Sphinx Col mostly cancels out the advantage of the higher start.)

The south end of Jefferson Notch Rd. is located directly opposite Mt. Clinton Rd. at a crossroads on Cog Railway Base Rd. (the road that runs from US 302 to the Cog Railway). The north end is on Valley Rd. in Jefferson (which runs between US 2 and NH 115; the jct. is 1.3 mi. west of US 2 and 2.9 mi. east of NH 115). The high point in the notch is 5.2 mi. from Valley Rd. on the north and 3.2 mi. from Cog Railway Base Rd. on the south. Jefferson Notch Rd. is a good gravel road, open in summer and early fall and closed in winter, but because of the high elevation it reaches, snow and mud don't disappear until late spring, and ice returns early. Drive with care, as the road is winding and narrow in places, and watch out for logging trucks.

Caps Ridge Trail leaves the parking area and crosses a wet section on log bridges. It ascends moderately, with one steeper section, up the lower part of the ridge, passing through several blowdown patches. At 1.0 mi., an outcropping of granite on the right provides fine views out to the southwest and up to the summit of Mt. Jefferson and the Caps Ridge ahead. Several potholes in this outcropping were formed by glacial meltwater.

About 100 yd. beyond the outcropping, the Link enters from the left, providing a nearly level but very rough path that runs 1.6 mi. to Castle Trail just below the Castles, making possible a very scenic, although strenuous, loop over the Caps and the Castles. Caps Ridge Trail follows the narrow crest of the ridge, becoming steeper and rougher as it climbs up into scrub. Views become increasingly frequent. At 1.5 mi., the trail reaches the lowest Cap after a steep scramble up ledges and runs entirely in the open from here. It skirts to the right of the high point of the first Cap, passes through a slight gap, and scrambles up very steep ledges to the second Cap. The trail winds up the ridge with somewhat less difficult scrambling to the highest Cap at 1.9 mi., descends slightly off its upper end, and then continues to climb steeply as the ridge blends into the summit mass. At 2.1 mi., the Cornice enters left, providing a very rough route to Castle Trail and Edmands Col, and then diverges right in 20 yd., providing a relatively easy shortcut to Gulfside Trail at Monticello Lawn and points to the south. Caps Ridge Trail continues climbing steadily northeast and then east over the rocks, keeping a little south of the ridge crest, to the summit of Mt. Jefferson (the high point is reached by a short scramble to the left). It then descends east 40 yd. to the base of the little conical summit crag, where Caps Ridge Trail meets Mt. Jefferson Loop just above the latter trail's jct. with Castle Trail near a large cairn.

Descending from the summit crag, Caps Ridge Trail leads slightly south of west.

BOUNDARY LINE TRAIL (MAP 1: F8)
From Jewell Trail (2,525 ft.) to:

Jefferson Notch Rd. (2,528 ft.)	0.8 mi.	50 ft. (rev. 50 ft.)	0:25
From Cog Railway Base Rd. parking area (2,495 ft.) to:			
Caps Ridge Trail (3,008 ft.) via Jewell Trail, Boundary Line Trail, and Jefferson Notch Rd.	2.6 mi.	600 ft.	1:35

WMNF This yellow-blazed trail connects Jewell Trail, 0.4 mi. from the hikers parking area on Cog Railway Base Rd., with Jefferson Notch Rd., 1.4 mi. south of Caps Ridge Trail. Boundary Line Trail thus provides a shortcut between the trailheads of Caps Ridge Trail and Jewell Trail or Ammonoosuc Ravine Trail (Section One), although Boundary Line Trail is lightly used and must be followed with care. It diverges left (north) from Jewell Trail 0.4 mi. from the Cog Railway Base Rd. parking lot and runs north, nearly level, closely following the straight boundary line between two unincorporated townships. At 0.5 mi., Boundary Line Trail crosses Clay Brook and then continues to its end at Jefferson Notch Rd.

MT. CLAY
JEWELL TRAIL (MAP 1: F8–F9)
Cumulative from Cog Railway Base Rd. parking area (2,495 ft.) to:

Clay Brook crossing (2,850 ft.)	1.1 mi.	400 ft. (rev. 50 ft.)	0:45
Gulfside Trail (5,400 ft.)	3.7 mi.	2,950 ft.	3:20
Mt. Washington summit (6,288 ft.) via Gulfside Trail and Trinity Heights Connector	5.0 mi.	3,900 ft. (rev. 50 ft.)	4:25

WMNF This blue-blazed trail begins at a parking area (Recreation Pass required; restrooms; plowed in winter) on Cog Railway Base Rd., 1.1 mi. east of its jct. with Jefferson Notch Rd. and Mt. Clinton Rd. (Cog Railway Base Rd. is the road that leads from US 302 to the Cog Railway Base Station at Marshfield.) Jewell Trail ascends the unnamed ridge that leads west from Mt. Clay and ends at Gulfside Trail, high on the west slope of Mt. Clay, 0.3 mi. north of the Clay–Washington col and 1.4 mi. north of the summit of Mt. Washington. The grade is constant but seldom steep, there are no rock scrambles, and the footing is generally good below treeline and only moderately rough and rocky in the last section below Gulfside Trail. In combination with Gulfside Trail and Trinity Heights Connector, Jewell Trail provides the easiest route to Mt. Washington from the west, featuring a great length of ridge walking above treeline with fine views, but this section is also greatly exposed to the weather and offers no shelter between the summit and treeline. In bad weather, or if afternoon thunderstorms threaten, it may be safer to descend from Mt. Washington via Lakes of the Clouds Hut and Ammonoosuc Ravine Trail, despite the steep and slippery footing on the latter. When the weather cooperates, descent by Jewell Trail offers much easier footing and thus may be preferred. The trail is named for Sergeant Winfield S. Jewell, once an observer for the Army Signal Corps on Mt. Washington, who perished on the Greely expedition to the Arctic in 1884.

Jewell Trail enters the woods directly across the road from the parking area, descends slightly to cross the Ammonoosuc River on a bridge at 0.1 mi. and then swings northeast and ascends at an easy grade. At 0.4 mi., Boundary Line Trail diverges left, and Jewell Trail ascends the crest of the low ridge between the Ammonoosuc River and Clay Brook, joining the old route of the trail at 1.0 mi. Here, a link path from the Cog Railway joins on the right (sign: "Cog R.R.").

Jewell Link. Jewell Trail can be accessed from the Cog Railway Base Station by this link path. Parking (fee charged, $10 per person in 2024; plowed in winter) is available in a designated lower gravel lot on the right (south) side of Cog Railway Base Rd. (sign: "Hiker Parking"), 0.4 mi. east of the WMNF trailhead parking area. Elevation is 2,630 ft. (The upper lots are reserved for Cog Railway customers.) Proceed on foot up the walkway on the left side of the access road, through a parking lot on the left, and walk up past the left side of the main Base Station building. The link path (sign: "Jewell Trail") starts on the left just beyond Platform A, 0.2 mi. from hiker parking. Elevation is 2,685 ft. Cross the tracks with care and descend a wooden stairway. In 40 yd., Jewell Link swings right behind a WMNF welcome sign and crosses the Ammonoosuc River (no bridge; difficult in high water). The unmarked but well-beaten path angles up to the left on the far bank and climbs by switchbacks, passes a closed former route on the right, and then ascends easily and swings left to meet Jewell Trail, 0.3 mi. from the Base Station, ascent 200 ft. (15 min.). From hiker parking, 0.5 mi., 250 ft., 0:20.

From the jct. with the link, **Jewell Trail** descends slightly to Clay Brook, crosses it on a footbridge at 1.1 mi., and then climbs northeast by long switchbacks. At 2.0 mi., the trail passes through a blowdown patch at the edge of the steep wall of Burt Ravine, which offers limited views. It then swings somewhat to the north side of the ridge and climbs east, staying well below the ridge crest until near treeline. Reaching treeline at about 3.0 mi., the trail zigzags at a moderate grade with rough, rocky footing up the ridge crest, which quickly becomes less prominent and blends into the slope of Mt. Clay. At 3.5 mi., Jewell Trail swings to the right, going away from what remains of the ridge, and angles up the slope at an easy grade to Gulfside Trail. To ascend Mt. Washington, follow Gulfside Trail to the right (south).

PINE MTN.
PINE MTN. TRAIL (MAP 5: E10)
From gravel pit on Promenade St. (801 ft.) to:

Pine Mtn. summit (2,404 ft.)	2.7 mi.	1,650 ft. (rev. 50 ft.)	2:10

WMNF This trail was reopened in the 1990s to restore an abandoned section of Pine Link that once connected an old route of the AT in Gorham with the Northern Presidentials via Pine Mtn. Reach the trailhead by turning west onto Promenade St. from NH 16 at a point 0.25 mi. south of its jct. with US 2, at the eastern edge of the Gorham business district. Follow this road through a residential area and then past a large cemetery on the right at 0.5 mi. from NH 16. The road becomes gravel and gets rough and narrow at 0.6 mi. and continues to the edge of a gravel pit at 0.7 mi. from NH 16, where cars may be parked on the left (sign for trail), just before a fork in the road. The road and parking may be plowed in winter. If not, hikers can use public parking in the business district or park in a plowed lot at the corner of Church St. and Railroad St. Parking in the lot adds 0.8 mi. round-trip to the hike.

Pine Mtn. Trail ascends on a narrow path south through the woods and in 0.1 mi. reaches a natural gas pipeline clearing used as a snowmobile trail. (In the reverse direction, look carefully for the left turn off the pipeline clearing; the trail sign is down at the lower edge.) The trail follows the brushy pipeline clearing right (west) for another 0.1 mi. and then turns left (south) into the woods (sign). Pine Mtn. Trail now follows an old road (also a snowmobile trail), bearing left at a fork in 50 yd. and bearing left at a second fork in another 200 yd. At 0.5 mi., the trail turns right off this road (sign) and passes through an old logging cut before swinging left onto a small ridge (arrow) and ascending. At 1.3 mi., the trail descends briefly to a swampy saddle, enters the WMNF, and angles up the northwest slope of Pine Mtn., crossing several old logging roads. At 2.1 mi., a spur path (sign: "View") leads 50 yd. left to a former viewpoint, which is now overgrown. At 2.3 mi., the grade eases and the trail swings left under utility lines; here, at a sign for Chapel Rock, a well-constructed side path ascends to the left and in 0.1 mi. reaches the northeast summit and the Horton Center worship area, where there is an excellent view from a rocky pinnacle called Chapel Rock; ascent is 100 ft. Enjoy the scenery and meditate if you wish, but please avoid disturbing any religious activities that may be in progress there. (*Note*: Public access to Chapel Rock is prohibited during the months of June through August while the camp is in session; the public is welcome to visit in the off-season only.)

Pine Mtn. Trail follows bog bridges under the utility lines for 60 yd. (the cliffs here are sometimes used for rock climbing by Horton Center guests; please share the trail) and then bears right into the woods at a sign and ascends to a 4-way jct. at 2.4 mi.; straight ahead (sign) yellow-blazed Pine Mtn. Loop Trail leads 0.2 mi. to Pine Mtn. Road. The portion of the old tractor road diverging sharply right here leads to the private Horton Center and is not open to the public. Hikers are requested to use Pine Mtn. Loop Trail and to not follow the road past the buildings of the Horton Center. Turning left here, Pine Mtn. Trail ascends the old tractor road (also signed as Pinkham Ledge Trail) 0.3 mi. to the summit of Pine Mtn., passing three signed side paths left to eastern outlooks: Chapel View, which leads 60 yd. to a ledge with an impressive view of Chapel Rock; Gorham View; and Angel View. From the viewless summit, where footings from an old fire tower remain, Ledge Trail descends 0.1 mi. ahead to the south cliffs and excellent views.

PINE MTN. ROAD AND PINE MTN. LOOP TRAIL (MAP 1: E10)
Cumulative from Pinkham B Rd. (Dolly Copp Rd.) (1,648 ft.) to:

Ledge Trail (1,800 ft.)	0.9 mi.	200 ft. (rev. 50 ft.)	0:35
Pine Mtn. summit (2,404 ft.) via Pine Mtn. Loop Trail and Pine Mtn. Trail	2.0 mi.	800 ft.	1:25
Loop to Pine Mtn. via Ledge Trail, with return via Pine Mtn. Trail, Pine Mtn. Loop Trail, and Pine Mtn. Road	3.5 mi.	850 ft.	2:10

HC This trail uses the private automobile road to the Horton Center on Pine Mtn. most of the way to the summit of Pine Mtn. The road begins a little northwest of the highest point of Pinkham B Rd. (Dolly Copp Rd.; closed in winter), opposite the Pine Link trailhead, where parking is available. This trailhead is 2.4 mi. from US 2 (at the foot of the big hill west of Gorham) and 1.9 mi. from NH 16 near Dolly Copp Campground. Pine Mtn. Road is closed to public vehicular use and has a locked gate but is open to the public as a foot trail to the summit, using Pine Mtn. Loop Trail and Pine Mtn. Trail for the upper part of the climb; hikers should watch out for Horton Center–affiliated cars along the road. Ledge Trail diverges from the road and runs over the top of the south cliff and to the summit; it is frequently used to make a loop over the summit.

The impressive views from the summit area include the much higher surrounding peaks—particularly Mt. Madison—and the valleys of Androscoggin, Moose, and Peabody rivers. The Horton Center, a private facility for renewal and education operated by the New Hampshire Conference of the United Church of Christ (Congregational), occupies a tract of 100 acres on the summit. The center consists of six buildings and an outdoor chapel on the northeast peak (not accessible to hikers from June through August while the camp is in session), which has excellent views and can be reached by a spur path from Pine Mtn. Trail. Please avoid disturbing religious activities that may be in progress. Hikers are requested to use Pine Mtn. Loop Trail and to not follow Pine Mtn. Road past the buildings of the Horton Center.

Pine Mtn. Road runs northeast from Pinkham B Rd., descends across a shallow col, and winds its way up the south and west flanks of the mountain. At 0.9 mi., Ledge Trail branches right to climb to the summit by way of the south cliff. Pine Mtn. Road now climbs more steadily, and at 1.5 mi. from Pinkham B Rd., the route to Pine Mtn. turns right into the woods on yellow-blazed Pine Mtn. Loop Trail; watch for a large sign just before the junction. Pine Mtn. Loop Trail climbs along the slope to the east of the road, bypassing the Horton Center and reaching a 4-way jct. at 1.7 mi. To the right, Pine Mtn. Trail (also signed as Pinkham Ledge Trail) leads 0.3 mi. to the summit and the upper end of Ledge Trail, passing three signed side paths left to eastern outlooks; reach the excellent views from the south cliff by descending Ledge Trail for 0.1 mi. Continuing straight from the 4-way jct., Pine Mtn. Trail leads 0.1 mi. to the side path to Chapel Rock. The trail leading sharply left from the 4-way jct. to the Horton Center is not open to the public.

LEDGE TRAIL (MAP 1: E10)
From Pine Mtn. Road (1,800 ft.) to:

Pine Mtn. summit (2,404 ft.)	0.6 mi.	600 ft.	0:35

WMNF This trail, sparsely blazed in yellow, runs to the summit of Pine Mtn. from Pine Mtn. Road (a private road, closed to public vehicles but open as a trail), making possible an attractive loop with a sporty ascent past excellent views, and an easy return. Ledge Trail diverges right from Pine Mtn. Road 0.9 mi. from Pinkham B Rd. (Dolly Copp Rd.), ascends through woods and swings right to the base of the south cliff; then it swings left up a ledge with a fine view south at 0.3 mi. It climbs steeply through woods to the east of the cliff with several easy scrambles and then swings left up broad glacier-scraped ledges to the cliff top, which provides beautiful views to the south and west. Ledge Trail then ascends gradually through woods for 0.1 mi. and meets Pine Mtn. Trail at the wooded summit, where footings from an old fire tower remain.

PLEASURE PATHS ON THE LOWER NORTH SLOPES
TOWN LINE BROOK TRAIL (MAP 1: E10)
From Pinkham B Rd. (Dolly Copp Rd.) (1,484 ft.) to:

End of path above Triple Falls (1,725 ft.)	0.2 mi.	250 ft.	0:15

RMC This short but steep yellow-blazed path gives access to Triple Falls from Pinkham B Rd. (Dolly Copp Rd.; closed in winter) 1.7 mi. southeast of US 2 and 2.8 mi. north of NH 16. Triple Falls are beautiful cascades on Town Line Brook named Proteus Fall, Erebus Fall, and Evans Fall. The watershed is steep, and the rainwater runs off very rapidly, so the falls should be visited during or immediately after a rainfall to get the best experience. Parking is at a pull-off on the north side of the road, just west of the bridge over the brook. The trail starts at a sign on the south side of the road just east of the brook. It climbs moderately and then steeply along the brook's bank, and at 0.1 mi. a side path leads 20 yd. right to a view of Proteus Fall (sign). Above here, the trail remains steep and runs along the edge of a gorge with a steep dropoff; use caution, especially in wet weather. Town Line Brook Trail climbs past Erebus Fall and soon reaches Evans Fall (sign). The trail continues another 50 yd. upstream and ends at an RMC trail sign.

SYLVAN WAY (MAP 1: E9)
From Memorial Bridge (1,425 ft.) to:

Howker Ridge Trail (1,625 ft.)	1.7 mi.	250 ft. (rev. 50 ft.)	1:00

RMC Sylvan Way departs from the Link at the east end of Memorial Bridge, 0.7 mi. from the Appalachia parking area, and leads over Snyder Brook to Howker Ridge Trail just above Coosauk Fall. Leaving Memorial Bridge, after 80 yd., yellow-blazed Sylvan Way turns left, away from Cold Brook, at the base of Cold Brook Fall, where a beaten path continues ahead up the brook. Sylvan Way descends across Beechwood Way at 0.1 mi. and then runs nearly level and crosses Air Line at 0.6 mi. and Valley Way 100 yd. farther. At 0.7 mi., within a space of 30 yd., Maple Walk enters left, Fallsway crosses, Sylvan Way crosses Snyder Brook on ledges 60 yd. above Gordon Fall, and Brookbank crosses. From here, Sylvan Way ascends gradually, crossing Randolph Path at 1.1 mi. Sylvan Way then passes through a brushy logged area and continues to Howker Ridge Trail.

FALLSWAY (MAP 1: E9)
From Appalachia parking area (1,300 ft.) to:

Valley Way jct. above Tama Fall (1,700 ft.)	0.7 mi.	400 ft.	0:35

RMC Fallsway is an attractive alternate route to the first 0.6 mi. of Valley Way, following close to Snyder Brook and passing several falls. From the east end of the Appalachia parking area, the yellow-blazed trail goes east for 60 yd. and then turns right onto a gravel road and crosses Presidential Rail Trail (Brookbank diverges left here; in reverse, cross the rail-trail and quickly turn left before reaching US 2), passes under power lines, and then enters the woods and continues straight ahead. At 0.2 mi. from Appalachia, Fallsway reaches Snyder Brook and soon passes Gordon Fall. In 60 yd., Sylvan Way crosses and Maple Walk enters right as Fallsway continues up the west bank of the brook in hemlock woods. The trail passes Lower and Upper Salroc Falls and soon enters Valley Way at 0.6 mi., below Tama Fall. In 30 yd., Fallsway leaves Valley Way and passes Tama Fall, where Brookbank enters left, and in another 60 yd., Fallsway ends at Valley Way.

BROOKBANK (MAP 1: E9)
From lower jct. with Fallsway (1,310 ft.) to:

Upper jct. with Fallsway (1,675 ft.)	0.7 mi.	350 ft.	0:30

RMC Brookbank follows the lower part of Snyder Brook on the opposite side from Fallsway. Brookbank leaves Fallsway on the left, 100 yd. from Appalachia, and follows Presidential Rail Trail east for 0.1 mi. to a bridge over Snyder Brook. Across the bridge, Brookbank turns right and in 70 yd. reaches a power line. Here, the trail turns right again and in 20 yd. swings left and enters the woods. It runs up the east side of the brook, passing Gordon Fall, Sylvan Way, Lower and Upper Salroc Falls, and Tama Fall. Above Tama Fall, the trail recrosses the brook on ledges and reenters Fallsway.

MAPLE WALK (MAP 1: E9)
From Valley Way (1,310 ft.) to:

Sylvan Way and Fallsway (1,400 ft.)	0.2 mi.	100 ft.	0:10

RMC Maple Walk diverges left from Valley Way a few yd. beyond the power-line crossing just south of the Appalachia parking area. It runs at easy grades to the jct. of Fallsway and Sylvan Way just above Gordon Fall.

BEECHWOOD WAY (MAP 1: E9)
From the Link (1,400 ft.) to:

Valley Way (1,850 ft.)	0.8 mi.	450 ft.	0:40

RMC This yellow-blazed path runs from the Link, 0.6 mi. from Appalachia, to Valley Way, 0.9 mi. from Appalachia, just below its jct. with Brookside and Randolph Path. Beechwood Way follows a good logging road with moderate grades. The trail leaves the Link and crosses Sylvan Way in 100 yd. and Air Line at 0.6 mi. After passing through a fine stand of tall sugar maples, Beechwood Way ends at Valley Way.

INDEX

Trail names in **bold type** indicate a detailed description found in the text.

Where multiple page references appear, bold numbering indicates the main entry or entries for the trail.

[Bracketed information] indicates which of AMC's White Mountains Trail Maps (sold separately) displays the features and where, by map section and letter.

A

Adams, Mt., 102–118
Air Line [1: E9–F9], **103–104**
Alpine Garden Trail [1: F9], **22–23**
Ammonoosuc Ravine Trail [1: F8–F9], **34–36**
Amphibrach [1: E9], **109–110**
Appalachian Trail (AT), xix, xxii, 2, 5
  Mt. Washington and southern ridges, 25–26, 29–33, 39–40
  Northern Peaks/Great Gulf region, 67, 71–75, 83, 85–87, 92–93
Appalachia parking area, trails originating from, 67, 80–81, 101–102, 103–104, 129

B

backcountry hazards, xxxi–xxxvii
Beechwood Way [1: E9], **130**
Boott Spur Link [1: F9], **20**
Boott Spur Trail [1: F9], **19–20**
Boundary Line Trail [1: F8], **123**
Bowman trailhead, trails originating from, 67, 81–82, 116–121
break-ins, xxxvii
Brookbank [1: E9], **130**
brook crossings, xxxv–xxxvi
Brookside [1: E9], **99–100**
Buttress Trail [1: F9], **90–91**

C

Camel Trail [1: F9], **24**
campfires, xxviii
camping, xxv–xxvii
camping regulations, xxvii
  Great Gulf Wilderness, 68, 70
  Leave No Trace principles, xxxvii–xxxviii
  Mt. Washington region, 9–11
  northern Presidential range, 69–70
  roadside campgrounds, xxviii

Caps Ridge Trail [1: F8–F9], **121–123**
Caribou-Speckled Mtn. Wilderness, xvii
Castle Ravine Trail [1: E8–F9], **118–119**
Castle Trail [1: E8–F9], **119–121**
Cave Mountain Path [3: H9], **60–61**
Chandler Brook Trail [1: F9], **87**
Chemin des Dames [1: F9], **108**
children, hiking with, xxiv–xxv
Clay, Mt., 123–125
Mt. Clay Loop [1: F9], **76**
Cliffway [1: E9], **110–111**
Clinton, Mt., 45–47
Mt. Clinton Rd. parking area, trails originating from, 28–33, 36–37
Mt. Clinton Trail [1: G8], **45–47**
The Cornice [1: F9], **77**
Covered Bridge Lane, trails originating from, 59–60
Crag Camp, 69
Crawford Cliff Spur, 30
Crawford Connector, 31
Crawford Path [1: G8–F9], **28–33**
Crew-Cut Trail [1: F9–F10], **27**

D

Daniel Webster-Scout Trail [1: F10–F9], **93–94**
Davis Path [1/3: H8–F9], **48–51**
The Direttissima [1: F9–G9], **22**
dogs, hiking with, xxv
Dolly Copp Campground, trails originating from, 82–84, 93–94
Dolly Copp Road. *See* Pinkham B Rd., trails originating from
drinking water, xxxvi–xxxvii
Dry River Cutoff [1: G8], **47–48**
Dry River Shelters, 11, 43–45
Dry River Trail [1: H8–F9], **43–45**
Dry River Valley, 43–48

E

Edmands Col Cutoff [1: F9], **76–77**
Edmands Path [1: G8], **36–37**
Eisenhower, Mt., 31–33, 47
Mt. Eisenhower Loop [1: G8], **33**
Mt. Eisenhower Trail [1: G8], **47**
Elephant Head, 37–38
Emerald Trail [1: F9], **117–118**

F

falls and injuries, xxxii
Fallsway [1: E9], **129**
following trails, xxii–xxiii
footwear, xxiv

G

gear, recommended, xxiii–xxiv
George's Gorge Trail [1: F9], **27–28**
getting lost, xxiii
Glen Boulder Trail [1: G9], **20–21**
Glen Ellis Falls parking area, trails
    originating from, 21–22
Glen Ellis Falls Trail [1: G9], **21–22**
Gray Knob cabin, 69–70
Gray Knob Trail [1: E9–F9], **113**
Great Gulf Link Trail [1: F10], **84**
Great Gulf Trail [1: F10–F9], **82–84**
Great Gulf Wilderness
    camping in, 68, 70
    trail descriptions, 82–93
Great Gully Trail [1: F9], **108–109**
Gulfside Trail [1: F9], **70–75**

H

Hayes Farm, trails originating from, 61–63
heat exhaustion, xxxiii
Hermit Lake Campsite, 11
Highland Center at Crawford Notch, 8–9
    trails originating from, 28–33, 42–43
hiker shuttle, xvii–xviii
hikeSafe Hiker Responsibility Code, xxi
Hincks Trail [1: E9–F9], **112–113**
history, xiv–xv
Howker Ridge Trail [1: E9–F9], **96–98**
hunting, xxxiv–xxxv
Huntington Ravine Fire Road [1: F9],
    17–18
Huntington Ravine Trail [1: F9], **15–17**
hypothermia, xxxii–xxxiii

I

Inlook Trail [1: E9], **99**
insects, xxxv
Iron Mtn. Trail [3: H10], **61–63**
Isolation Trail [1: G9–G8], **55–56**
Israel Ridge Path [1: E8–F9], **116–117**

J

Jackson, Mt., 37–40
Jackson area hikes, 61–63
Jefferson, Mt., 76, 118–123
Mt. Jefferson Loop [1: F9], **76**
Jefferson Notch Rd., trails originating from,
    67, 121–123
Jewell Trail [1: F8–F9], **123–125**
Joe Dodge Lodge, 7–8

K

Kelton Trail [1: E9], **98–99**
King Ravine Trail [1: E9–F9], **106–108**

L

Lakes of the Clouds Hut, 9, 11
    trails originating from, 23–24, 34–36
Mt. Langdon Trail [3: H9], **56–57**
Lawn Cutoff [1: F9], **24**
Leave No Trace principles, xxxvii–xxxviii
Ledge Trail (Pine Mtn.) [1: E10], **128**
Liebeskind's Loop [1: F9–F10], **28**
lightning, xxxiii
The Link [1: E9–F8], **80–81**
Lion Head Trail [1: F9], **14–15**
The Log Cabin (shelter), 69
Lower Bruin [1: E9], **102**
Lowe's Path [1: E9–F9], **114–115**

M

Macomber Family Information Center, 8
    trails originating from, 37–39, 41
Madison, Mt., 93–102
Madison Gulf Trail [1: F9], **85–87**
Madison Spring Hut, 68
    trails originating from, 70–75, 91–93,
    105
Maple Walk [1: E9], **130**
maps and navigation, xi–xii
Mizpah Cutoff [1: G8], **41**
Mizpah Spring Hut, 9
    trails originating from, 37–41, 46–49

Monaway [1: E9], **111**
Mt. Monroe Loop [1: F9], **33–34**
Montalban Ridge, 48–60. *See* also Davis
  Path
Mount Washington Auto Road, 4–6
  trails originating from, 85–87
Mount Washington Cog Railway, 6
  trails originating from, 34–36, 123–125
Mt. Langdon Shelter site, 11, 57

N
Nauman Tentsite, 11
Nelson Crag Trail [1: F9], 18
NH Route 16, trails originating from, 22,
  52–55, 61, 67, 82–84. *See* also Pinkham
  Notch Visitor Center
northern Presidential Peaks
  huts/camping in, 68–70
  region description, 65–67
  road access, 67–68
  trail descriptions, 70–130
  See also Adams, Mt.; Clay, Mt.;
    Jefferson, Mt.

O
Old Jackson Road [1: F9], **26**
Osgood Cutoff [1: F9], **93**
Osgood Tentsite, 70
Osgood Trail [1: F10–F9], **91–93**

P
Parapet Trail [1: F9], **94–95**
Mt. Parker Trail [3: H9], **58–59**
parking fees, xvii–xviii
The Perch (lean-to), 69, 113, 117
Perch Path [1: F9], **113**
Pine Link [1: E10–F9], **95–96**
Pine Mtn., 125–128
Pine Mtn. Road/Loop Trail [1: E10],
  126–127
Pine Mtn. Trail [5: E10], **125–126**
Pinkham B Rd., trails originating from, 67,
  78–79, 95–98, 126–127, 128
Pinkham Notch Visitor Center, 7–8
  trails originating from, 12–22, 25–28
Pleasure Paths, 128–130

Presidential Rail Trail [1: E9–E8], **81–82**
Presidential Range-Dry River Wilderness, xvii
  camping in, 10–11
  trails in, 43–59
Promenade St., trails originating from,
  125–126

R
Randolph East parking area, trails
  originating from, 78–79, 81–82
Randolph Path [1: E9–F9], **78–79**
Raymond Path [1: F9], **25–26**
Rocky Branch Shelters (#1 and #2), 11, 54
Rocky Branch Trail [3: G10–H9], **52–55**
Rollo Fall Path [1:E8], **121**

S
Saco Lake Trail [1: G8], **42–43**
Saco River, trails originating from, 56–57
Saco River Trail [1: G8–H8], **2**
safety, xix–xx
Sam Willey Trail [1: G8], **41**
Sandwich Range Wilderness, xvii
Scar Trail/Loop [1: E9], **104–105**
search and rescue, xxxi–xxxii
Shapleigh Bunkhouse, 8–9
Short Line [1: E9], **106**
Six Husbands Trail [1: F9], **89–90**
Southside Trail [1: F9], **24**
Sphinx Trail [1: F9], **88–89**
Spur Trail (Mt. Adams) [1: E9–F9],
  111–112
Stairs Col Trail [1: H9], **52**
Mt. Stanton Trail [3: 10–H9], **59–60**
Star Lake Trail [1: F9], **105**
storm damage, xx–xxi
Sylvan Way [1: E9], **129**

T
Town Line Brook Trail [1: E10], **128**
trail maintenance, xxxvii
Trinity Heights Connector [1: F9], **25**
trip planning, xix–xx
Tuckerman Crossover [1: F9], **23–24**
Tuckerman Ravine Trail [1:F9], **12–14**

U

US 2, trails originating from, 67, 114–115.
  See also Appalachia parking area
US 302, trails originating from, 37–40,
  42–45, 48–49, 51
Upper Bruin [1: F9], **102**

V

Valley Way [1: E9–F9], **101–102**
Valley Way Tentsite, 70, 102

W

Wamsutta Trail [1: F9], **88**
Washington, Mt., 1–25
  auto road, 4–6
  camping near, 9–11
  cog railway, 6
  huts and lodges, 7–9
  safety on, 2–4
  summit buildings, 4
  trail descriptions, from Pinkham Notch,
    12–22
  trail descriptions, southern and western
    ridges, 28–36
  trail descriptions, upper cone area,
    22–25
  trails descriptions, northern ridges,
    70–75
  See also Mount Washington Auto Road;
    Mount Washington Cog Railway
Watson Path [1: E9–F9], **100–101**
Webster, Mt., 37–40
Webster Cliff Trail [1: G8], **39–40**
Webster-Jackson Trail [1: G8], **37–38**
Westside Trail (Mt. Washington) [1: F9],
  24–25
White Mountain National Forest, xvi
  forest protection areas (FPAs) in, 10
  history, xv
  wilderness and scenic areas within, xvii
wildlife, xxxiv
Wild River Wilderness, xvii
Willey House Station site, trails originating
  from, 41
Winniweta Falls Trail [3: G10], **61**
winter hiking, xxviii–xxxi

ABOUT AMC IN NEW HAMPSHIRE

The Appalachian Mountain Club's New Hampshire Chapter has more than 10,000 members and offers hundreds of trips each year. Well-trained and dedicated leaders guide hiking, paddling, skiing, and climbing excursions. The chapter is also active in trail work, conservation projects, and instructional programs. You can learn more about this chapter by visiting outdoors.org/community/chapters. To view a list of AMC activities in New Hampshire and other parts of the Northeast, visit activities.outdoors.org.

AMC BOOKS UPDATES

AMC Books strives to keep our guidebooks as up-to-date as possible to help you plan safe and enjoyable adventures. If we learn after publishing a book that relevant trails have been relocated or route or contact information has changed, we will post the updated information online. Before you hit the trail, visit outdoors.org/books-maps and click "Book Updates." While hiking, if you notice discrepancies with the trip descriptions or maps, or if you find any other errors in this book, please let us know by submitting them to amcbookupdates@outdoors.org or to Books Editor, c/o AMC, 10 City Square, Suite 2, Boston, MA 02129. We will verify all submissions and post key updates each month. AMC Books is dedicated to being a recognized leader in outdoor publishing.

AMC Books are published by the Appalachian Mountain Club (AMC), a nonprofit with the mission to foster the protection, enjoyment, and understanding of the outdoors. **Since 1876** we have been working to protect the mountains, forests, waters, and trails you love in the Northeast and Mid-Atlantic regions.

Join us in this work by becoming an AMC member! **When you join AMC, you can:**

- Take pride in knowing that you are supporting outdoor recreation and conservation in the Northeast and Mid-Atlantic

- Enjoy thousands of outdoor activities

- Receive up to 20% off merchandise, books & maps, and stays at AMC destinations

Scan the QR code to sign up!

AMC Books

AMC's Best Day Hikes in the White Mountains, 4th Ed.
Robert N. Buchsbaum

Whether readers want a short family outing or are avid hikers looking for a full[-]excursion, *AMC's Best Day Hikes in the White Mountains* makes it easy to find the per[fect] hike for all skill levels. This new edition clues in readers to 60 of the greatest day hike[s on] the some of the Northeast's best and most famous hiking trails, from Tuckerman Rav[ine] to Crawford Notch to Flume Gorge, with five brand new hikes included in this editio[n].

$19.95 • 978-1-62842-137-8

Best Backcountry Skiing in the Northeast, 2nd Ed.
David Goodman

Thirty years after his first guidebook became a cult classic among Eastern pow[der] seekers, David Goodman has revised and expanded his "bible of Northeas[t] backcountry skiing" for the next generation of winter adventurers. From thrilling [day] trips to hut-to-hut wilderness journeys, this is the only comprehensive guide to the b[est] backcountry ski and snowboard tours in New Hampshire, Maine, Vermont, New Y[ork] and Massachusetts.

$21.95 • 978-1-62842-124-8

Southern New Hampshire Trail Guide, 5th Ed.
Compiled and Edited by Ken MacGray with Steven D. Smith

This comprehensive trail guide covers New Hampshire hiking trails south of [the] White Mountain National Forest, including the state's beloved Lakes Region [and] Seacoast. Every trail description provides turn-by-turn directions, making route find[ing] straightforward and reliable, while suggested hikes feature icons showing kid-frie[ndly] trips, scenic views, and more.

$23.95 • 978-1-62842-115-6

This Wild Land
Andrew Vietze

Almost twenty years ago, Andrew Vietze made an unexpected career change: f[rom] punk rock magazine editor to park ranger at Baxter State Park in Maine. From midn[ight] search-and-rescue missions to trail maintenance to cleaning toilets, Baxter ran[gers] do it all… and over the decades Vietze has seen it all. In *This Wild Land*, Vietze tell[s his] story with humor, action, and an eye for the compelling details of life as a park ran[ger,] making it the perfect read for outdoor and armchair adventurers alike.

$18.95 • 978-1-62842-132-3 • ebook available

Find these and other AMC titles through booksellers and outdoor retailers. Or order directly from AMC at outdoors.org/books-maps or call 800-262-4455.